FLIGHT MAPS

FLIGHT
MAPS

ADVENTURES WITH NATURE
IN MODERN AMERICA

JENNIFER PRICE

BASIC
B
BOOKS

A MEMBER OF THE PERSEUS BOOKS GROUP

"A Brief Natural History of the Plastic Pink Flamingo" was first published by the Phi Beta Kappa Society in *The American Scholar.*

Copyright © 1999 by Jennifer Price.

Published by Basic Books,
A Member of the Perseus Books Group

FIRST EDITION

Designed by Rachel Hegarty

A CIP catalog record for this book is available
from the Library of Congress.
ISBN 0-465-02485-8

99 00 01 02 /RRD 10 9 8 7 6 5 4 3 2 1

To my parents—Elmer and Madelon Price.

CONTENTS

LIST OF
ILLUSTRATIONS

INTRODUCTION

It is perhaps our most impressive safety advance ever—A Volvo that can save your soul.

—TV commercial for the Volvo
All-Wheel-Drive Cross Country, 1998

Fish spend 24 hours a day, 365 days a year, playing together in the water. The divorce, crime, and stress rate . . . is roughly zero.

—TV commercial for
Bayliner leisure boats, 1997

Flight Maps records my travels through American history and culture to pursue what began as a simple question: "What does nature mean to me?" I have found myself in an abundance of unexpected places, which have included forests, not always safe, of more questions. Can a Volvo Cross Country save your soul if it takes you to a stunning mountain range? Why, in the late 1890s, did a lot of Americans decide that a whole stuffed tern on a woman's hat was no longer a lovely thing? Why do backpackers cart plastic pink flamingos into wilderness areas? Does PBS really "give you the whole wide world?" My questions have led me to the

VOLVO TV AD

most entrenched depths of human power, angst and desire. I have toured the archives and artifacts of 1980s mall-architecture manuals, eighteenth-century cookbooks, and John Waters movies. You do not need the $40,000 All-Wheel Drive Volvo to visit these places. A VCR, a remote control, a library card and a knack for parking-lot navigation have been more useful than hiking boots, a sport-utility vehicle or anything with Gore-Tex.

I had never planned to become a Thoreau of the mall. And why watch TV to ask what nature means? This book is rooted in my deep uneasiness with entrenched American definitions of nature. Like so many suburban baby boomers, I discovered wild places on vacations and at summer camp—in my case, in the Rocky Mountains and in the vista-laden, sunset-riven, geologically stunning American Southwest. As a teenager, I began to watch birds. As Roger Tory Peterson has said, "birds have wings, and they do things," and the things they do continue to guide me on hikes and camping trips through places so quiet and clean and uninhabited and wondrous that they seem to hold the potential—and it is a certainty emblazoned and reinforced in American nature writing—to, well, rescue one's soul. And for less than $40,000. I embraced Nature as the Last Best Places. I defined my experiences in Nature as more Real and Essential. I set Nature in stark contrast to everything modern and urban, and used Nature to articulate the social confusions and ecological destructions of modern urban American life.

But in the cities and suburbs where I actually lived, I felt increasingly uneasy, because these everyday places seemed irredeemably *anti*-Natural. They were un-Real, Nature-destroying, inescapably irreverent. How to live here? Because I defined the Nature I loved as Out There, I saw everything built in the cities—roads, bridges, buildings, violins—as Nature destroyed. If you think of nature as the place where you save your soul, then how to sustain your soul in the life to which you return? If I define Nature as Out There, then how can I use nature In Here without destroying it? I toyed, like many, with retreating to a backcountry Alaskan cabin. Instead, I have joined the proliferating calls to reenvision the spaces we inhabit as places where people must *use* nature. I even moved to Los Angeles. And I have tried to see modern American life as something we literally create—for worse, and potentially for better—from the nonhuman natural world. In *Flight Maps*, I try to come to terms with my cherished definitions of Nature.

Why do it at the Mall of America? My interest in the crossroads of nature and popular culture began as vague curiosity: "Gee, I wonder if the penguin on this coffee mug means anything to me at all." And if you had told me, ten years ago, that I would think very hard about the plastic pink flamingo, I'd have been worried. But the ratio of plastic to real flamingos in the United States is 700 to 1. In the late-twentieth-century era of industrial technologies, global markets, and mass communications, Americans' most everyday encounters with the natural world take place through mass-produced culture. Like so many Americans, I encounter scads of copies of wild nature at a daily clip—on my shelves, on walls of stores, on TV, in stores, on billboards, in magazines, on lawns. Yet "What does a pink flamingo mean?" is a question that nature writers, historians, anthropologists and K-mart shoppers alike have hardly asked. As I've dug into such questions with more method than madness, I have become ever more firmly convinced that they offer peerlessly clear insights into what Nature means and why. "There's a lesson here," as the Bayliner TV ad ends. But I do not think it is that fish—tuna, for example, that a shark is chasing—lead stress-free lives. Rather, I think it is that many Americans— and especially my affluent post–World War II generation of baby boomers—have used a vision of Nature as a not-modern Place Apart powerfully to understand, navigate, enjoy, critique and, ultimately, to evade the defining hall-marks, troubles and confusions of modern American life.

We patrol a strict boundary between Nature and not-Nature with a hefty set of desires. I think that the boundary is not just for nature-lovers, but has worked alike for people, like Woody Allen, who prefer to be "two with nature." And why we call buildings, boats and Volvos anti-Nature points to the biggest desire of all. Ultimately, I will venture, the well-off baby-boomers have used a very American idea of a Nature Out There to ignore our ravenous uses of natural resources. If I don't think of a Volvo as nature, then can't I buy and drive it *to* Nature without thinking very hard about how I use, alter, destroy, and consume nature? As a group, the affluent baby boomers have been hungry in equal measure for Nature as Meaning and nature as resources. I think we want to save our souls from consumerism, and from the sins and costs of modernity, but at the very same time, we want to enjoy all of modern life's social and economic benefits fully. These exacting desires, and the messy contradictions, stay mostly undercover. Yet TV ads and the Mall of America are unusually good places to look for them—exactly because in these places, such as the Volvo TV ad, we define Nature as a Place Apart but also so obviously and rabidly consume. Wilderness areas, hiking trails, ranches and farms: the places where American nature writers have commonly gone to ex-amine Americans' connections to nature are, I'll argue, actu-

BAYLINER TV AD

ally harder to read. Even urban parks and backyard gardens yield our secrets with more hesitance.

In any society, visions of the connections between what's human and what's not human are basic and powerful guides with which people navigate the social and ecological world around them. Americans have long deployed a Nature Out There as a basic and meaningful conceptual map. After the 1950s, baby boomers adapted Nature to their own desires, and used it enthusiastically to canoe through the postwar era—but we hardly invented it. So I begin with two origin stories: in the 1870s and 1880s, the astounding extinction of the billions-strong passenger pigeon flocks testified dramatically to the destructive potential of fast-expanding markets; and in the late 1890s, the vehement campaign that the first Audubon Societies waged against the fashions of stuffed birds on women's hats set the cornerstone for both modern conservation and a twentieth-century nature-lover tradition. The first story charts the history of a destructive hunger for resources, and the second the history of a fierce quest to make nature meaningful. As the third of the five essays—at the book's physical, chronological and interrogative center— I have planted a brief history of the plastic flamingo, because I am now convinced that the checkered postwar chronicle of the infamous pink lawn creature speaks more forcefully than most any other thing, person or text about the powerful definition of Nature as a Place Apart. These three histories in turn suggest how and why we got to where we are in the 1990s: a decade and zeitgeist in which nature stores hawk Ansel Adams calendars and inflatable penguins in mothership shopping malls, and multimillion-dollar boat companies advertise yachts on TV using New Age guitar music and no-stress fish who commit no crimes and never divorce.

Can a Volvo, even an All-Wheel Drive, save my soul? Most of us, even Volvo lovers, have to doubt it. But neither will the powerful conviction that nature is a Place Out There, and all that is not modern. The American nature-writing tradition is inquisitive, reverent, skeptical of modernity, respectful of details and deeply American. I have been searching for real meanings in the natural world. I wish fervently to discover and strengthen my connections in an era when they feel so tenuous—and to sort out a critique of modern life and its alienations. I have meditated wholeheartedly on pigeon pies, warblers on women's hats, *Dr. Quinn, Medicine Woman* and the dire fickleness of lawn-ornament fads. I have traveled also through Andy Warhol prints, turn-of-the-century hat shops and the nation's largest shopping malls in an effort to arrive at useful meanings, reestablished connections and honest desires. The travels have been at once unsettling and reassuring. The details have been consistently wondrous.

MISSED CONNECTIONS
ᝆ THE PASSENGER PIGEON ᝆ
EXTINCTION

They say that when a flock of passenger pigeons flew across the countryside, the sky grew dark. The air rumbled and turned cold. Bird dung fell like hail. Horses stopped and trembled in their tracks, and chickens went in to roost. "I was suddenly struck with astonishment at a loud rushing roar, succeeded by instant darkness," the ornithologist Alexander Wilson wrote after he encountered a pigeon flock along the Ohio River in the early 1800s: "I took [it] for a tornado, about to overwhelm the house and everything around in destruction." Wilson sat down to watch the flock pass over, and after five hours, he estimated that it had been 240 miles long and numbered over two billion birds.

Since the extinction of the passenger pigeon in 1914—which would seem nearly as astonishing as the flocks themselves—Americans' collective memory of the species

SHOOTING PIGEONS IN IOWA
from *Leslie's Illustrated Newspaper,* 1867

has grown vague. We tend to confuse the birds with the domestic carrier pigeons, still very much in existence, that served as messengers during the two world wars. The passenger pigeon, or "wild pigeon," looked like a large mourning dove, and ranged across the eastern half of the continent from Quebec to Texas. It did not perform feats of heroism in wartime, but by all accounts was hard to miss, and was one of North America's more riveting natural wonders. In 1831, John Jay Audubon wrote about a forty-mile-wide pigeon roost he had seen in Kentucky. "Some persons have thought fit to consider my account of this species as fabulous," he defended himself several years later, "[but I] could easily have obtained corroborative statements." Like Audubon, many chroniclers claim they had witnesses. Others claim sobriety. Some refuse to try: "too strange to describe"; "beyond the power of this pencil to portray." A typical wild-pigeon roost blanketed hundreds of square miles of forest. The underbrush died, the trees were entirely denuded of their leaves, dung piled up inches deep, and century-old trees keeled over under the cumulative weight of the nine-ounce birds.

We know the exact day of the extinction: the last passenger pigeon died on September 1, 1914, in the Cincinnati Zoo. The last of seven captive birds, she was named Martha. In the wild, however, the species was effectively extinct by 1900. The number of birds had declined rapidly, almost in an instant, from billions in the 1870s to dozens in the 1890s. *What happened?* At the time, people weren't exactly sure. In fact, many refused to believe it: thirdhand reports circulated that ship captains had spied the flocks over the Gulf of Mexico, and there were putative sightings in Chile, Bolivia and along the coast of Russia. "They went as a cannon-ball is dropped into the ocean," the game dealer Edward Martin wrote, still mystified in July 1914, "now in plain sight, then a splash, a circle of ripples—and nothing." It was "as if the earth had swallowed them."

Others charged angrily that game dealers and commercial hunters such as Martin had destroyed the pigeons. Since the 1860s, as the rapid westward expansion of rail lines linked the still-rich game haunts of the rural Midwest to fast-burgeoning eastern cities, market hunters had been harvesting game in unprecedented numbers. By all accounts delectable, pigeons were also the target of choice in the newly popular sport of trap shooting. As market hunters cleared the game birds of the Midwest literally county by county, the pigeon hunts became notorious: at a famous 1874 nesting in western Michigan, four hundred market hunters shipped out twenty-five thousand pigeons every day for five to six weeks. By 1890 the game business had driven eskimo curlew, golden plover and other species to the brink of extinction. Buffalo herds vanished exactly in these decades, and their sudden decline met with the same disbelief: surely the enormous herds must have fled to Canada or other more hospitable climes. The bison, we know, never left the Great Plains in any numbers. And the passenger pigeon would never recover. "No other bird," the naturalist John Muir waxed nostalgic in 1913, "had seemed to us so wonderful." The next year Martha died, and she was taken to the Cincinnati Ice Company, frozen in a three-hundred-pound block of ice, and shipped to the Smithsonian. And while Edward Martin still harbored a faint hope that some birds might "yet be hidden in the vast forests of the Amazon," the extinction finally persuaded many Americans that the continent's wildlife was finite and that much of it had been destroyed.

An extraordinarily active posthumous phase of the pigeons' history had already begun. My choice of the story of this extinction to launch a wide-ranging inquiry into Americans' connections to nature follows a well-established tradition. By 1900, American conservationists had already begun to invoke the loss of the pigeon flocks as one of our most devastating encounters with nature. The birds' disappearance fueled a reckoning, an inquiry. After 1914, a stream of essays, histories, children's books and novels about these birds would appear—and the stories continue, because the wild pigeons, if they are congregating at the South Pole, waiting for us to reform our ways, still haven't returned. Civic groups have erected monuments to the pigeons in Michigan, Wisconsin and Pennsylvania. "No living man," Aldo Leopold wrote in 1949 in *A Sand County Almanac*—the post–World War II environmentalist bible—"will see again the onrushing phalanx of victorious birds, sweeping a path for spring across the March skies."

What happened? We will never know the exact causes. Hunting, deforestation and disease have been the preeminent theories—in that order. With the hindsight of ecological science, we do know that the very species that look most inalterably abundant—the great auk, the Carolina parakeet, the passenger pigeon—can in fact be unusually vulnerable to population declines, since the enormous groups in which they live are so often essential to their survival. Hunting may have driven these flocks below a minimum population threshold—in combination, perhaps, with disease or the destruction of forest habitat.

Still, the postmortem on wild pigeons not surprisingly has focused not on their biological weak points but rather on *us.* As the refrain of a 1973 folk song asks, "God, what were we thinking?" What we *do* know is that in the late-nineteenth century Americans' encounters with nature changed. As urban populations exploded, the economic uses of natural resources increased exponentially, and the destruction of game species became a bellwether for our ties to nature in the coming century. Extinction stories beg naturally for morals—even for the dinosaurs: were they overconfident? too carnivorous?—and the passenger pigeon has been the most spectacular modern extinction. Leopold wrote his elegy to the species for the 1947 dedication of a monument to Wisconsin's last pigeon. The stone lies in Wyalusing State Park, just south of the site of the great 1871 nesting—seventy-five miles long, where the game business had shipped out 1.5 million birds—and the plaque condenses the standard moral of this story into a single sentence: "This species became extinct through the avarice and thoughtlessness of man."

My own version is longer. Who exactly drove the pigeons to ruin? What were their *specific* motives? To find the meaning in the extinction, I haven't looked for timeless human failings such as "man's avarice." Rather, I've looked at Americans' fast-changing connections to the wild natural world, as urban populations exploded and market networks grew rapidly more complex. Above all, in pursuit of my own question—"What does nature mean to me?"—I've looked for the changing meanings of passenger pigeons in people's lives. Before the extinction, what did the pigeons mean: what did people do with pigeons, and say about them? What did the flocks mean in the 1870s and 1880s? And what did they mean after?

To get to the moral you have to go back to the fable, to the once upon a time, to tales about everyday life. In the 1870s, market hunters were netting pigeons in Wisconsin. Farmers were leaving their fields to work for the hunters. Sportsmen in Chicago were signing up to compete in weekend trap shoots. People were shopping for pigeons in the outdoor markets in New York City, and chefs at restaurants like Delmonico's were deciding which vegetables to serve with pigeons and how to prepare the sauce. The sky was dark. The air was rumbling. What were these people thinking?

Pigeon Years

In the early 1700s, when pigeon flocks flew over Philadelphia, Americans were climbing onto the rooftops with sticks and knocking the birds out of the sky. For people who preferred to use guns, pigeon shooting was particularly fine just west of Broad Street. By 1720, city officials had legislated a fine of five shillings for shooting pigeons in the streets. In 1727, Quebec authorities passed a similar act

> because . . . everyone takes the liberty of shooting from his windows the threshold of his door the middle of the streets without thinking of the passer-by the old people the children who cannot take shelter . . . from the danger to which they are exposed by . . . people of whom the greater part know nothing about the handling of guns.

Little expertise was required, however, since a shot into the sky generally brought down enough meat for dinner. The Quebec ordinance also made leaving work to shoot pigeons a criminal act. During one pigeon flight in 1821, the constable in colonial Toronto arrested lawyers, the sheriff, and much of the town council before he gave up and proclaimed open season in the town square.

When pigeons flew over settlements, people followed. Fields tended to lose their farmers, shops their shopkeepers and schools their children. "Here they come!" the Kentucky settlers around Audubon had cried. Where pigeons nested and roosted, hundreds of people converged on the site, which was not entirely a safe thing to do. The overhead flocks precipitated a mixed hail of dung, branches, whole trees and bludgeoned birds. The uproar, like a "hard gale at sea," rendered inaudible the firing of one's own shotgun. Depending on the season and local custom, American colonists shot pigeons, netted them, knocked them down with sticks, ignited pots of sulfur beneath them, or chopped down trees stacked with eighty or a hundred nests apiece. In Tennessee, settlers set fire to the nest trees and returned later to gather up the squabs, the young pigeons, that had toppled to the ground, roasted alive.

Pigeons didn't show up near any one settlement very often. Foraging for the heaviest crops of seeds and nuts, especially beechnuts and acorns, the flocks migrated up through the northern colonies in the spring to nest, and back south in the fall. In most beech and oak species, a stand of trees produces a bumper crop every two to ten years. Around Niagara in the 1700s, the flocks came every seven or eight years, and the settlers called these "pigeon years." For weeks, pigeons glutted the town markets. The colonists broiled and roasted pigeons, stewed them in gravy and jellied them in a calf's-foot broth. They salted the birds away in barrels for the winter. Eventually people would long for feathers and the stench of poultry to lift from the air, but for a while the pigeons provoked spontaneous revelry in the streets. When the English traveler Andrew Burnaby arrived in Newport in autumn 1759, and could find hardly any fare at the taverns besides pigeon, he had stumbled upon a "pigeon year" in southern Rhode Island. Above all, colonists made pigeon pot pies. After the extinction many former pigeon hunters would reminisce about pot pie with as much regret and fondness as for the birds themselves. A good pot pie had five or six pigeons inside, and stuck in the middle, "three feet nicely cleaned, to show what pie it is."

What were colonists thinking? What exactly did pigeons mean? In retrospect, environmentalists often have pinned the later devastations of game animals to a utilitarian, Judeo-Christian view of nature that European immigrants brought to New World lands; and I agree, the colonists thought of the pigeons as useful to humans and as economic resources. The first English reports on New World landscapes in the 1600s read a lot like marketing lists. In the case of game, the rough, muddy colonial roads (English travelers complained endlessly about potholes) kept the early markets small and local—pigeons jostling in the back of a wagon for two days would make better compost than pie—though even by the mid-1600s, the very first generation of colonists had destroyed game populations near the large settlements. Yet there were farmers, shopkeepers, boys and girls who were thinking about nothing *but* pigeons for weeks at a time. The colonists appreciated pigeons in other ways, too. They valued the wildlife and lands around them for many reasons at once. Wild pigeons were economic resources to shoot and eat and to sell. They were also a natural wonder, and an occasion for celebration.

In fact, the wild pigeons fueled the widely shared conviction that Americans could never deplete their resources. While in the 1990s, that logic may be hard to grasp, colonists perhaps would have had to summon even greater imaginative powers to envision the comparatively empty, devastated landscapes that have become so familiar to us. Six-foot lobsters in the surf, rivers swarming with salmon and covered with ducks, woods "abounding with deer, and the trees with singing birds": the abundance of North American wildlife in the 1600s and early 1700s sounds almost as biblical today as it must have seemed to European settlers (with decidedly more biblical turns of mind) who left behind Old World lands that had been overhunted for centuries, and where the upper classes held game preserves under strict control. While even the first settlers depended primarily on domestic European crops and livestock, they supplemented freely with wild game. Occasionally, when the crops failed due to drought or an early freeze, colonists relied on hunting as an essential stopgap. Reports to England seldom failed to mention the free and abundant game, or the wild pigeons: "I have seen them fly as if the airy regiment had been pigeons, seeing neither beginning or ending, length or breadth of these millions of millions."

To shoot and eat a game bird in the American colonies became a defining New World act. Think of Thomas Morton in Massachusetts in the 1620s, reporting back that he had seen a thousand geese "before the mouth of my gun," and had fed his "dogs with as fat geese there as I have ever fed upon myself in England." The geese were American. So was their easy abundance, their impressive lard-to-bone ratio, their frequent presence on the table, and not least, one's freely held, unregulated right to shoot them. Going off to shoot pigeons or geese, and hauling strings of them back home, became activities resonant with one's experience of daily American life. The hunt meant so much more than mere utilitarian gain. To go hunting was to tap into the continent's bounty, to supplement the table, to exercise your skill with a shotgun, perhaps to band together with neighbors after plowing. You also expressed your rights or ideals in a fledgling polity. Hunting was at once an ecological, economic and political thing to do, a social event and a sport. It was like telling a story to yourself, *about* yourself. Not actually a story told out loud: the hunt was more a cultural play, a story acted out in the course of day to day living, about your relationships to birds but also to one another—a story about where you lived, who your neighbors were, how you made a living and what you believed. In the course of their encounters with pigeons—as they invested nature with small worlds of meaning—people were also doing a great deal of thinking about themselves.

You could make especially emphatic meanings with pigeons. A waterfowl hunt brought together a few neighbors, but a pigeon hunt, which mobilized an entire county, enacted a more powerfully meaningful story about the social ties that knit these rural communities together. Likewise, to bag "thirty, forty, and fifty pigeons at a shot" was practically to caricature your political claims to American game. And if settlers relied on other game animals during lean times, the pigeon hunts, when necessary, enacted a more dramatic cultural play about the weak points of the colonial economy: in 1769, during a widespread crop failure in Vermont, pigeons staved off starvation for thirty thousand people for six weeks. Above all, more than any other piece of the New World, pigeon flocks symbolized the continent's natural bounty. The salmon, geese and lobsters inspired believe-it-or-not reports, but the pigeons' abundance seemed quite literally biblical, like "the quails that fell round the camp of Israel in the wilderness." Eventually the pigeons' disappearance would symbolize Americans' rapid conversion of a landscape of abundance into one of scarcity. The pigeons would narrate that story with special effectiveness, too.

Pigeon Years Every *Year*

In the seventeenth and eighteenth centuries, European settlers were just one of many human groups who encountered pigeons. Until the late 1700s, colonists inhabited far smaller regions of eastern North America than did Native Americans. Some if not all indigenous societies east of the plains used wild pigeons intensively, and thought about them deeply. And some parts of the nonhuman natural world, no matter the humans, seem inevitably to carry unusual doses of meaning. The Senecas, of what is now western New York and

Pennsylvania, have left the best historical record as pigeon hunters. In Seneca legend,

> a white pigeon once flew into the forest lodge of a noted old man, the Wild Cat. White Pigeon informed the old man that all the various tribes of birds had held a council at which it had been decided that the wild pigeons should furnish a tribute to mankind, because their Maker had selected the wild pigeons for this important duty.

Like the colonists, Senecas believed that pigeons were put on earth for humans to use. Yet their stories and worlds of meaning were different, and apparently more sustainable: pigeon flocks had been nesting on Seneca grounds for hundreds of years. The group's history dates to at least A.D. 900, and pigeon bones have been found at archaeological sites.

An Iroquoian group, the Senecas were major parties in the 1700s to the warfare among the British, French, Iroquois and Americans. Of the many white captives they adopted, a few—such as Horatio Jones, who was captured as a teenager—recounted the pigeon hunts in memoirs, or "captivity narratives," that became an early-American literary craze. One spring, around 1782, a runner arrived in a village on the Allegheny River, shouting, "Pigeons, pigeons!" "All was now bustle and confusion," Jones remembered, "and every person . . . at once set out" on a two-day trip north to a pigeon nesting on the Genesee River. As Seneca bands from all over converged on the site, they built huts to "[afford] a fair shelter" for several weeks. The men chopped down small trees—toppling squabs so stuffed with beechnuts that the young birds occasionally exploded on impact—and women and children either bludgeoned the squabs, pinched their heads at the temples or wrung their necks. "It was a festival season," Jones would write, "and even the meanest dog in camp had his fill of pigeon meat." Senecas boiled pigeons and stewed them. They dried the birds in smoke and packed away thousands in bags and baskets. Sometimes they served them in bunches of a half dozen, tied together by the necks and with the bills pointing out—perhaps, as the colonists did with pot pies, to show what kind of dish it was?

At first glance, these events appear remarkably similar in act, method and meaning to pigeon years in the colonies. Senecas killed uncountable numbers of birds, using expedient methods. They ate and thought about nothing but pigeons for weeks, and enjoyed it immensely. A pigeon hunt was a large-scale social affair—not like the fall deer hunt or the maple harvest in early spring, when the clans split into families. In fact, the Senecas sometimes used "pigeon time" to conduct tribalwide business, such as the allotment of planting grounds to clans. In the evenings, people gathered to sing, dance and tell tales. Horatio Jones arranged his own marriage at a pigeon nesting. Hunting pigeons was much more than the simple act of killing and eating pigeons. In Seneca society, too, the hunt was a featured economic, social and political event.

In the long view, the hunt and its meanings look very different. Senecas dispatched scouts to find a nesting every single year, while colonists hunted pigeons only when the flocks happened to fly near. The clans hunted for a few specific weeks, in the spring, when the squabs fledged. And Senecas never killed adult birds. As White Pigeon had emphasized to Wild Cat, "*young pigeons* were to be taken in the proper season"—an injunction that, whether intentional or not, encouraged Senecas to keep the adult breeding population intact. The pigeon hunt was part of the Senecas' annual subsistence cycle. The nestings occurred at a critical time of year, after maple sugar harvest and before planting, when winter grain stores were depleted or scarce. For Senecas and colonists alike, a pigeon hunt enacted stories about everyday life. The Senecas' hunts, however, narrated a different economic livelihood, of traveling across watersheds to exploit seasonal wild resources. Seneca pigeon time was shorter, regular, predictable, vital.

According to tales the clans retold in the evenings, they had

learned these songs . . . from a superior people [the pigeons] and so we must cherish this ceremony. We have learned, too, that in dancing we must always make the circuit of the fires in one certain direction, namely, from the right toward the left.

Downstream along the Hudson River, colonists were swapping tales about how many birds they'd killed with one shot.

The Senecas were playing too, but they were playing by rules. Like the daytime hunting frenzy, the nightly revelry was more deliberate: if the pigeons had been put on earth for humans to use, and agreed to this destiny, the people owed these songs and dances in return. The colonists' stories showed no such restraint. Pigeons, pigeon killing and pigeon revelry all contributed critically to making the Seneca world work as it should. To the settlers, pigeons meant many things, but in the colonial world of markets, towns and farms, game birds served no absolutely vital economic, spiritual, social or political purpose: in eighteenth-century cookbooks, you can find many more recipes for chicken.

To say Indians historically were more "connected" to nature has become a truism—as if somehow, after European conquest, the continent of North America lost its meaningfulness, like steam into the desert air after a hard rain. Yet colonists made the nonhuman world around them highly meaningful. Both societies used pigeons intensively. Both put pigeons to human purposes and valued them through human eyes, whether stewing birds, selling them or enacting and enjoying the pigeon hunts as an understanding, or story, about the ties to people and to nature that knit that world together. All humans are connected to nature: white Americans, like all people, have always made nature meaningful. What changes is not the fact of connection, or the amount of meaning, but the content of each. European immigrants brought utilitarian markets, that would encourage overintensive use of resources; in the 1800s, Senecas, too, would participate in the pigeon and game markets. Regardless, people's connections to specific wild resources were not essential. As the webs of varied meanings reflected, the colonists' ties to pigeons were expendable.

An Almighty Dollar a Dozen

In the 1780s and 1790s, the Iroquois, who had allied themselves with the British during the Revolution, ceded much of their land in treaties with the new American states. As early as the 1750s, pigeons already had become scarce on the eastern seaboard. New and improved roads, canals and eventually railroad lines rapidly expanded the markets west. Game depletions followed in the wake of new transport routes. And the meanings of wild pigeons changed as market hunters and urban consumers encountered pigeons, too. In the early 1800s, market hunters shipped passenger pigeons from upstate New York on schooners down the Hudson River. In the 1840s, hunters shipped wagonloads of pigeons to New York City over the new Newburgh and Coehecton Turnpike, across former Seneca lands. As late as 1833, settlers with pigeon fever were shooting at flocks in Chicago's mud streets, and as late as 1864, the citizens of St. Paul were brazenly ignoring laws against the discharge of firearms in the center of town. By 1870, however, the only wild pigeons in Chicago, New York or St. Paul were piled in the stalls of outdoor city markets, shipped by rail from the last region where large flocks still nested, in the still extensive forests of the northern Midwest.

Pigeon fever erupted in Sauk County, Wisconsin, late in April 1871. Also in Columbia, Juneau, Adams, Monroe and Jackson counties. The pigeons nested across a swath of southern Wisconsin ten to twelve miles wide and roughly seventy-five miles long, from the oak groves of Black River Falls to the dells of Baraboo. "Never in the history of the La Crosse Valley," reported the newspaper in Sparta, on the nesting's northern edge, "were such myriads of pigeons seen, making the whole valley resound with the noise." Near Kilbourn, on the southern edge, "a stranger would have thought it about war-time. . . . [everyone] had a gun or wanted to borrow one." One merchant sold over sixteen tons of shot. The La Crosse Valley had entered pigeon time.

The Milwaukee–St. Paul Railway had extended its lines to Kilbourn in 1857, Sparta in 1858, and Black River Falls in 1870. "Hardly a train arrives," the *Wisconsin Mirror* reported, "that does not bring hunters or trappers. . . . Pigeons are shipped to all places on the railroad, and to Milwaukee, Chicago, St. Louis, Cincinnati, Philadelphia, New York and Boston." Pigeons were selling for fifty cents a dozen in Milwaukee, and two dollars in New York. By 1870, as the swiftly expanding game business made market hunting a feasible (if difficult) career, hundreds of specialized "pigeoners" were tracking pigeon flocks through the Midwest. At the La Crosse Valley nesting, the pigeoners hired local farmers to drive wagons and hunt. They shipped pigeons in ice to game dealers in the cities, and sent live birds to sporting clubs for trap shoots: they stayed up all night hammering together barrels. When the squabs fledged, they snapped off the heads and loaded the fat bodies into wagons. They filled the express trains to capacity and made special arrangements to ship the birds east on midnight freight trains. Packing pigeons thirty dozen to the barrel, they shipped more than twenty barrels daily from each of half a dozen stops on the railway line.

A pigeon hunt was still a sociable event. The flocks still drew huge crowds and provoked a single-minded massive frenzy. Over one hundred thousand people—roughly equal to the resident population of the six counties—converged on the valley. Farmers were still stuffing pigeons into pot pies—although it was "no longer fashionable to have the feet of the pigeons sticking out of the slit in the top of the paste" (according to one Philadelphia cookbook, but the new rules may not have achieved hegemony yet in the rural Midwest). However, the varied meanings of the pigeons had changed. In the evenings, there must have been fewer conversations about pot pie, and far more about wholesale prices, railway express charges and daily rates for wagons. By 1871, the meanings of pigeon fever centered squarely on money.

Money: twentieth-century laments have made it the chief culprit. These scenes of market hunting in the Midwest quickly became the cause and meaning, the root and moral center of the extinction. In 1907, the sportsman William Mershon bitterly blamed the demise of wild pigeons on "the greed of man and the pursuit of the almighty dollar." Sponsors of the 1947 monument to Wisconsin's last passenger pigeon —"the avarice and thoughtlessness of man"—sited the stone strategically just south of the La Crosse Valley. In fact, while the 1871 nesting was one of the first nestings in the northern Midwest that hunters tapped as vast cash faucets, an 1878 nesting in Emmett County, Michigan, just south of the remote upper peninsula, would be the very last, before the flocks vanished. But "the greed of man"? Pigeons still meant far more than economic gain. And the meaningful reasons people convert birds into cash are far more varied and complex.

As money, what did pigeons mean? In Sauk County in 1871, the "almighty dollar" was more almighty than many of the local farmers, for their part, would have liked. Since the 1850s, declining soil fertility across southern Wisconsin had diminished the viability of wheat as the area's staple crop. Amid statewide ventures to diversify in the 1860s—Wisconsin dairies emerged from this crisis—farmers in Sauk County had tried planting hops, just when the hop louse devastated hop fields in the East, and few Americans wanted to go without beer. Kilbourn, the county seat, flourished as the world's center for hops production—until 1868, when the hop louse arrived and ruined hundreds of farmers, many of whom in their enthusiasm (and greed?) had failed to reserve even an acre of land to raise grain for personal use. While settlers in the 1700s had feared disastrous crop failures as a danger to subsistence, most of these local Wisconsin pigeon hunters feared the dangerously volatile markets. For Sauk County farmers, as for all people, to hunt pigeons was to play out an understanding of one's time and place—and one's role in the world—and the market hunts told a story most effectively about the uncertainties of the cash-based economy in which most farmers were now firmly enmeshed. After the Civil War, as new rail lines connected rural counties to large eastern markets, farmers all over the Midwest were diving deeply into debt to invest in new machinery to boost production, and many lost their gambles in market crashes such as the Panic of 1873. The wild pigeon hunts, of course, told the story even more emphatically. "Altogether," sighed the editor of the *Sparta Herald,* "it seems likely that we can 'live on pigeon pies' for a while, whether we are able to 'read our title clear,' or not." When the pigeons arrived as plentiful and well-timed as manna during a severe agricultural depression, they made dramatically obvious the opportunities and drawbacks of being a market player.

As for the pigeoners, the itinerant hunters, these men pursued livelihoods that were even more precarious. Hunters were the least-well-paid players in the game business, which was not hugely profitable to begin with. During other seasons, they hired out as farmhands or pork packers. Men who hunted for a living were traditionally scorned as lower-class layabouts who eschewed steady work. According to H. Clay Merritt, a very industrious hunter who personally cleaned out entire midwestern counties, this reputation was undeserved. But Merritt and his colleagues didn't eschew money, either, and compared to most game species, pigeons were like cash that grew on trees. Pigeons were what hops had been to the farmers—closer to the main chance than you usually could get. Of the stories embedded in full-time market hunting, the pigeon tales may have been especially gratifying to enact.

Without doubt, avarice had something to do with the fortunes, and the meanings of the pigeon hunts, in the La Crosse Valley in 1871—but the pursuit of money was not powered solely by greed. As money, the pigeons still meant many things. They were still expendable—even more so, as a commodity interchangeable with every other. In these webs of meaning, however, the meaning of every pigeon had changed. In the 1700s, colonists had turned pigeons into pie, soup and feather pillows. But in the 1870s, people converted the birds into cash. And they converted the cash into seed, plows, shotguns and powder. On May 18, 1871, the Juneau County newspaper, the *Mauston Star*, with notices for six foreclosure sales, ran advertisements for land, flour, feed, wagons, saddles, milling, boots, shoes, threshing machines, feed grinders, wallpaper, pianos, tobacco, fly killer, gargling oil, Dr. Crook's Wine of Tar, coffins, fire insurance and pain-free dental work—to name just a few things the pigeons might have meant or become that day.

What were people thinking? There is a world of difference between thinking of a pigeon as pigeon pie and thinking of it as cash or a plow. You could convert any game bird, like any crop or pig or deer or bucket of milk, into a plow. As cash, the value of a wild pigeon had become more abstract. The bird and its meaning had lost some uniqueness—and the pigeons, if anything, had always meant something highly unique. As the writer Leah Hager Cohen has described commodification: We "strip objects . . . bare of their original identities," and "find we *can* compare apples and oranges." Market players disconnected the meaning of a pigeon from many specifics of a pigeon—the bird's habits, its taste. That pigeon, you could say, lost some of its "pigeonness." At the scenes of the market hunts, as people converted pigeons to cash, they invested the pigeons with meanings that did not say much specifically about the birds themselves.

Urban Character

As La Crosse Valley pigeons traveled to New York City, the disconnections of meaning only multiplied. Since 1914—as the infamous scenes of the market hunts were cemented in American memory in books, songs and stone—the trap shooters and restaurant goers at the other end of the rail line have drawn scant attention. Yet a quieter, more urban, still abundant set of encounters lies behind the extinction. The urban consumers were thinking about pigeons, too.

Trap shooting—a sport in which contestants shoot at targets launched into the air—began in England in the late-eighteenth century and arrived in the States by the 1830s. The first American sportsmen used tame or wild pigeons, in fact anything aloft in North America in sizable numbers, whether quail, starlings, pigeons or bats. Wild pigeons quickly became the preferred target. The contestants shot pigeons from "ground traps" that simply set the birds free, or "plunge

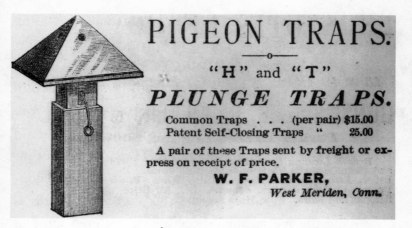

ADVERTISEMENT
in A. H. Bogardus, *Field, Cover, and Trap Shooting,* 1874

traps" that sprung the birds into the air. Match rules specified the distance between shooters and traps, and the number of birds to shoot at. The sport still has adherents (today's clay disk targets are called "clay pigeons"), but its heyday, in the 1870s and early 1880s, coincided exactly with the last great pigeon nestings in the northern Midwest.

By 1871, shooting matches were common weekend entertainment at sporting clubs and fairgrounds throughout the country. Without question, hundreds of thousands of pigeons (or more) from the 1871 nesting in southern Wisconsin became targets, though it can be tricky to guess exactly which birds went where. In late April, shooters competed in cities including Buffalo, Toledo, Milwaukee and Washington, D.C. When E. Osborn, a major Chicago game dealer, shipped orders to New York and Boston by rail from Tomah, one stop down the line from Sparta, some may have gone to the New York State Sportsmen's Association, which received 10,800 birds for shooting matches at its annual May convention in Utica. "The shooting was capital," reported the New York City sporting journal *Spirit of the Times*, whose coverage of the convention focused on the moves of sportsmen, not pigeons. The "most intense and exciting" events were the double-bird shoot—in which contestants shot at two birds at once—and the special final shoot, which featured some of the country's best marksmen, including the new national champion Captain Adam H. Bogardus.

Bogardus, from Chicago, had erupted onto the midwestern shooting scene in the late 1860s by winning a match in which he shot at his traps from a speeding buggy drawn by galloping horses. In 1869, he won a wager that he could shoot five hundred birds in eleven hours—which he did with two hours to spare—and became the first trap shooter to hit one hundred consecutive pigeons. In 1870, after defeating a Chicago shooter who had challenged "any man in Illinois," Bogardus moved on to compete within the eastern shooting fraternity and captured the national trophy just days before the Utica convention. At this point, he was issuing regular challenges in the sporting journals:

> I hereby challenge any man in the world to shoot a match at pigeons—A.H.B. (*Turf, Field, and Farm*)

ADVERTISEMENTS IN *Chicago Field*
(above) 1877, (below) 1875

While no man stepped forward from any of the larger continents, he defended his title successfully through the rest of the decade. He was "a champion of champions, willing to shoot anywhere," a competitor would recall, "at pigeons, blackbirds, snowbirds, blocks of wood, glass balls, anything so it was in the air and moving."

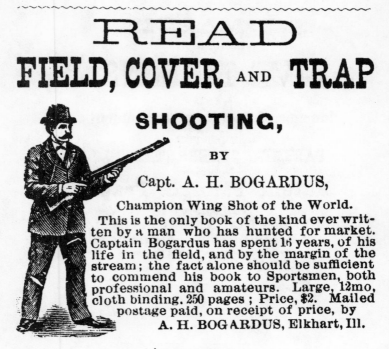

READ
FIELD, COVER AND TRAP
SHOOTING,

BY

Capt. A. H. BOGARDUS,

Champion Wing Shot of the World.
This is the only book of the kind ever written by a man who has hunted for market.
Captain Bogardus has spent 16 years, of his
life in the field, and by the margin of the
stream; the fact alone should be sufficient
to commend his book to Sportsmen, both
professional and amateurs. Large, 12mo,
cloth binding, 250 pages ; Price, $2. Mailed
postage paid, on receipt of price, by
A. H. BOGARDUS, Elkhart, Ill.

ADVERTISEMENT
in *Chicago Field,* 1877

You could say Bogardus and his fellow trap shooters put a
new twist on an old American pastime of shooting pigeons
in the cities. Yet these events and their meanings look completely different and new. To begin with, the festivities were
newly exclusive. To ship live pigeons from the Midwest was
expensive. The birds cost about two dollars per dozen, and
suffered a high die-off rate: only 8,000 of the 10,800 birds
shipped to the Utica convention arrived "in good condition." A wild-pigeon shoot was the most elite form of the
trap shoot, which was itself the most elite of the target-

shooting sports. As game birds were shipped into the eastern cities, they entered the social circles—and the worlds of meaning—that could afford to pay the cost of the trip.

"Pigeon shooting . . . captivates nearly everyone who participates in it": within these circles, the meanings of the pigeon shoot by all accounts were powerful. "It would not . . . be wise," cautioned *The Dead Shot*, "to examine with too close a scrutiny the charm it possesses." To forge on nevertheless, what was the appeal, exactly? Pigeon shooting had always meant much more than killing pigeons. For the famous shooter Albert Money, nothing "[brought] out the points of a man's character more than pigeon shooting." An accomplished trap shooter was "nervy, high principled, a whole souled fellow who can be a good fellow amongst good fellows." "Perfect coolness and prompt dexterity," agreed *The Dead Shot*. "A man of cool, calm, and collected demeanor." "Character, coolness, and determination." "Both cool and cautious." Pigeon shooting, according to all the manuals, elicited and cultivated good, cool character in men. Bogardus himself, in the opinion of his editor, was a man "of the most resolute and persistent character . . .no fatigue subdued him, no misfortune disheartened him."

Not all sportsmen were comparably entranced. Many embraced field shooting as the more conducive venue for building male character: in wilder haunts, this tended not to work well with wild pigeons, which required hardly more sight than skill to shoot. And sportsmen's eloquence on the vast appeal of field sports reads somewhat differently:

Capt. Money's Position at the Traps

Captain Albert Money—
"Character, Coolness, and Determination"

The heart beats with renewed vigor, the blood courses through its usually sluggish channels with a quickened pace, and the whole animal as well as intellectual economy becomes sharpened and revivified under exciting and healthful influences.

Field shooters enthused less about coolness and more about physical vigor and self-reliance. Sportsmen's schemes for cultivating male character differed on the finer points. Still, all resonated with the anxious certainty, widely shared among late-nineteenth-century American men of money, that manhood was at once absolutely essential and critically endangered in a fast-changing social and economic era. Trap shooters, who typically were middle-class men and who competed to excel in the market economy, emphasized control and discipline. A trap shooter was "as cool as can be, and could not be moved, not if a house was to fall on him." Field sportsmen, whose chosen pastime was more expensive, hewed more to an old-wealth faith in superior breeding among the twin tides of immigrants and newly minted self-made men. And there was widespread anxiety about the end of the frontier, which Americans had long mythologized to have shored up male virility and American character in the past. Shooting pigeons had always been an act of imagination. In the 1870s and 1880s, as sportsmen made the trap shoot a popular theater in which urban American men of money met and told themselves stories about who they were, they used pigeons in their schemes.

Post-extinction, the scenes at the trap shoots—their power, their excitement, their meaning—pale next to the flockside scenes of dung-bespattered, blood-encrusted market hunters, whose philosophy of pigeon shooting invoked the self-control of a feeding frenzy. In fact, I think the trap shoot's most telling twist of meaning lies in the very absence of the flocks, from both the tournament fields and the conversations. Trap shooters, so voluble on the subjects of character and manhood, said remarkably little about the pigeons themselves. You can find scattered remarks in the manuals—"they [are] rapid fliers, full of erratic swoops and dives and better sport than the tame pigeons"—and in the tournament reports in the sporting journals: "Those that escaped the shooters . . . made a bee line from the trap close to the ground. . . . Those that flew to the right or the left of the trap were commonly killed." Contestants engaged in a modicum of discussion about the flight patterns of individual pigeons. It was exactly the wild pigeon's wily flight habits, apparently, that made it the target of choice. A challenging test of cool demeanor, the fast-flying pigeon told the trap shoot's story especially well.

An individual pigeon, though? It was a strange and novel concept in the history of human encounters with the species. At Seneca campsites and in farm counties—even at the great midwestern nestings, where market hunters converted pigeons to cash—people talked about nothing *but* the birds. The wild pigeons' phenomenal flocks, the species' most obvious fact of natural history, had always told the human stories so beautifully. And reports on pigeon shooting had once read differently:

> Imagine a thousand threshing machines accompanied
> by as many steamboats with an equal quota of R.R.
> trains passing through covered bridges and you possibly
> have a faint conception of the terrific roar following

**TO SPORTSMEN AND SHIP-
PERS OF GAME.**
AUSTIN & CO., 347, 348 AND 455
WASHINGTON MARKET, NEW YORK,
desire to call the attention of Shooters and Shippers
generally to the fact that they are dealing more especially in Snipe, Woodcock and other Western Game
(in season). Trial shipments requested. Prompt returns made on all shipments. Reference, North River
Bank, New York.   7-17-1y

ADVERTISEMENT
in *Chicago Field*, 1877

the monstrous black cloud of pigeons as they passed in
rapid flight.

An afternoon trap shoot transpired one pigeon at a time. It
was an orderly, clean and only moderately loud and celebra-
tory event. It may have been exciting, but it was definitely
not a pigeon year. Trap shooters were telling meaningful
human stories with pigeons, as people always had. But a trap
shoot wasn't really *about* pigeons at all.

Sportsmen would later deny, even, that trap shooters
played a major role in the pigeons' disappearance. As Bogardus and his acolytes shot pigeons at distant clubs and fairgrounds, they did not see the birds disappear from a nesting
flock in the northern Midwest. At a trap shoot, people who
used pigeons intensively lost track of pigeon natural history.
They also lost track of their own connections to pigeons—
and of the consequences.

BALLOTINES OF SQUABS À LA MADISON

Ballotines of Pigeons à la Madison

The city dwellers who dined on pigeons have drawn little or no attention since the extinction. Practically speaking, these scenes and their meanings are the most elusive to reconstruct. Unlike colonists, Seneca captives, market hunters, and trap shooters, in the 1870s these restaurant goers generally failed to write about their encounters. The major Chicago game dealers such as E. Osborn shipped by far the greatest numbers of pigeons to eastern game markets. Yet to find these birds demands a measure of guesswork.

To follow a squab from the La Crosse Valley to the fork of a New Yorker in May 1871, one might well begin with an eight-mile wagon ride one morning from the northwest edge of the nesting to the Sparta rail depot. The squab is packed in a barrel with ice and shipped on the 3:00 P.M. Milwaukee-St. Paul express train to Milwaukee and then south to Chicago, where the barrel is transferred to the Chicago, Burlington & MO express train to New York City. A driver for the American Merchant's Union Express picks up the barrel at Grand Central Station and delivers it to a game dealer, who has purchased the pigeons from a Chicago dealer on commission. The largest, best-stocked game stalls in New York were in the Washington and Fulton outdoor markets. Fulton Market was home to the dealer Amos E. Robbins, who supplied New York's finest restaurants, most notably Delmonico's. Each morning, Lorenzo Delmonico himself arrived at the market at 4:00 A.M. to choose the very best of the day's selection. The squab is fresh. It travels in his wagon from Fulton and South Streets up Broadway to Fourteenth Street and is unloaded in the restaurant kitchen on Fifth Avenue before 8:00 A.M.

So far the trip has taken about two days. The bird still has some distance to travel, much of it cultural, before it enters the dining rooms. It may become a "pigeon à la Lombardy," handed from one chef to another as it is cleaned and boned, simmered in wine and stock, and garnished with sweetbreads, ham, mushroom heads and a velouté sauce. Its journey takes another day, maybe two, if it becomes a "ballotine of squab à la Madison," en route to which the chefs bone it; stuff it with truffles, pork, liver, ham and pistachios; coat it with madeira; bake it in a mold; ice it with pâté and truffles; arrange it with eleven other squabs on a revolving stand, which is garnished with truffles and stuffed tomatoes, topped with a vase of cut vegetables, and set onto a stand made of wax and veal fat molded into the shapes of shells and griffons; and decorate it with larkskins filled with pâté, mushrooms stuffed with foie gras, and glazed truffles and jellied tongue.

Fine dining had arrived on the American scene. In the early 1800s, pigeon recipes had been simple how-to affairs:

> For a pie, cover each pigeon with a piece of fat bacon
> to keep them moist. Season as usual, and put eggs.

And places to eat, called "eating houses," differed little from the eighteenth-century taverns that the English traveler Andrew Burnaby had found in Newport, where the proprietors served the dish of the day and little else. English travelers in the colonies complained as much about the food as the roads. What we define as restaurants, with written menus and separate tables, cropped up in the 1830s in eastern cities. By the 1850s, elegant new hotels in New York City were adopting the menus and precision sauces of French cuisine. Chefs ordered game birds—which had been scarce in New York since the early 1800s, when the eastern countryside was hunted out—to pepper these new menus generously. An Everyman food in the country, game from the Midwest became a shipped-in delicacy in distant cities. Like live pigeons sent to the sporting clubs for trap shoots, the birds therefore were swirled away into the wealthier social circles, which consumed them by the Chicago, Burlington & MO trainload. A regulation-size French dinner consisted of ten to twelve courses, many of which featured game dishes and included a separate roast-game course, after the sherbet.

No establishment was more intrinsic to the rise of fine dining in this country than Delmonico's. The original two Delmonico brothers nearly single-handedly introduced restaurant protocol and the French language to American eating with a small café in 1832. For thirty years, they set the trends for a growing cadre of competitors. For the next thirty years, after the Civil War, they dominated the field. In the 1870s, while the pigeon business enjoyed its own glory days in the Midwest and Bogardus challenged the world's men, Delmonico's operated out of the four-story mansion on Fourteenth Street and Fifth Avenue, and then, after 1876, beneficently bedecked five-story quarters on Fifth Avenue and Twenty-sixth Street, within five blocks of a half dozen of New York's finest hotels. The scenes that transpired at these two sites were peopled by an extraordinary number of the well-born and famous. Presidents past, present and future ate there, as did most of Tammany Hall. General Grant ate "ballotines de pigeons" there in March 1873, and Governor Tilden dined on "cotelettes de pigeonneaux Signora" in July 1876. Mark Twain, William Dean Howells and most of the New York literati frequented the restaurants, as did opera singers, actor Edwin Booth and the theater crowd, *New York Herald* mogul James Gordon Bennett and a good number of Bennett's cronies in the New York Yacht Club, along with much of the Ivy League, the city's leading banker August Belmont, and every nameless millionaire from the mutually repellent ranks of the old guard and the nouveau riche.

In 1871, Sorosis, the founding club of the late-nineteenth-century "woman's club" movement, held their regular luncheon meeting at Delmonico's on May 1 in a private room upstairs. Delmonico's catered an in-house dinner on May 5 for the Atalanta Boat Club, and at the end of May catered an honorific banquet for the city's chief justice, which was attended by the mayor, U.S. senators and other political luminaries. It's a fairly safe bet that Delmonico's served pigeons at one or more of these gatherings, and I'll wager on Wisconsin pigeons from the oak forests southeast of Sparta. It's impossible to know for sure: the *New York Herald*, which reported on all of these events, fails to mention the menus. The Sorosis women, we know, engaged in a group discussion of the question, When does frankness cease to be a virtue? The mayor toasted the chief justice as the "terror of evil-doers at the Tombs," and the Atalanta Boat Club members likely were talking about the upcoming annual June regatta. And as they ate through the roast game course and the rest of these meals, urban restaurant goers were telling stories to themselves about what kind of people they were. They were different, of course, in gender, political ties and favorite pastimes, but tended to be the kind of upper-class women who worried about women's virtue and public persona, and the sort of men who sailed private schooners up to Newport for the weekend. All were the sort of people who dined at Delmonico's on the trademark game dishes of haute cuisine. And not one of them expected to see pigeon feet sticking out of her ballotines à la Madison, to show what kind of dish it was.

The stories these diners told as they encountered pigeons said next to nothing about the pigeon flocks. And in contrast to the trap shoot, the individual pigeons here did not even convey the stories and their meanings especially well: if only because the birds resembled their domestic relatives in Washington Square, wild pigeons defined the lower heights of haute cuisine. In these scenes, the pigeons can be hard, really, to find at all. Assuming pigeons were there, and armed uncannily with the knowledge of which people had them, you still have to pry below layers of ham, truffles, labor-intensive sauce and wax griffons—and even then, who could identify the payload? And of course, diners at Delmonico's never personally removed the birds from the flocks before they ate roast pigeon. The wealthy restaurant goers—among the most numerous users of pigeons— would acknowledge even less responsibility for the game markets and their own encounters than the trap shooters. What were the diners thinking about pigeons? Even more germane, what were they *not* thinking? The disconnections between meanings and natural history, and meanings and uses, had become very strange and decidedly modern. Americans had converted the pigeons to cash, shipped the birds far from their oak and beech forests, and transformed them with epicurean visions. And in the course of the journey, pigeons had gone from being the most extraordinary bird on the continent—and in many people's lives—to passable, ordinary, indistinguishable.

Senecas, too, had told fantastic tales, about Wild Cat and talking pigeons. They had experienced pigeon hunts as social, political, ecological and economic narratives of their own lives. It is an intrinsically human endeavor to use one's encounters with nature to define one's place imaginatively in a particular human and natural world. We continue to do it. Americans have always done it. But until the 1800s, human narratives about pigeons were all firmly anchored to the most basic, obvious facts about the species. At the trap shoot, and even more at Delmonico's, the whole complex imaginative process was becoming detached from its natural moorings. City folks drew nature inarguably and creatively into their lives, but in the process lost track of some things about nature and about their connections to it. Americans' meaningful encounters with pigeons had become peculiarly free-flying.

Only the Oaks Will Remember

In 1880, when pigeons arrived in small numbers in western Michigan to feed on the heavy beechnut crop, the five hundred pigeoners waiting for them left to search for "the main body." The rest of the pigeons never came, and game dealers barely filled advance orders from shooting clubs. By summer, the larger tournaments were forced to substitute domestic pigeons. The tame birds, though, tended to flutter to the ground and walk away: they had always been more pedestrian flyers. By 1890, people had begun to write about pigeons in the past tense: "I have often stood in the farm-yard, gazing in rapt admiration, as the setting sun was darkened by the traveling flocks. We miss them more than any other birds." Others were more optimistic. In 1896, an Ontario resident who had not seen the species in twenty-five years spotted a flock of nine pigeons and wrote to G. C. Tremaine Ward, who had solicited reports on new sightings and replied, "we might expect to see them again, in large numbers."

The trap shooters were not willing to wait. They embarked on a quest for a more dependable target. They tried the iron "gyro pigeon" favored by English shooters; but it flew too straight, and tended not to break or even drop when hit, which left American sportsmen dissatisfied. Bogardus designed and marketed a glass ball that enjoyed popularity for a few years—particularly when "some thoughtful person filled it with feathers"—but it did not always shatter, and sprayed the grounds with broken glass when it did. The goal of all the new devices appears to have been twofold: to approximate the flight of a wild pigeon, and to let the shooter feel he had hit something. Eggs were tried before trap shooters settled on the "clay pigeon," which smashed into bits, "so nearly resembled the actual motion of the birds," and had a zero die-off rate when shipped. The men of character missed pigeons a little, but not for long. The trap shoot and its meanings, while sustained for awhile by the wily flight of the wild pigeons, didn't in the end depend on it.

Meanwhile, the market hunters were searching for substitutes for pigeons in the game bird business. Golden and upland plover proved popular among eastern epicures; eskimo curlew was especially popular, and by 1890 would be hunted to the brink of extinction. The pigeoners and game dealers must have missed the pigeons a little too, if only as a source of cash that for a brief time had been so easy to harvest. But there were other sources of cash—like most commodities, the birds were replaceable—and the wild pigeons proved no more essential than as targets at the traps. At Delmonico's, patrons may not even have noticed the pigeons were gone. While epicures predictably have left little or no record of how they reacted to the sudden absence of wild pigeons from their lives, it's a safe guess that most people simply began to order the curlew. The meanings of one's cotelette

ADVERTISEMENT
in *Clay Pigeon and Wing Shooting,* 1884

did not compel attention either to its disappearance or to one's own complicity. The pigeons, always an unassuming presence in haute cuisine, vanished from it quietly.

Farmers noticed. They had been noticing for decades, as the pigeons retreated steadily westward. The pigeons had never come every year, but when the flocks failed to come year after year, their absence was acutely felt. "Even now," William Mershon wrote,

> I fall to day-dreaming and seem to hear myself saying in those golden boyhood days: "Mother, I am going for pigeons to-morrow morning! We'll have pigeon pot-pie to-morrow."

> The sight of such immense flocks of these birds, so beautiful and so desirable for the table, made Pigeon shooting the most fascinating of all game hunting.

These paeans to pigeons, written in 1901 and 1905, joined a stream of recollections being published around the turn of the century. And while others missed the pigeon's cash value, taste or wily flight patterns—those single, fungible traits so readily furnished by curlews or clay disks—these authors lament the loss of everything about the species. In rural counties, pigeons only rarely had been deemed essential, but they had been nothing if not a phenomenon that was unique and memorable. Pigeon flocks were irreplaceable, and so were pigeon years. Rural Americans, who had done most of the hunting and had always known the pigeons best, missed both.

At first, the market hunters blamed the pigeons. The birds must have flown north, or perhaps south: they had chosen to leave. People began to report pigeon sightings in Utah, California, Mexico, Russia, near ships out over the Atlantic and on the shores of Lake Titicaca. The claimants insisted that they (or someone who knew a person they knew) had known the pigeons well and *knew* how to tell a passenger pigeon from a mourning dove. For two decades before Martha died, a collection of writings accumulated that now read as a kind of preliminary postmortem: pet theories, purported sightings, rewards announcements (all futile), the reminiscences, eulogies and protests that eulogies were premature. And the blame was flying. Many blamed "man's greed." Most of the early critics, however, fingered the market hunters more directly.

Sportsmen fired the harshest volleys. In incensed editorials in the sporting journals, they decried the market hunters as "murderous netters" who engaged in a "nefarious, inhuman, and destructive business." "It wasn't done by sportsmen," fumed William Leffingwell, a Chicago authority on field shooting: "no man having the heart of a sportsman could go into a roost of pigeons and strike down the innocent fledgeling [*sic*] with a club." Leffingwell and other sportsmen had invested deeply in the conviction that the purpose of hunting was to cultivate character, not profit. Real men shot a few birds, and shot them well—and market hunters, who shot birds the wrong way, defaulted badly on both manhood and character. Even trap shooters devolved blame onto the market hunters. Of course, all these sportsmen were the sort of men who enjoyed sufficient wealth and leisure to pay a trap-shoot entry fee, or to decamp from the city for a weekend to shoot a few birds well. In our encounters with nature, we tell stories about who we are but also who we *are not*—about social ties that divide communities as well as knit them together—and upper- and lower-class men, urban and rural, defined themselves in part by the ways they did and did not hunt. As intensive markets generated widespread wildlife declines in the 1880s, sportsmen spearheaded the attack on commercial hunters. If the conflict was about conservation, it was as much a class war.

How many pigeons had trap shooters killed? How many had Leffingwell and the sporting journal editors eaten in fine restaurants in Chicago and Manhattan? And most pertinent, in the late nineteenth century, how many urban sportsmen's livelihoods were tied to the all-out harvest of the continent's natural resources for the benefit of urban consumers whose role in the overuses of natural resources simply was less visible? Consumers' failure to see their own powerful connections to pigeons owes much to the commodification and distance that characterize modern encounters with nature. But the failure to make connections is also convenient. And convenience, too, will prove to be an enduring modern desire. Market hunters mounted only a limited defense: uneducated on average, they were less prone to write for publication. But, as the game dealer Edward Martin pointed out, the pigeoners hadn't chased the birds "until but a dozen lived, pursued these to the last pair and shouted in unholy glee, 'I've done it! I've done it! I've exterminated the pigeons!'" All these Americans maneuvered within the same economy, in which game animals, ultimately expendable, were marketed intensively and across great distances. In 1904, H. Clay Merritt, who wrote one of the very few accounts by a market hunter, surveyed the empty land-scape the hunts had left behind and chalked it up to "progress"—an idea that has hardly gone undisputed but an analysis that is more precise than "man's greed" and more tele-scopic than "heartless, unpitying men who murdered [the birds] in their babyhood."

As the pigeons disappeared, they began to take on new meanings. For many Americans, the flocks were becoming icons of the past in a time of rapid change. "Alas," as the Michigan businessman Mershon wrote in his memoir "My Boyhood Among the Pigeons," "the pigeons and the frosty morning hunts are gone, no more to return." At the turn of the century, nostalgia ran rampant among a new generation of urban professionals, who had moved into the growing cities after being raised on farms and had rapidly developed urban angst. The vanishing pigeons carried echoes of bygone times, much as later generations would rue the demise of drive-ins, radio serials and baseball without night lights and Astroturf. Shooting pigeons and making pigeon pies had been in part an understanding of a certain rural world, and onetime pigeon hunters now understood the loss of the flocks as the loss of that larger experience. What could be a more perfect or meaningful symbol? When a young Mer-shon had gone out pigeon hunting with his dogs Sport, Bob and Ranger, he'd gone off to shoot a bird that soon would be as irretrievable as his childhood.

Sightings continued. For years, the U.S. Bureau of Biological Survey (the precursor to Fish and Wildlife) sent their staff ornithologists out to chase down leads. In 1929, a pair was reported in northern Michigan; and a flock of fifteen was said to have been sighted near Indianapolis. Purported sightings and survival theories were mutually encouraging. In 1939, a *Saturday Evening Post* feature on the extinction drew "scores" of letters from readers who had sighted pigeons or heard of sightings in many places, from northern Wisconsin to Bolivia, and who proffered theories, including that the pigeons had flown to another planet. As recently as 1955, a letter in *Newsweek* proposed that the wild pigeons had interbred with the domestic birds, so that "their strain lives on in the pigeons that we see on the city streets." Who knows? Maybe some wild pigeons did fly south to Argentina or north toward the midnight sun, and perhaps a few stragglers survived for a while and occasionally were spotted by someone who knew a passenger pigeon when she saw one. Maybe the pigeons that trap shooters failed to hit in the 1870s flew off into the urban wilds and found mates. But as Duane Young, an ecologist, pointed out in 1953, we have scant evidence to "support the hope that the pigeons had gone west in the true American spirit of liberty to get a new lease of life." Sightings dwindled. As time went on, personal recollections were published less often. The people who had known pigeons best left their meanings and memories with grandchildren.

The Wisconsin memorial was erected in 1947, and in 1957, Michigan designated a state historical marker in Emmett County at the 1878 site of the last great nesting. The historian A. W. Schorger sorted through the great profusion of writings about pigeons to publish the first book-length account of the species' natural history and extinction. The pigeons passed into the official channels of history. Memory since then has taken more mediated forms. "In recent days we've been thinking now and again about the passenger pigeon," wrote *The New Yorker*'s editors in 1976, moving through what had become the standard benchmarks of this history—the unbelievable flocks, the gory scenes of market hunting in the northern Midwest, and the story of Martha—and closing with an excerpt from Leopold's elegy to pigeons.

> Trees still live who, in their youth, were shaken by a living wind. But a decade hence only the oldest oaks will remember, and at long last only the hills will know.

And if the pigeons had always been deputized to help Americans think meaningfully about themselves—about our political ideals, our relationships to each other and the past—we've used these new stories above all to question our approach to nature. We made the extinction a modern parable, with a moral that cautions against destructive ways of thinking about nature. "The avarice and thoughtlessness of man," Schorger called it on the memorial plaque. "Greed"

Passenger pigeon monuments

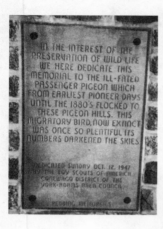

Hanover,
Pennsylvania.
*Dedicated by
the Boy Scouts of America*

Wyalusing State Park,
Wisconsin

Oden,
Michigan

Duane Young agreed. *Life* called it the "rapacity of mankind." "The best example known of the relentless power of man's stupidity." "Supreme irreverence for life." "Wanton greed." "The epitome of bestiality."

And yet our own stories, I'm convinced, can be more specific and useful. They have lost a great deal of personal relevance in the telling. As we've connected to pigeons across the long-distance routes of parable and memory, we've lost track of much of the history, and a large measure of the moral. After a century, it isn't surprising. Like so many of these laments, the 1973 folk song, for example, dwells on Martha. It begins:

> Oooooh, high above the trees . . . like rainbows
> They landed soft as the moonglow
> In greens and reds they fluttered past the window
> Ah, but nobody cared or saw

Nobody saw? Fluttered? Birds can be lovely, delicate things, but this particular species could change the wind speed and ambient temperature. The pigeons once had been compared to hurricanes, tornados and threshing machines. But you may think "moonglow," and notice green and red touches on the wings, if you visit Martha, a lone pigeon, at the Smithsonian's natural history museum—where she shares a display case with an eskimo curlew, a trumpeter swan, and other casualties and near-casualties of the late-nineteenth-century markets. "There will always be pigeons in books and in museums," wrote Leopold, "but book-pigeons live forever by not living at all." Martha lacks pigeonness. And the stories we tell about her species have lost track of a few things about pigeons.

A much older paean to the pigeons once captured the species much better:

> When I can shoot my rifle clear
> At pigeons in the sky
> I'll say good-by to pork and beans
> And live on pigeon pie

On the no-pigeons side of the extinction, the essential poetry here is easy to miss. But the song evokes a pigeon year. And to create pigeon years from pigeons was once inevitable. It was essentially human, when faced with the remarkable flocks, to draw the birds aggressively into one's world and to use them for multiple purposes that included telling powerful stories about that world. The colonists and market hunters hardly used the pigeons with due restraint. Yet at least, unlike the urban consumers, they knew they were using the birds— and to use natural resources more sustainably, first you have to recognize you are using them. At the most, the pigeon hunters knew, as Senecas did, that their ties to nature were transformative and multifaceted—at once economic, aesthetic, utilitarian, imaginative. Modern paeans have rued the loss of the pigeon flocks, a natural wonder. But we lost pi-

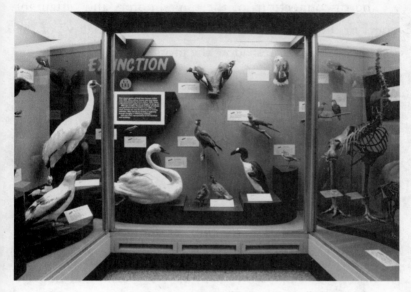

MARTHA IN THE SMITHSONIAN "EXTINCTION" EXHIBIT
Birds of the World, National Museum of Natural History

geon years too, a wonderfully complex, integrated human connectedness to pigeons.

The disconnections of the trap shooters and restaurant goers in the cities—not the "avarice" or "bestiality" of the market hunters—foreshadow the most common late-twentieth-century American encounters with nature. Most of us do not personally snap the heads off the poultry we eat. We don't personally harvest the abundance of natural resources we use. All of us consume nature from within cities or markets, where nature arrives commodified, transformed, already dead, and way out of ecological context. We connect to nature long-distance geographically, through a complex maze of economic networks. Our connections to nature are highly mediated. To recognize one's own involvement in resource-intensive markets, and to make nature meaningful in ways that tell us about these connections, can be difficult—especially when we so thoroughly enjoy the fruits of those markets. Why try very hard? Convenience makes it doubly hard to navigate our ties to nature. And this, as much as the avarice of man, is the moral of the pigeon's story: the specific, modern constellation of intensive overuses of nature, urban long-distance connections and strangely unmoored meanings. In the late nineteenth century, once upon a time—if you cut through a convenient haze of memory—well-off Americans, especially, continued to use nature to tell meaningful stories, but began to lose track of nature in the process, and of their daily connections to it.

As the market hunter H. Clay Merritt proposed, what really happened was "progress": the transition to a more urban, long-distance, economically expanding high-technology world. In the 1870s, progress in America meant shooting the wild pigeons by the millions for profit. But it also meant the removal of the pigeon feet from the pigeon pie. After that happens, how do we know what kind of pie it is?

2

WHEN
WOMEN WERE WOMEN,
MEN WERE MEN,
AND BIRDS WERE HATS

In 1886, the ornithologist Frank Chapman set out on a fact-finding expedition across Manhattan to Fourteenth Street—into the heart of the women's fashion district—where he counted every bird species he could identify on women's hats. In two afternoon trips, he saw the stuffed wings, heads, tails and bodies of three bluebirds, two red-headed woodpeckers, nine Baltimore orioles, five blue jays, twenty-one common terns, a prairie hen, a saw-whet owl—Chapman was a talented birder—and 132 other birds. There were forty species in all. A few years earlier, the wild pigeons had vanished into the earth (or the sky), and a theory of a pigeon refuge in Czechoslovakia already sported not much more hope than evidence to support it.

In the 1890s, a national conservation movement was on the verge of erupting. A growing number of Americans were now ready to argue against the devastations of resources and to convert their laments into action. And out of an impressive array of serious ecological threats in North America that might have incited a great many people to organize—sport hunting, egg collecting, subsistence hunting, deforestation, water pollution and the ongoing ravages of the game markets—women's bird-hat fashions ignited the first widespread public protest. In the late 1890s, outraged Americans across the country founded state Audubon Societies to combat the feather trade, and waged the first real national grassroots conservation crusade. The members of the societies forged new meanings. On the brink of a new century, how did they reach out, across the widening distances between the cities and the wilds, to make nature newly valuable and meaningful? How, and why, did they set out to restrain the overuse of natural resources?

The hats, not necessarily the gravest of the threats in retrospect, were an obvious epidemic. For centuries, birds had cycled in and out of fashion as women's hats in the United States and Europe, but since the 1880s had established virtually a permanent perch. The plumes of egrets, the heads of owls and even eight to ten warblers per hat: every species seemed vulnerable. Hats sported eagle feathers, whole hummingbirds, and sparrow wings pointing up "in a most . . . perky fashion. . . ." "That there should be an owl or ostrich left with a single feather apiece hardly seems possible," the *Harper's Bazar* New York reporter commented on the 1897 winter hat season. The fashion magazines of these decades burst with as many birds and feathers as a Peterson's field guide. In the late 1890s, entire terns and pheasants became especially popular—with the head draped over the front brim—and the white dorsal feathers of the snowy egret reigned as a hallmark of high hat fashion. "It will be no surprise to me," a Chicago reporter remarked in 1900, "to see life-sized turkeys, or even . . . farmyard hens, on fashionable bonnets before I die."

Like the game markets, the feather trade devastated a raft of wild bird populations. And like pigeons, many of the most sought-after species nest in large colonies, and were therefore dangerously easy to destroy. At Cape Hatteras in 1896, the plume hunters shot all but one in a hundred terns. The remnant populations today in reddish egret, gull-billed tern and roseate spoonbill colonies date back to the bird-hat markets. Snowy egrets and great white egrets were nearly decimated. Just as the game business had swept through the Midwest in the 1870s and 1880s, the millinery trade in the 1880s and 1890s cleaned out tern, heron, gull and egret rookeries up and down the Atlantic coast, from Maine to the Florida Keys.

LATEST LONDON   MILLINERY STYLES

———   ———

OCTOBER   1896

SELECTED FOR THE MILLINERY TRADE REVIEW

The state Audubon Societies rapidly enrolled large memberships. They drew audiences of as many as a thousand people to public lectures, such as Chapman's "Woman as Bird Enemy," and distributed hundreds of thousands of leaflets, such as "Save the Birds!" "Woman's Heartlessness," "An Appeal to Women," and "A Word for the Owl." A rancorous debate raged in newspapers and magazines across the country. And in 1900, after just four years, Congress responded by passing the landmark Lacey Act—the first federal conservation measure, which prohibits the interstate shipment of wild species killed in violation of state laws—and set aside the first national wildlife refuges. The blowup over the bird hats had engendered the creation of new organizations, laws, preserves and policies. The campaign seemed to redeem the pigeon fiasco. And the societies went on to serve as a pillar of both a fast-growing conservation movement and a twentieth-century American nature-lover tradition.

There was something remarkably explosive about dead birds on women's heads. The bird-hat debate was a catalytic episode and a prophetic series of events for our own twentieth-century efforts to value nature and to regulate our uses of it. This is a strange story, and not widely known. In the annals of the environmental movement, the battles that John Muir, Theodore Roosevelt and Gifford Pinchot waged for national parks and forests in the early 1900s have prevailed as the heroic tales. Why Americans decided to save places like Yosemite is a more familiar question. But the bird-hat campaign marks an even earlier, essential shift into new ways of thinking about nature. Why did so many people decide that a dead pheasant on a woman's hat had become less lovely rather than entirely unthinkable? What were *these* people thinking? To find the meanings and prophecy in the bird-hat episode, you have to make that question resonate with the fierce and compelling logic with which people asked it in the 1890s, when it was new.

The Audubon Societies

In fact, I think the bird-hat episode's very strangeness is the reason it has not endured well in historical memory, and points directly to what is most compelling about the story. And I'll begin with the most basic, least remembered and most suggestive fact—that the great majority of the founders and members of the Audubon Societies were women. The story of this campaign features a comparatively obscure and largely female cast of protagonists: Mrs. Augustus Hemenway, Miss Minna B. Hall, Mrs. Orinda Hornbrooke, Jennie June Croly, Celia Thaxter, Mrs. T. K. Noble, Olive Thorne Miller, Mrs. Morris F. Tyler, Helen Winslow and many others. Most of these women were not bird-watchers. They did not own hiking boots. They never, ever wore shorts or knickers. And their heroics—and meanings—now often seem as quaint and alien as the bird hats themselves.

The first Audubon Society was founded in Massachusetts in January 1896, after Mrs. Augustus Hemenway read an article that described the market hunters' raids on the egret rookeries in Florida. As pillars of Boston society, Harriet

Hemenway and her husband avidly enjoyed public service, and have left their name on the Hemenway Gymnasium at Harvard. That winter afternoon, Mrs. Hemenway asked her cousin, Miss Minna B. Hall, to tea. The two women combed through the Boston society register and set out to contact the most fashionable ladies in the city to organize a boycott of the bird hats. They invited the women to a set of afternoon teas, and convened a more formal meeting of prominent Boston women and men, who organized to work for reforms in the feather trade and for bird protection in general. The group took its name from a similar group that the prominent sportsman George Grinnell had founded in New York in 1886. Grinnell's Audubon Society, however, had grown too fast for him to manage, and in 1888 had collapsed under the weight of its own success.

The new societies had staying power. "A score of ladies met in Fairfield on January 28, 1898, and formed [a Connecticut Audubon Society]," the new national Audubon magazine *Bird-Lore* reported, as women organized societies in states from New Jersey and Rhode Island to Tennessee, Iowa, Texas and California. As in Massachusetts, men joined the clubs. The rosters of honorary vice-presidents boasted Grinnell, Chapman and Theodore Roosevelt in New York, and in the District of Columbia the secretary of agriculture, the Surgeon General and a Supreme Court justice. Yet in nearly every state, women founded the clubs, and asked male scientists and civic leaders to sign on in the leadership. In Massachusetts, Hemenway, Hall and the others drafted William Brewster, head of the American Ornithologists Union (one of the first U.S. scientific groups), as their president. The North Carolina club, which the ornithologist T. Gilbert Pearson founded, was the major exception. On average, men made up half the leadership, and women 80 percent of the membership. The "local secretaries," who managed the everyday organizing work in the towns, were almost all women.

Men or no men, their fans and detractors alike tended to perceive the new groups as women's clubs—as much as or even more than as new clubs for conservation. In Bridgeport, Connecticut, for example, where the newspaper reported Audubon news on the "Woman's Own Page," the local secretary stocked the membership cards at the Woman's Exchange. The Woman's Club of Keokuk founded the Iowa Audubon Society. The national journal *Club Woman* endorsed the Audubon campaign as "not the least important work being done by women's clubs to-day": "A dead bird's body ... on a fashionable hat ... is positively repulsive," the editor Helen Winslow wrote—but "anything to be in the fashion, even if we have to wear our grandmother for a chatelaine ornament." Even in North Carolina, where Pearson wishfully conceived of his new club as "gentlemen and their families," the Raleigh newspaper referred to it as "the Honorable T. Gilbert Pearson and his legion of women ... backers." And the secretary of the Connecticut Federation of Women's Clubs, as she invited the state society to join, assured the Audubon secretary that male members would be no obstacle.

A "woman's club": that did not mean merely a group of women in the same room. As in all eras, a women's club or group has meant rather women who band together *as* women. What *that* means, of course, depends absolutely on the reigning definitions of the era—and in the late-Victorian 1890s, both women's groups and their mandate as women were especially well defined. The "Woman Club movement" had emerged in the 1860s out of a tradition of women's volunteer temperance and moral-reform societies that dates back to the early nineteenth century, and from women's more secular experiences with activism during the Civil War. The club movement constituted a major branch of the larger "woman movement," or "organized womanhood," that thrived as one of the major social developments in the late 1800s. The first clubs had gathered to study literature (such as Sorosis, the pioneer, possibly pigeon-eating New York club that met at Delmonico's), and had combined paper giving and formal discussion with social events. In the 1870s, the club movement had expanded rapidly into the arts, general study and social reform. By the 1880s, women's clubs had sprouted in every American town. The clubs staked out a broad middle ground between religious temperance societies and more radical suffrage groups, and attracted members from both ends. They drew from the ranks of the upper and middle classes, and like the exclusive, twenty-five-member Saturday Morning Club in New Haven, who sponsored biweekly public lectures and held parties on their husbands' yachts, tended to be at once serious minded and socially

"Snap Shots at Prominent Ornithologists. No. II."

FRANK CHAPMAN AND HIS LEGION OF WOMEN
from *Condor* magazine, 1901

prestigious. A century later, many women's literature and arts groups—my mother's Ladies' Friday Musical Club in St. Louis included—date back to this active era. But the club movement enjoyed its heyday in the late 1890s—exactly when the Audubon Societies were forming. And the meanings of women's clubs are an essential context for the new meanings of birds.

"Organized womanhood": the thousands of women in these clubs organized exactly around a mandate of womanhood. How did club women act *as* women? What did club life mean? The movement grounded its raison d'être in the middle- and upper-class Victorian code of "separate spheres"—a set of gender definitions that linked female and male innate character to social destiny. Women embraced these definitions to varying extent, but few rejected them completely. According to the code, the masculine, naturally "competitive, aggrandizing, belligerent, and self-interested" instincts destined men to the rough-and-tumble public sphere of business and politics. The feminine "moral, nurturant, pacific," "pious [and pure]" character destined women— or *Woman*—to the domestic sphere, where she pursued motherhood as her most important duty. By tending to children's moral education, Woman maintained the morals of *all* American society. Not that any of this sounds outdated entirely. Yet as the historian Rosalind Rosenberg has written about this mind–body formula, "at no time was that idea ever more fervently held or more highly elaborated than it was in America after the Civil War." The expansive nineteenth-century literature on the gender gap could fill a few bookstores, and make *Men Are from Mars, Women Are from Venus* read like a milquetoast entry. "The home is first in woman's heart," Olive Thorne Miller, a future Audubon leader, explained in her 1891 handbook for club women. "Home is—and will ever be—the chosen kingdom of woman . . . the instinct that makes her the home-maker of the race." And what about men? In theory at least, the "separate spheres" code defined men and women in equal measure, but the morally challenged sex actually seems to have inspired less verbiage. This literature betrays an acute preoccupation with the distaff half. The sportsmen and trap shooters, the first chapter's quasi-heroes, so obsessed with the requisites of male character, seem to have played more in their own corner. Everyone waxed large about what and where women, or Woman, should be.

And ironically, the powerful ideal of domestic woman-hood—which Audubon women such as Miller touted—had always pointed women in two directions. It rooted them to their homes, but it outfitted them at once with an excellent reason to venture into a public arena that suffered so logically from a deficit of moral talent and enthusiasm. Since the early-nineteenth-century temperance groups, society women had extended their duty as keepers of the moral flame to the public sphere, and by the late 1800s had staked out a wide range of social reform causes that many women termed "national housekeeping." As Jennie June Croly, founder of Sorosis and president of the General Federation of Women's Clubs, explained: "While we have none of that greediness which is characterized as 'wanting the earth,' the earth really seems desirous of placing itself in our charge." Women's clubs lobbied for better working conditions in factories. They taught hygiene courses, founded libraries and kindergartens, and spearheaded campaigns to preserve natural areas, including the Palisades on the Hudson River and Mesa Verde National Park in Colorado. Museums, health clinics, local public colleges, settlement houses, employment bureaus, school lunches, street cleaning, city playgrounds: at the turn of the century, women's reform efforts paved the way for much of what we enjoy as urban culture and expect of modern government. In the 1890s, the state and national club federations established committees on civics, village improvement and industrial conditions, as well as art, literature and education, and convened meetings that featured odd combinations—well, not odd at the time—of teas, recitals, and lectures on everything from philanthropy and refuse disposal to home economics, prison reform and feminine character. But whether the women read history books or bought garbage cans for city streets, "one and all," as Miller enthused, were "doing the same work." The thousands of diverse clubs, Croly wrote, shared a single, overarching cause: "a new and more glorious womanhood." The "great army of club-women mothers" were "[marching steadily] toward the united womanhood" by two routes: first, by "self-improvement" or education, and second, through the deployment of women's special talents and knowledge, thereby improved, to improve the larger society. As a latter-day club woman has written, these women "studied the universe at one meeting and planned how to reform and regulate it over the teacups afterward."

This is the atmosphere into which the Audubon Societies emerged and set to work. The late 1890s saw a frenzy of new clubs: women founded a great many reform-oriented clubs, especially, between 1895 and 1899; and many women worked on causes in two or three different clubs. In 1896, when Mrs. Hemenway, who taught classes for working-class women in the Women's Industrial and Educational Union, read about the mass destruction of birds for the feather trade, how logical it must have seemed to found a club to tackle the issue. How logical it must have sounded to join. In Connecticut in 1898, the officers for at least eleven women's clubs also were active in the societies. Think of Mrs. Edgar H. Fox and Mrs. T. K. Noble, Audubon members who had founded the Central Club in Norwalk in 1896 and thereafter became, respectively, the local Audubon secretary and the president of the Connecticut Federation of Women's Clubs. Or picture the Audubonite Mrs. E. S. Morse chairing a new committee on bird protection at an 1898 Massachusetts club federation meeting, and another meeting eight months later on the problems of poverty, labor, crime, disease and infant mortality. You can almost see the issues interweave in the datebooks of these women and in the piles of literature on their nightstands and coffee tables. In New Haven, Mrs. Arthur T. Hadley, Miss Caroline White, and five other Audubon women belonged to the Saturday Morning Club, which ran a lecture series that drew twenty-five Audubon women—including Study Club, Fortnightly Club, YWCA and state federation leaders—every other week to the Church of the Redeemer, where Mrs. Morris F. Tyler, an Audubon member and Fortnightly Club leader, was an active member. In conversations among clubmates, wives and husbands, bird protection had to become "not an isolated affair . . . but [related] to all other movements of the age." You

JENNIE JUNE CROLY

"While we have none of that greediness which is characterized as 'wanting the earth,' the earth really seems desirous of placing itself in our charge."

can practically see the bird-hat campaign become the mission of this confident army of late-Victorian middle- and upper-class women: "ready, alert, systematic." You can see it become the cause of organized womanhood.

We can trace the first Audubon Societies forward to the Ladies' Friday Musical Club as much as to the modern Society, the Sierra Club and any other modern conservation group. *Womanhood:* in the 1890s, it was a far more explosive topic than bird protection. (Isn't it still?) In the last Victorian years, the greater rigidity of women's roles was fortified, too, by the anxiety that these roles faced serious attacks. As women and men made birds meaningful—just as people did with wild pigeons, and as all people do in their encounters with nonhuman nature—they at once defined themselves and their place in the world. Any piece of nature, as it becomes meaningful, travels through complex human social webs. Early conservationists, too, even as they argued against overuses of natural resources, were at once telling themselves who they were.

And the societies' activists were wealthier urban Americans who hewed to a powerful and comprehensive gender code, which they used to define morality. Why did the bird-hat issue erupt? Not surprisingly, the one conservation issue that they united around happened to be the sole issue in which women were the most visible players. The definition of Woman as the keeper of morality made this one issue resonate at a higher moral volume than any other. What more perfect catalyst? At a time when many Americans were ready to embrace conservation as a moral issue, the women's bird hats acquired broad moral overtones far more efficiently than game hunting or water pollution. Would mass devastations of bird populations to decorate men's hats have triggered such outrage? The hats became entangled exquisitely in the fervid middle- and upper-class beliefs in what made men men and women women.

Women, especially, took on the feather trade in the name of womanhood. They took it on for birds too—but the volcanic dialogue about womanhood became a kind of familiar conduit into the newer, more uncharted subject of conservation. The radical suffragists were gaining ground. The New Woman lay just ahead. The topic could only get more explosive.

The Conservation of Womanhood

"Do women who wear birds ever stop to think what an injury to the . . . moral influence of our sex they are inflicting?" Mrs. Orinda Hornbrooke demanded in *Club Woman*. As Audubon women made birds *and* a vision of moral womanhood meaningful, they set forth a few new arguments for bird protection that most of us have never heard. A dead pheasant or Baltimore oriole on a new hat posed a serious threat to the cause for which club women had such great ambitions. The gravity of the threat matched the magnitude of their hopes. "The Federation may become a mighty factor in the civilization of the century." "The twentieth century, with beckoning hand, awaits our coming." The excitement, the sense of promise, the confident plans about what moral, educated women could accomplish together: they infuse the club manuals, *Club Woman*, the conference programs, the minutes of club meetings. "The greatest power for humanitarian work that the world has ever known." "The electric thrill of the mighty movement of our own times." Even to a late-twentieth-century skeptic with little sympathy for Victorian morés, it can be contagious: as the women's historian Anne Firor Scott has testified, too, it is not hard to be "carried away by the women's own infectious enthusiasm for their work." At the brink of a new century, club women aimed to exalt Emerson's dictum—"Civilization is the power of woman for good"—to complete realization. Or more simply: "She who rocks the cradle rules the world."

Not everyone in the societies appealed, like Hornbrooke, to women as the morally progressive gender. Some men, especially, chastised the hat-bearing women not so much as morally lapsarian but as "fatuous," "brainless or heartless," "shallow and foolish" and "feather-headed . . . in more ways than one." The separate-spheres code had always made space for women in two directions from men's sphere: Above and Below. If women and men were different, exactly *how* was a matter for contestment, and the same disengagement from the public pursuits of business and politics that made women natural guardians of morality could also render them (how could it not?) unfortunately petty, ignorant, vain, selfish and thoughtless. Club women generally had to tackle these definitions of Woman as a serious threat to the cause. The bird hats constituted a highly visible setback—as serious, perhaps, as the brash New Woman. One male magazine editor and Audubon member blamed the destruction of birds on the "selfish [and murderous] vanity of women." "Pause a moment, well-meaning sisters of 'little knowledge,'" *Bird-Lore* scolded women. Or as a *New York Times* editorial reprimanded, "If woman would but think!" Imagine Mrs. Hemenway or Mrs. T. K. Noble reading any of these at breakfast. Imagine, too, the displeasure with which Mrs. Hornbrooke informed *Club Woman* readers about a well-meaning woman who had asked for and received a physician's certificate stating that the bird on her new hat had died a natural death. These lines of attack struck an especially raw nerve. As Olive Thorne Miller had written with such confidence in her 1891 club handbook, "The frivolity that has existed among women is greatly diminished." Club women meant to exalt and deploy the moral side of womanhood, but also to make the petty side obsolete. To them, the trivial image of womanhood was like the dark side of the Force.

And few topics evoked the nether definitions of womanhood more effectively than hats: spring, summer, fall and winter hats, and morning, afternoon and evening hats. Walking and traveling hats. Church, garden, mourning, golf and carriage hats. Women's elite fashions—which achieved such byzantine dimensions in the late nineteenth century, when they became the stuff of Edith Wharton novels—mandated a devotion to hats that can now seem wondrous in a more hat-free age. Hats proliferated in a stupefying variety of styles that changed as often as the weather, and by the 1890s they had become at once fashion's major feminine accessory and its superego. Hat shops populated nearly every fashionable block of Fifth Avenue, from Twenty-sixth to Fifty-ninth Street, and often featured elegant parlors and showrooms, where the activities flourished as a metonym for the arcane mysteries of womanhood: "If there's anywhere on earth a man looks out of place and a perfect fool, it's in a millinery store." The baffling taxonomy of hats and the picayune rules of hat etiquette—"a hat very often is spoilt for want of the proper tilt on the head"—fed the subterranean reaches of women's sphere like compost. And since the 1880s, women's hats had been piled so high with feathers, birds, fruit, flowers, furs and even mice and small reptiles that they seemed literally to match the hat's metaphoric size as a target. In the 1890s, hat jokes abounded:

> "Is my new hat all right?"
> "Yes, dear, you look like a laundress carrying home her day's work on her head."

> "So you've bought another hat already, have you? What did you pay for it?"
> "Nothing."
> "Well, that's cheap! How did you manage it?"
> "I told the milliner to send the bill to you!"

It was at this time that jokes about not being able to see over women's hats at the theater became serious complaints.

In sum, the fact that bird hats were *hats* made them doubly evocative as a threat to the cause of moral womanhood. As the societies tapped into a volcanic dialogue about who women are, hats already had become a chief energy source in that conversation. What did club women think about hats?

How might Mrs. T. K. Noble or Olive Thorne Miller have reacted when the *Standard Designer* reported in April 1897 that the "feminine mind"—the object of so much high-minded energy and optimism—was "at the present season intent upon the selection of the Easter hat and bonnet"? At the 1900 General Federation meetings, one speaker stated flatly that "a federation should stand for a certain dignity . . . utterly incompatible with the . . . wearing of a hat." In official photographs of club leaders, Mrs. Noble, like most of her colleagues, has chosen to remain hat-free. Of course, the societies branded the wearers of *bird* hats vapid and frivolous as inevitably as if the milliners had embellished each mound of owl heads, egret tails, hummingbirds, ribbons, hydrangea branches, plums, cherries and terns with a big red bull's-eye.

And yet, the hat was more complex. It could be a dilemma in one's self-definitions, because club women, while serious and high-minded, at once identified themselves so essentially as high-class—and what signified a well-off society woman more visibly than fashionable dress and exactly the right hat? In theory, every woman, rich or poor, was born with natural moral gifts. In practice, the separate-spheres definitions of Woman as morally superior favored wealthier women over working-class women, who had to work outside the home in men's businesses. Just as the elite sportsmen's definitions of true manhood envisioned the lower-class market hunters as less masculine, the club women's definitions of a separate and true womanhood, however optimistic and well-meaning,

Where the Finer Hats are Shown.

WANAMAKER MILLINERY DEPARTMENT
on Broadway

tended to exalt the virtues of society women. They made lower-class women less moral and less respectable, and therefore less feminine. And less fashionable. If hats could represent a threat to higher womanhood, women also used them as a sign. Among the hat jokes, one can find quite a few that make fun of working-class "maids" who stick chicken feathers in their hats to imitate society women, as well as an occasional joke about club women:

> She feared her paper might fall flat,
> Her theme was far from bright:
> So donned her newest frock and hat
> And thus came through all right.

A few women objected that fashion made women "vain, use-less, and empty-headed." Yet to most club women, fashion and hats were more ambiguous symbolically. The editor of *Club Woman*, Helen Winslow, also wrote a column on women's clubs for the fashion magazine *Delineator*. The St. Louis Pioneers Club (the precursor to my mother's club) staged a debate on whether "the desire to dress according to fashion should be encouraged." Croly herself, the General Federation president, had edited the major fashion magazine *Demorest's Monthly*. In 1900, typical issues of *Harper's Bazar* featured the Paris hat fashions, notes on women's clubs, a cover story on Croly, and a comment on Mrs. John Jacob Astor in the "New York Society" column: "Her hats are small, very smart-looking, but quite inconspicuous." Hats might symbolize the dark side of the Force but also woman-hood at its best, in which case the tilt of one's hat could be a very serious matter. Like the terrain of the late-Victorian definitions of separate womanhood—at once promising, elit-ist, changing—hat shopping was a minefield of propriety, pettiness, progressiveness and panache.

As the societies navigated every part of this terrain in the course of the bird-hat debate—and as these particular hats fell out of moral favor—bird hats became lower class by de-fault. Their detractors inevitably branded them as "vulgar and in bad taste." As the Audubon Societies shoved dead birds out of fashion and into ignominy, they demoted the hats, as *Bird-Lore* sneered, "to the 'real loidy' who . . . with hat cocked over one eye . . . haunts the cheaper shops, lunch[es] on beer . . .

rides a man's wheel, chews gum, and expectorates with seeming relish." As with most arguments against bird hats, the societies called wearing a bird hat an unwomanly thing to do. And since failures of womanhood would spell the inevitable moral downfall of the rest of society, this was easily the most serious social transgression a woman could make.

In 1896, transgressions against womanhood were far more troubling than those against nature. As American elites made birds meaningful across long distances—just as with passenger pigeons—the meanings of the birds themselves seem to have gotten lost along the way. The new bird lovers often talked much more about women than birds. Even as urban consumers revalued wild nature and worked for resource conservation, their discussions reflected the disconnections endemic to modern urban life. How did these societies launch a new dialogue on nature? It was a conversation these urban elites were already having—and the ways that bird hats so perfectly tapped into every part of it—that steered them with such enthusiasm into a new conversation about birds.

The Conservation of Birds

Even when the founding Audubonites talk about *birds,* and the more bird-oriented reasons to save them, the conversations say just as much about who women are (and men too, by counterdefinition). What did Audubonites *say* about birds? A great deal. What new meanings did they create? The societies' efforts to save birds do appear just as valiant as their efforts to conserve womanhood. The bird lovers set forth new arguments for bird protection with such fierce persistence that they made these ideas widely familiar. The new nature advocates created a language for twentieth-century conservation. Yet even these ideas said as much (and often more) about the deep meaningfulness of definitions of Woman.

Why save the birds? "The exquisite purity of their plumage," Chapman enthused, attracted "every lover of the beautiful." Birds, many agreed with him, were beautiful. "What marvels of grace! . . . How lovely . . . [and] delicate. . . .What music of motion . . . [and] brilliance of color!" The destruction of such God-given beauty would "reduce the glad and joyous earth to an oppressive silence and gloom." A few Audubonites argued that birds actively campaign on behalf of beauty on earth—"every [tern] works hard and tirelessly," a member wrote to the *New York Times*, ". . . [to clear] our harbors . . . of material repulsive to human eyes"—but most embraced birds' more passive aesthetic virtues. The arguments pivoted out of, around and through definitions of womanhood. After all, the bird-hat fashions had begun (so the story goes) in the court of Louis XVI in the late 1700s, when the feminine paragon Marie Antoinette stuck a few feathers through her hair and set off a craze that imparts fresh meaning to "big hair," and *tout de suite* had the *au courant* ladies of Versailles piled so high with feathers that they had to tilt their heads out of the carriages they rode in. The fashion sparked enthusiasm because French elites defined beauty as a shared essential attribute of both women and birds; and a century after, the equation thrived as a credo in American fashion and in American elites' definitions of womanhood. No wonder Chapman's lecture "Woman as Bird Enemy" attracted an audience of a thousand. Beauty was intrinsically avian *and* feminine. It made women women and birds birds—and it is exactly why birds became women's hats.

In the late Victorian decades, as well, the "natural look" stormed into women's high fashion and made bird hats doubly powerful as statements of femininity. Nature, many people began to assert, is the source of true beauty: in an era of rapid social and economic change and mobility, the use of Nature to set human standards was becoming a powerful hallmark of modern thinking. Milliners in the late 1890s piled women's hats not only with birds but with real flowers, sea mosses, leaves, grasses and medium-sized animals. "Nature made her beautiful," as one anti-Audubon man argued in the *New York Times*, and "the earth and the sea give up their gems for her. Let the air do the same." And the societies were delivering a crash course in a new women-beauty-birds calculus. If a live tern was naturally beautiful, like Woman, a dead tern on a hat was ugly, a desecration of nature's beauty and a travesty of womanhood. Women remained complicit at considerable risk. "The place for dead birds," Helen Winslow objected, "is not above a pretty woman's face." "I believe it is woman's sacred mission," the Iowa club woman Margaret T. Olmstead argued, "to be the conservator of beauty and not its destroyer." At the least, the hats were "inartistic." At worst, they were "a disgusting sight." "Dead and mutilated bodies." "Charnel houses of beaks and claws, and bones and feathers,

A KILLING HAT.

[" The dealers declare that the demand for birds of every description will this year be greater than ever." —FASHION PAPER.]

Westminster Gazette
1901

and glass eyes." "Does any woman imagine these withered corpses . . . are *beautiful?*" The new Audubon arguments reduced the lovely fashions of Marie Antoinette to an anti-feminine bone pile.

A second, equally common argument for bird protection popularized the great economic value of birds. Since 1883, the American Ornithologists Union had been researching the significant role that birds play in the control of insect pests—mostly in an effort to reverse farmers' habit of shooting birds on sight. The Audubon Societies, with many AOU scientists in their leadership, quickly coopted the argument. "Have the milliners, with their petty interests," William Dutcher, a leading ornithologist, demanded, "any right to jeopardize the safety of the agricultural interests?" Congressman John F. Lacey himself, as he engaged in the debates on the Lacey Act, brought worm-ridden apples onto the House floor so that his fellow Representatives could see the dangers firsthand. The economic arguments sounded scientific, fact-based, rational. They sounded *masculine*, and their proto-ecological validity aside, swiftly became essential weapons in a campaign that was widely perceived to be run by women. The arguments made a cameo appearance whenever the feather-trade forces charged the societies with ignorance or foolishness: It's the economy, stupid, the Audubon men inevitably retorted. Women, too, advanced this argument. As an Audubon woman argued to the Iowa State Federation of Women's Clubs, "Birds are an important factor in Nature's plan for preserving the balance of vital forces." To argue conservation for economic reasons was to be rational, progressive and well-informed. It was to be a man who sounded like a man, or a club woman who had rejected Woman's trivial side. These definitions and antidefinitions of the separate characters of women and men, as much as the AOU research itself, gave the economic arguments their persuasive force—and made the new arguments resonant and more meaningful.

At least some members of the societies championed birds as remarkable models for human behavior. Patience, ingenuity, bravery, industry, dignity, "generosity, unselfish devotion . . . the love of mother for offspring": you could find every one of these traits, new conservationists argued, among chickadees, geese, herons and warblers. Dead herons, of course, made ineffective examples. These defenses of birds were rooted in the popularity of turn-of-the-century moral-istic nature stories, in particular a subgenre of bird stories au-thored mostly by women, including Olive Thorne Miller and many other members of the literary Meridian Club in New York. *Citizen Bird, Little Brothers of the Air,* "The Feath-ered Ishmaelite": the stories gave moral mothers the tools with which to educate children. And if the economic argu-ments enjoyed an unmistakably male ring, these arguments sounded just as recognizably distaff. The bird stories them-selves were rooted in the nineteenth-century tradition of "sentimental" women's fiction, also well-populated by women authors (Harriet Beecher Stowe's *Uncle Tom's Cabin* is an enduring example), that showcased moralism, piety, ma-ternal teachings and domestic ideals. The feather-trade forces immediately dubbed the birds-are-us arguments as senti-mental. "Much has been said about 'mushy sentiment,'" the scientist and Audubon leader J. A. Allen objected during an extended debate in the *New York Times* letters section in 1897, as he reassured the public that "[the campaign] is in the hands of ornithologists . . . fully conversant with the facts of the case." A kind of arms race played out, with gender-loaded weapons, as some Audubonites hailed birds as moral exem-plars, the societies' adversaries charged "sentimentalism," and Audubon leaders returned fire with prepackaged lectures on the American farm economy. The milliners themselves re-peated *sentiment* like a mantra—if not "wearisome bosh"—as the quick successes of the women-led Audubon crusade converted their condescension and vague amusement to horrified disbelief.

If many Audubon leaders chose to downplay the "sentimental" argument, they were even more mortified by humane activists' claims that to kill animals for any purpose at all is un-Godly and wicked. The religious Humane Movement—that began in England in the mid-nineteenth century and has evolved into the modern Humane Society—had battled slavery, vivisection and cruelty to animals, and logically took up the bird-hat crusade under their banner. "Can it be pleasing to a merciful God," one advocate objected in the *New York Times*, "to see the little creatures he has made . . . slaughtered by thousands [for] . . . the daughters of Eve?" But in the 1890s, the argument sounded radical and unacceptable to most men and women, however bird-loving or God-fearing. Not that the anti-Audubon forces didn't try to pin it to the societies and attack it. "There is very little that woman wears that does not cost life," the *Millinery Trade Review* ventured, "and if these Audubon notions were to be carried to extremes, we blush to think of the possibilities of her future appearance." The milliners set forth the specter of that most unwomanly Victorian-era woman: the Naked Woman. They tried to use the definitions of Woman to their advantage. Yet the acknowledged extremism of the humane activists' arguments rendered even that valiant effort ineffective. Everyone knew, an anti-Audubon man conceded in a letter in the *Times*, that "killing is the law of nature"—"except the vegetarians, and they, being obviously mad, do not count."

Still, even rationalists such as Frank Chapman and J. A. Allen shared the activists' enthusiasm for "civilization"—a cause for great allegiance among the middle and upper classes at the Progressive turn of the century. A great many scientists, club women, Humane Movement members and other new conservationists argued for bird protection in the name of its steady advance. To kill birds per se might not be uncivilized or wrong. But to kill birds to make women's hats? That was newly barbaric. That women—the very upholders of civilization—wore the hats made it of course particularly objectionable. How could such women still "[feel] wholly superior to the Red Men, who decorate themselves with their neighbors' scalps?" The reigning definitions of civilization, like the definitions of Woman, had always favored certain people over others: white over nonwhite, Western over non-Western, upper class over working class, and wealthy white women, who embodied the separate moral womanhood, over all others. The men in the Millinery Merchants' Protective Association offered to stop using birds from civilized countries: "this, however, will allow [the use of] the birds of China, Japan, India, Africa . . . and the islands where no white men . . . penetrate." Sportsmen, too, rallied for civilization, saying the lower-class market hunters "should be compelled to leave the country and seek society among savages"—but no one seemed to pay much attention. Most people saved their vitriol for civilized Woman, and her responsibility to raise civilized men, who came less naturally to civilization but were educable.

Audubon Society members often disagreed. They sank their energy into the cause of bird conservation for different reasons. In practice, these diverse arguments often merged. "Without our bird friends to protect us," Mrs. Hornbrooke wrote, "the insects that buzz and sting and creep, and crawl and slime, will have their way in the world"—which evoked at once the perils of a bird-free farm economy, a sentimental affinity to birds, and the imminent destruction of Western civilization. The societies did not create one, unified new language for conservation. They made all these arguments common currency in the late 1890s. Some have endured better than others. All sound at least a little familiar. At the time, the arguments drew in scientists, club women, sportsmen, nature writers and humane activists, who split divisively over the meanings of birds and nature but unified around the deeply meaningful definitions of who women are.

And no aspect of the feather trade dramatized these meanings more flawlessly or vividly than the raids in south Florida on the snowy egret rookeries—which had first incited Mrs. Hemenway to action. The egret plumes, which women's hats had featured in abundance since the 1880s, were the long, soft, beautifully white dorsal mating feathers that male and female egrets grow only in the spring breeding season. The plume hunters raided the nesting colonies soon after the eggs hatched, when the parent egrets' refusal to abandon their nests made the adults effortless to shoot. Or in the words of Mrs. Hornbrooke,

Egret plumes . . . are the nuptial dress. . . . The birds must be taken . . . when the young birds are hatched . . . for at that time the solicitude of the parent birds is greatest. . . . When the killing is finished . . . the slaughtered birds are left in a white heap to fester in the sun and wind in sight of their orphaned young that cry for food and are not fed.

Imagine Mrs. Hemenway reading *that*. In the context of Victorian norms for women, marriage and motherhood, the scenario was evocative, to say the least, and the "harrowing descriptions" "published *ad libitum*" spread with efficacious speed. Each rendition featured the same guideposts: the bridal dress, the parental devotion, the starving young and of course, the crowning horror—that it was all done *in the name of Woman*.

"The ground is strewn with the mutilated corpses of mothers!" "A woman . . . guilty of such cruelty would be no true woman, but a feminine monster." How could moral womanhood go so thoroughly awry? Women were exploiting the natural instinct of motherhood to kill mothers and children: as an argument against the bird hats, the scenario was more compelling than the specter of cornfields without avian protection, or even an earth without avian beauty. "Cruel thoughtlessness." "Murderous vanity." "An act . . . never . . . followed by even the most savage race of men dealing with their most hated enemies." "Why, to obey a fashion, do [women] lower the standard of civilization, when as women they should stand for every movement in its advance?" This was the most vain, antimoral, selfish, uncivilized, low-minded threat of all. The argument eluded charges of radicalism and sentimentalism as the different Audubon constituencies rallied in unanimity. "This is one of the moral questions," the naturalist Herbert Job wrote, ". . . classed with the opium traffic and the slave trade . . . to which there is but one side." "In the name of humanity, of womanliness, of motherhood, we ask women to refuse to wear the aigrette." Serious club women, hardened scientists, incurable sentimentalists and mad vegetarians all agreed. "The reproach against womanhood will continue until . . . the last brood of nestlings [has] starved, while the mother-bird dies with bleeding breast." The anti-Audubon forces, for their part, could post only the weak objection that "human ingenuity" might invent a way to secure the aigrettes "without inflicting starvation upon the baby herons."

Why save the birds? For their beauty, economic value, potential as role models, and status as God's creatures—but mostly, for womanhood. In fact, and doubly suggestive, few people ever mentioned the *male* egrets. One might conclude from this passionate debate that the father birds, like their human counterparts, had gone off to work. Yet in egrets, as in all heron species—as Allen and Chapman and others must have known—the male and female share parental duties. The sexes build the nest together and take turns as they incubate the eggs and feed the nestlings. Half the "mutilated corpses" strewn on the ground were actually *fathers*. The gender relations of egrets look less like a model for Victorian separate spheres than like the post–1960s two-working-parent family—and the egret fathers less like avian Teddy Roosevelts than a paradigm for the sensitive New Age man. And in heron species, larger chicks often peck smaller chicks to death and shove them from the nest. As exemplars for human behavior generally, snowy egrets, like most animals, tend not to conform that well to human expectations. How did the Audubon Societies make nature newly meaningful? The Audubonites popularized reasons to save and value species that inhabited distant wild places. Yet even when they told stories specifically *about* birds, the meanings often still conveyed little about how these species actually mated, ate, slept, had sex, bred, migrated, fought off predators. Like the urban pigeon consumers, the new conservationists, too, set that twentieth-century precedent of disconnection.

Economics

The new meanings lost track of the birds themselves. But just like the affluent trap shooters and Delmonico's patrons, the conservationists also lost track of people's *uses* of birds—and of economic networks.

Because the debate had never been about manhood or men. Women were supposed to feel the worst. Women had to rescue the baby egrets. And women, not men, were to blame. The finger-pointing at the consumers is an intriguing reversal from the sportsmen's attacks on the pigeon hunters. Yet, it worked an evasive magic that was closely related. As the societies shifted this conservation issue into women's sphere of morals and civilized behavior, they effectively shifted it *away* from men. More to the point, they spirited it away from men's *sphere* of business and economics exactly at a time when economic growth was accelerating at a modern pace. And that, too, made the bird-hat issue singularly bewitching to a wide audience. If not quite as invisible as snowy egret fathers, the men came close. "The dried and ghastly head and beak," as "Woman's Heartlessness" author Celia Thaxter charged, was "dragged down to point to the face below, as if saying, '*She* did it!'"

In a letter to the *New York Times,* one woman set forth a rare objection.

> We never kill the blithe songsters. . . . Do we not scream at the mere sight of one of those deadly weapons? . . . We wonder who does destroy them? Not the men, of course. . . . We wish someone would find out who the guilty ones are. We should like to know also . . . who prepares the birds for the millinery market and does the importing, and offers them for sale. It is all very queer.

The bird hats were the product of an international network of market hunters, milliners, wholesalers, importers, manufacturers, buying agents, commission merchants, factory

workers, sales clerks and, finally, the society women who purchased the hats—and who were as likely to have killed or
stuffed or sold an egret as to have climbed Mt. Everest on
their last vacation. Among the men on this list, only the market hunters drew any serious attention. "If women would not
buy these slaughtered remains," as Herbert Job explained,
". . . men would not shoot the poor things . . . so . . . the responsibility . . . must be laid to women"—which left that interesting black hole in between for everyone else. The
societies branded the market hunters "a harmful class of selfish people," "the wretches who are paid to do the rough
work" and "rough, untaught men" of "barbarous stupidity"
and "no refinement of feeling." It could not have helped that
the south Florida coast in these decades had a notorious reputation as a rough-and-tumble refuge from civilized society—a frontier image that Key West still thrives on. And if
the hunters had been shooting egrets for men's hats, they
likely would have had to endure a great many more lectures.
Here, the women's visibility saved them from the fate of the
game hunters in the Midwest: "What can we expect of men
and boys while women set such an example of brutality?"
Regardless of culpability, you could not expect these men to
stop of their own accord. In the highbrow Victorian gender
scheme, lower-class men languished at the bottom rung of
civilized society. These men had little innate moral sense to
appeal to. They were hopeless.

The more affluent businessmen were not hopeless. They
were blameless. They were not immoral. They were amoral.

"The part the men agents play is that of supplying the demand," an Audubon advocate wrote in 1898, and most people seemed to agree: "Woman wants." The millinery district in New York City dominated three full blocks of lower Broadway, where an army of merchants operated a huge and profitable international industry. And yet the societies met all this economic energy and effort with virtual silence. Why? Mabel Osgood Wright, president of the Connecticut society, set forth one of the few explanations that appears: "Why should we expect the milliner with a living at stake to be more moral than the woman?" "The milliner . . . *must* keep well in the front with novelties in the push of trade-rivalry." The businessmen, everyone seems to agree, are trapped by economic forces beyond their control. And these forces take two forms: Fashion and the Market.

"Suddenly," Chapman stated, "as a result of causes too mysterious for the mind of man to comprehend, Fashion claimed the terns for her own." "What fashion decrees," his AOU colleague Witmer Stone likewise marveled, "must, of necessity be followed." As a force on the male sphere, fashion, a.k.a. "Dame Fashion," conjured the trivial face of womanhood and motives for which men had no explanation. Men, women and all the Progressive forces of Reason acceded to its power. The fashion magazines in the 1890s report on each new season's hat styles not as if men had created and marketed them but as if they had just arrived by courier from another planet. Even the milliners abdicated any efforts to control the trends: "Dame Fashion," the *Millinery Trade Re-*

view explained, "is dictatorial in what shall be used in the trimmings of hats." What could businessmen do about that? Fashion was the feminine mystery: it was female vanity and frivolity, the target of men's jokes, the reason you couldn't see in the theater. The merchants and manufacturers couldn't begin to comprehend it, much less take responsibility for it.

The market operated according to unseen dictates, too, and was equally unstoppable. "The milliners," as Mabel Wright defended them, had "a perfectly good right as business men to protect their invested capital." Far from mysterious, the market was ultrarational, powered not by the men who engaged in it but by the economic logic of the "Invisible Hand." It was soulless. The health of the American economy, even, required that the market be left to operate according to the neutral laws of self-interest and competition. Women's sphere was powered by sentiment and morals. Men's sphere was ruled by logic. In the Gilded Age, the Invisible Hand enjoyed great popularity as a metaphor. Of course, many critics before and since have defined American capitalist markets, like all others, as completely rooted in human intention—which people create and run, for better and worse, with their whole minds, hearts and souls—and have defined self-interest as a mechanism that operates separately from the greater economic good. The metaphor mystifies the economic decisions that market players make, and the differential power we wield. It confounds responsibility for the consequences of markets, for people and for nature. The market and Dame Fashion were like the yin and yang of

THE DESPOT OF APRIL.
"FASHION RULES THE WORLD."—BY HY. MAYER.

"Fashion Rules the World"
Godey's Magazine, 1897

men's immunity in the feather trade. Both were deliberate human inventions, in which men were fully complicit. But the nature lovers' definitions of women and men routed responsibility away from the masculine moiety.

The one issue that captured the public imagination was also the single issue that implicated Woman—and Woman was not only a widely shared obsession, and a lightning rod for moral debate, but also so conveniently above, below, outside and beyond market forces. Why *did* this issue erupt? In 1896, the American economy was poised on the brink of tremendous increases in production and consumption—and therefore the harvest, industrial transformation, marketing, purchase and use of natural resources. And the new conservationists, as businessmen and wealthy consumers, used more resources than most. In a highly useful shift from the pigeon laments, the societies made a set of long-distance links between nature and consumers starkly visible. They wrestled with the destructive consequences. They battled successfully for laws against overuses of resources. But by centering the problem on women and women's sphere, they exempted the harvest, manufacture and marketing stages from the heart of the discussion, and from their collective diagram of their connections to the wilder realms of nature. And if they reeducated one generation of consumers, they consigned the looming threat of modern consumer*ism* to the sidelines. What these early conservation advocates all agreed on, really, was that it was wrong for higher-class women of superior morals to let lower-class men kill mother egrets, particularly for mothers and by taking advantage of maternal instincts, and especially if the baby birds were left to starve. That was a powerful cause to rally around, for two chief reasons. It coopted a remarkably powerful social conversation about who women and men are. And it left the fast-expanding markets, and people's enjoyment of them, conveniently on the edge of the picture.

If the bird-hat story has a moral for my own generation of well-off baby boomers, it's double-edged. The episode set a major cornerstone in the foundation of modern conservation. And it set a twentieth-century precedent by which wealthier Americans made nature meaningful and valuable, yet failed to grapple with the vast economic networks by which we transform nature into everyday life.

Politics

The Audubon women did not just talk about conservation of birds and womanhood. They went to work. The men, in any case, passed the solutions, like the blame, straight to their better half. "It is to the women themselves we must look for any real result." "It lies in the power of women to remedy a great evil." Or as Frank Chapman began one of his lectures to a packed New York audience: "Ladies and gentlemen—more particularly ladies." Men could stop shooting egrets. They could refuse to design or market the bird hats, and could enact laws to regulate the trade. But they could not effectively tackle this problem. To shore up the sands of womanhood was not a job for men.

As it happened, women ran a vast network of volunteer groups for exactly that purpose. The societies turned to the ready-made membership, tactics and organization of women's clubs. If the bird-hat issue erupted mostly due to gender archetypes and economic convenience, this women's network at once made a woman-centered issue an enormously practical one to tackle. The societies appointed local secretaries to organize an Audubon club in every town. The women set up traveling libraries—a standard club activity—on birds and bird protection. They spoke to women's clubs and hosted teas. They visited schools, to work for "home enlightenment through the great army of club-women mothers," so that every child—as *Harper's Bazar* reported—might answer the door and yell, "Mama, there's a woman with a dead body on her hat who wants to see you." The women publicized "White Lists" of milliners who sold feather-free hats—a tactic they borrowed from the Consumers' Leagues, which also were founded and run mostly by women—and organized bird-free millinery shows. The Audubon women engaged in the effective, well-organized, late-nineteenth-century middle- and upper-class politics of womanhood.

The men in the societies also set to work. While women ran the committees on schools, education and traveling libraries, men took charge of lectures, bird charts and legislation. Chapman, Pearson, William Dutcher and other AOU ornithologists conducted surveys of nesting grounds. Pearson had traveled the marshes of the mid-Atlantic coast in the 1880s, talking to plume hunters and documenting population declines; and after 1900, he inspected wholesalers' stock, and prowled the Raleigh railway station in search of illegal bird shipments. The leaders met privately with legislators and wrote to newspaper editors. They negotiated with the Millinery Merchants' Protective Association. The men worked hard. They traveled the privileged halls of men's sphere and spoke man to man within them. And while women brandished the language of morals, they brandished science, reason and the law.

These men often claimed the women's work was more important. While this deference can sound condescending or at best diplomatic, that likely says more about my own, 1990s rejection of "women's work" as a separate category. The Audubon men accessed formal avenues of power and

WOMEN AND MEN
IN THE CONNECTICUT AUDUBON SOCIETY, 1923

stamped the movement with the essential cachet of male authority. But the Audubon women built the movement—and the women sustained it. Through organizing and education, the women created the public support necessary for Congress to enact new laws. They created exactly the grassroots structure that Grinnell's short-lived Society a decade earlier had lacked. The mostly male AOU, too, had been battling the feather trade since the 1880s, but would make little progress until they joined forces with the women-led societies. Of the two kinds of gatherings that Mrs. Hemenway hosted at her elegant Boston home—teas for fashionable women, and meetings of state Audubon leaders—the teas were quite likely more pressing. When Chapman declared that "the salvation of the heron rests solely in woman's hands," he arguably absolved himself and his male colleagues too readily. He also simply may have been right.

The societies made quick progress. Thousands of women responded enthusiastically: some "burned their feathers." In May 1900, within four years after Harriet Hemenway and Minna Hall had convened for tea, Congress passed the Lacey Act—and conservation gained an essential foothold. In triumph, Mabel Osgood Wright celebrated in *Bird-Lore*:

> Let us credit the law *and* the lady, and hope that the two are standing with locked hands, as they . . . form a twentieth century alliance in the cause of Bird Protection, as they have so often done in other things that elevate the race.

That she granted half the credit to men sounds at best diplomatic. Regardless, to women such as Wright, the twentieth century beckoned far more brightly.

The Twentieth Century

In Steve Martin's 1993 play *Picasso at the Lapin Agile*, set in a café in 1904, Elvis stops in from the future and tells a young Einstein and Picasso, who are matching wits, that the new century will fail to happen as they have envisioned it. The "Age of Regret," he tells them—but these two avatars of the coming century see a "future . . . driven by light" and a "Modern wait[ing] to be met." Other people at the café, too, see "images sent through the air," "people being carried in giant airplanes," and "vast quantities of information . . . stored in very small spaces." Relativity. Ideas traveling at light speed. A "brief craze for lawn flamingos." The very collapse of time and space. None of this yet seems to augur any regret.

After 1900, the code of separate spheres unraveled. Not completely. But the rigid boundaries around a separate, morally superior Womanhood succumbed to such pressures as new white-collar jobs for urban middle-class women and the very educational advances that women's clubs had worked so hard to achieve. The women's club movement receded steadily from the vortex of middle- and upper-class women's activities. The exigency of the clubs' volunteer reform work subsided, too, as the Progressive-era government, as a response in part to the clubs' lobbying efforts, translated many of the women's social and environmental campaigns into legislation. As part of that process, Congress passed the Lacey Act and enacted a set of federal regulatory controls on American markets. And while in the 1930s, the more destructive consequences of ceding control of markets to an all-rational Invisible Hand would call forth the more aggressive New Deal regulation—and many new measures for wildlife and soil conservation—the power and legitimacy of that metaphor has continued to wax and wane.

In 1905, the state Audubon Societies joined to create the National Association of Audubon Societies—shortened in the mid-1940s to the National Audubon Society—and impounded the snowy egret from the *Millinery Trade Review* as their emblem. Into the 1920s and 1930s, they lobbied for protective legislation, created their own network of refuges, and founded and led major recovery programs for bald eagles, roseate spoonbills and whooping cranes. In the 1940s, they staked a major presence in the post–World War II environmental movement, whose substantial victories since have included a recoding of the Lacey Act in the far more powerful Endangered Species Acts of 1966, 1969 and 1973. In 1991—snapping at the heels of their own centennial—the society embarked on a fresh quest for younger members and for a sharper political edge. Image consultants advised the main office in New York to avoid such terms as "oldest organization" and "birds"—and the president, Peter Berle, scrapped the snowy egret logo for a green rectangle. "We want to be Greenpeace," an editor of *Audubon* explained, "but we don't want to parachute off bridges." The bird-hat campaign has gotten stranded, like a unified moral womanhood, in the late nineteenth century—as quaint and tame and strange—though women and their campaign to save birds once had enough politics and sharp edges to spare. Society histories still celebrate Mrs. Hemenway and a few of her cohorts as women who made key contributions to early conservation. But how did these early advocates act, think and speak *as* women? Mrs. Hemenway, Helen Winslow, Mrs. Orinda Hornbrooke and Mrs. E. S. Morse were so much more than activists with more estrogen. Women were conservation pioneers. But womanhood, and its meanings, remains the essential key to the effectiveness and the meaningfulness—and the limits—of the pathbreaking campaign these women waged against bird hats.

As we make nature meaningful, we say a great deal about who people are, are not, can be, should be. What makes women women and men men? The sportsmen who shot pigeons cared deeply about this question. And this age-old query has continued to be paired with this age-old practice. If Elvis had dropped into Mrs. Hemenway's parlor from the future, would she have asked him to stay to tea? Or Robert Bly and Clarissa Pinkola Estés, with ideas about men drumming naked in the woods and women running with the wolves? Their gender visions might have been irreconcilable—or maybe not. Yet think of Teddy Roosevelt's "strenuous life," Boy Scouts and Girl Scouts, and men's hunting clubs in the early 1900s, just after the bird-hat debate. And think of ecofeminism, Bly's Iron John, the Marlboro Man and *Dr. Quinn, Medicine Woman*—all very popular and powerful stories about women, men and nature—in the 1980s and 1990s. The Victorian calculus still endures, even: try reading the supermarket magazine *Victoria,* for example, with articles—"Living in Nature's Sweet Embrace: Where Only Birdsong Marks the Hours"—that can be as eye-widening as the *National Enquirer.* But whether late Victorian or New

You've come a long way, ladies!

THE AUDUBON SOCIETY TELLS THEIR HISTORY
In special anniversary issue of *Audubon,* 1973

Age, these nature stories all share a distinctively modern twist: they all tell us remarkably little about nature. And some of these omissions, even if only half willful, are extremely convenient.

And civilization? The club women's Big Project, for a new and better civilization in the brand-new century, ran into a great deal of trouble almost immediately. The landmarks of modern twentieth-century American life—urbanism, consumerism, capitalism, rationalist efficiency, technological progress—have never suffered for lack of enthusiasm since

tropical whites

A dress that displays its maker's trademark tour de force. OPPOSITE PAGE: Azzedine Alaïa's skintight knit, banded with peekaboo straps. About $1,260. Alaïa New York; Caron Cherry, Coconut Grove FL; Alaïa chez Gallay, Beverly Hills. THIS PAGE: More white—a treetop display of egrets roosting in mangroves. Details, more stores, last pages.

WOMEN AND EGRETS IN THE '90S

Fashion spread, *Vogue*, 1990

ACTRESS AND ESTÉE LAUDER
MODEL ELIZABETH HURLEY
in *People Weekly,* 1998

SPRITE-DRINKERS
RULE THE WORLD
in *Us,* 1994

the early 1900s. But we have matched an entrenched optimism with an equally deep anxiety—which *also* defines the modern era—as so many Americans have rejected or questioned the regnant ideals of "progress" and "civilization," and by the 1990s have threatened to wreck the project entirely on the shoals of relativism and postmodernism. As a major strand of countermodern skepticism, so many Americans have objected to the devastating consequences of modern life for the nonhuman natural world. After 1900, a search for truth and meaning in the world's wilder haunts took form in an expansive back-to-nature movement. And it became a major refrain in the postwar environmental movement.

This is my legacy. Like many baby boomers, and as a "nature person," I have turned to nature to critique modern life, and like the early foes of bird hats I have advocated restraint on the uses of resources. But we also have inherited the modern, convenient failure to make nature meaningful in ways that tell us *about* nature, and about our own economic connections to it. And these disconnections have haunted deeply the modern search for meaning, as in the twentieth century, so many Americans have turned to nature to assuage their doubts about modern life, and as consolation for regret.

3

A BRIEF NATURAL HISTORY
OF THE
PLASTIC PINK FLAMINGO

The plastic pink flamingo? What can a lawn ornament that sells for $7.95 (for a pair) at K-Mart really mean? "Nothing," had always been my own answer—but the pink creature turns out to be packed with surprising resonance and revelations for what *nature* has meant to Americans in the twentieth century. The bird's history speaks beautifully to my own generation of well-to-do baby boomers in particular—about our own meaningful, post–World War II exploits, and our specific failures of connection. It's especially eloquent about big, broad definitions

of Nature. And yet, the pink flamingo? As the environmentalist and nature writer Terry Tempest Williams has branded
it, "our unnatural link to the natural world?"

My faith in the meaningfulness of the plastic birds dates
back to a day in 1992, when after I had made disparaging
comments about the flock of birds in the yard of our rented
house, my housemate Kathy responded that she had moved
in because she liked them. An avid outdoorswoman, Kathy
told me she had traveled with a friend who had a pink
flamingo named Eudora and who had taken the bird backpacking, mountain-biking and cross-country skiing across
the Sierras and Alaska. Our houseguest Phil chimed in that
he had taken a pink flamingo on spring skiing trips in Colorado. I began to ask around. Another friend had stolen pink
flamingos off lawns on drunken late-night outings in high
school. A literary agent told me about a *New Yorker* editor
with a well-known collection. My thesis advisor remembered an NPR story on a kidnapped pair that had sent back
postcards from the Eiffel Tower. Between two commentators
for a 1992 paper I presented at an American history conference, the geographer had kept a flamingo that a scholar of
landscape architecture had brandished at the start of a lecture
(as the nadir of poor taste) and handed to him in the front
row; and the British historian loved them. My neighbor had
created a pink flamingo installation for an art show at college. A friend's family gave the birds as joke gifts to each
other at Christmas. Everyone seemed to have a pink

flamingo story to tell. Eudora herself had gotten left behind accidentally one summer in a cabin at Donner Pass. In memoriam, Kathy took one of ours on a winter kayaking trip to the Baja; and in the spring, she drafted all the birds as croquet wickets for her bring-your-own-Jell-O lawn party.

The plastic flamingo has been a compelling and pervasive object in American post–World War II culture. A cheap polyethylene replica of a real bird species that no longer even inhabits the United States, it has achieved fame and notoriety as a popular lawn ornament, the symbolic excrescence of bad taste, a travel companion, and even an objet d'art. The human stories around the plastic creatures have raged wildly and abundantly. Why put them on lawns? Why steal them *off* lawns? Why take a fake pink bird up a ski lift? And why put it in a backpack, where the allotment of every square inch is so remarkably careful? The deepest meanings of each of these flamingos, I've become convinced, owe their logic and fervor to deep meanings and big definitions of nature. The story of the pink lawn bird is the tale of how Americans converted a plastic object into the very symbol of what is artificial. It is a story of the meanings of Artifice. And that is a history, at the same time, of the meanings of Nature. In the 1990s, Nature has never seemed so urgent a place to turn for meaning, and the plastic flamingo has never sold as well. The two developments—and Nature and Artifice—are locked together absolutely in the same history.

Nature and Artifice

The plastic flamingo was invented in 1957, but lawn ornamentation has a prehistory that dates back many millennia—
to the stone gods of the ancient era, at least, that Greeks
and Romans planted in their gardens. I'll begin in mid-
eighteenth-century England, where the bird's meanings and
anti-meanings sink definable roots. At that time, a new
English school of landscape architects rejected the established
French and Italian ornamental traditions as too artificial, and
engineered a "naturalistic" revolution in landscape design. Led
by the great architect Lancelot "Capability" Brown, they created a new, more "natural" lawn aesthetic that would rival the
geometric gardens of seventeenth-century Versailles as a paradigm for the future, and would cast a great shadow forward
on American landscapes, American lawns, and the dos and
don'ts of American yard art. The new practitioners turned the
estates of English lords and aristocrats into rolling expanses of
meadows, trees, lakes and streams. And in these bastions of
Nature, the outdoor statuary, and all obvious signs of human
artifice, received a tenuous welcome. At Versailles, the royal architects lined the avenues and parterres with unprecedented
quantities of dragons, satyrs, lions, swans, wolves, nymphs and
Greek Gods, in marble, bronze and gilded lead. Across the English Channel, the natural landscapes featured rustic her-
mitages and a modest handful of stags or dogs—but nothing
so nonnative as a flamingo—in stone, and the gray-earth

shades of plain lead. Brown and his followers far preferred to deploy real animals such as sheep, cattle and, best of all, native deer. In their zeal to perfect the human-free aesthetic, they invented the "ha-ha," a deep, narrow trench that kept the ruminants on site as handily as a fence or hedge but created the vision of an unaltered expanse.

Natural versus artificial. Nature and Artifice. And yet, to turn an estate into Nature required great efforts of human intervention. As Brown's minions fanned across the English countryside (and by the mid-1800s, had blotted out geometry from nearly every large landholding), they constructed hills where the ground was flat, and dug new lakes. They planted tens of thousands of trees on each estate, chopped down entire groves of others, added dead trees back in for effect, cropped vast acreages of new grass and excavated ha-has. They made rivers bend and meadows roll. They made sunlight dapple. In some cases, they evicted longtime tenant farmers and razed their villages. It is tricky to say whether the "nature" they left behind them contained less "artifice" than the geometric avenues and precision topiary of Versailles—or less human labor and capital to maintain. The architects created not nature itself, in all its diversity, but an idea or definition of Nature—as a place that is absolutely free of humans and human artifice. They adhered, at the same time, to a definition of Artifice—as human invention that is absolutely free of nature. Just as American pigeon users would do a century later, they made nature meaningful, but in the process were losing track both of nature itself and of people's aggressive uses of it. Here, the very *definition* of Nature betrays a set of unmoored meanings. These estates of Nature were in fact an even mix of nature and artifice. Yet the English revolutionaries—as Brown's famous protegé Humphrey Repton enthused—set out to "conceal every interference of art, however expensive" and to "[make the landscape] appear the production of nature only."

Why? The blandishments of this definition of Nature as anti-Artifice have been enduring. Eighteenth- and early-nineteenth-century England—where the idea achieved an early power—was a seedbed of modern urbanization, industrialization and market capitalism, and saw the privatization and enclosure of once-common agricultural lands. As cities and new rural grids and fences expanded to dominate the landscape, many people began to define Nature as a realm that was yet untouched—as a sort of polar opposite. They defined Nature not as the parts of the natural world that humans use or change, but as the nature that humans *do not* use. Nature: a Place Out There, it was fast coming to represent everything that life in early modern England was not. It was not urban. It had no industrial factories. It was a place without economic activities, and a nonpopulated refuge from social upheaval. While early urban Americans would use pigeons and bird hats to define the world and their place within it, in the 1700s in English cities and towns there emerged a broad definition of Nature itself, which people used to order, define and navigate the changing landscape—social and natural—of the modern era.

Above all, as people in the throes of becoming modern converted nature into a Place Apart, without change, they appealed to Nature as a timeless source of authority. If humans didn't change or inhabit Nature, then wasn't it a separate, universal source of Truth—free of all human control? In the late 1700s and early 1800s, *natural* emerged as a potent watchword. Hume and Burke propounded "natural" theories of moral philosophy and politics. Adam Smith described the new market-based economy as a "natural" set of laws. Gainsborough painted a "natural" aesthetic. Wordsworth sought aesthetic and spiritual truths in Nature. Even etiquette manuals lauded the value of "naturalness" in manners and posture. If many people in early modern England defined Nature as not human in an increasingly human-made world, they at once designated it as an absolute source of authority in a society marked by rapid changes. Capability Brown translated this definition of Nature powerfully into concrete form, as a meaningful idea you could walk around in.

In fact, what claimed the authority of Nature more boldly and effectively than ownership of a vast expanse of Nature itself? *Who* claimed the authority of Nature? And who used Nature to define themselves? The urban poor and working classes were confined to the cities. And the rural peasants could hardly afford to treat nature as a place where one never farms or hunts. Only wealthy landowners enjoyed this definition—urban merchants who purchased country retreats, and landed aristocrats who could afford to take prime agricultural lands out of production. A Brown masterpiece made as definite a statement of social power as Versailles. If Louis XIV had declared his power of the throne through the rigid control of nature, English estate owners used rivers and hills to declare their wealth and power *as natural*. At a time when market capitalism and social mobility were eroding traditional social categories and patterns of deference, these wealthy elites called on Nature to buttress their authority. In these decades, many landowners hired Gainsborough and other artists to paint their families lounging, in "natural" and therefore naturally better postures, in their own vast and natural landscapes.

Ironically, in this era of explosive economic growth, these wealthy elites also happened to be exactly the humans who were using and changing nature by far the most. They were exactly the people who were losing track of their aggressive uses of nature. The definition of Nature as a Place Apart doesn't merely allow you to ignore your economic connections to nature (as urban American bird-hat foes and trap shooters conveniently did); it also actively *erases* them. All in all, English elites used a definition of Nature—a map of the ways that human and nonhuman nature are and are not connected—as a powerful conceptual tool. They used it to define the hallmarks of modern life. They used it to buttress their social status—to claim what's what and who's who. And they used it, consciously or not, to erase and evade their own, personal uses of resources. English landowners claimed Nature as their own. And much of the future history of this idea of Nature will unfold as a battle among the more monied so-

cial classes in particular—over who gets to claim the authority of Nature, and for what purposes.

The plastic pink flamingo was two centuries away. Meanwhile, in the late 1700s, French and Italian landowners were
hiring English architects to dig up their exquisite gardens
and convert them into Nature. Across the Atlantic, a few
wealthy and sophisticated Americans, such as Thomas Jefferson, also copied the English landscapes. In the United States,
people took to the natural aesthetics like birds to the sky.
After all, Americans have always embraced a meaningful vision of Nature both as countermodern and as a source of social and political authority—from the Puritans' "city on a
hill," to Jefferson's pastoral ideal that wed rural roots to re-
publican independence and virtue, to Thoreau's faith in
wilderness as an antidote to overcivilization. From national
myths of the American West to the remarkably literal Mount
Rushmore, Americans have made Nature a powerful source
of authority for American identity.

After the Revolution, landowners began to inscribe this
vision into their lawns. In the early Republic, the English
school found its great native apostle in Andrew Jackson
Downing, a nurseryman in upstate New York. As the Adam
of landscape architects in the United States, Downing reigns
as a key figure in American intellectual history. In the 1840s,
he made meadows roll, rivers meander and trees clump ir-
regularly on country estates throughout the Hudson River
Valley, where the famous "Hudson River school" of land-

scape painters committed similar visions to canvas. And he approached the question of outdoor ornamentation with a prudent dose of caution. "Vases, urns," "rustic baskets" and "other harmonious accessories": he deployed these only near the manor. A bit farther away, he planted "rockwork" and wooden "moss houses." On the farther reaches of one's lands, however, human artifice had to cede entirely to Nature. A vase way out there, he admonished, "[does] violence to our reason or taste." Downing planted trees and constructed hills to hide the sight of roads and towns. Like his English mentors, he landscaped a definition of Nature that, while heavy with human values, aggressively erased the economic connections that people made to nature. He set up a strict barrier between Nature and Artifice. At his own residence in Newburgh, he instructed his grounds staff of all-too-visible humans to use "invisible hands" to mow the lawns at night.

Downing's real passion was to design landscapes for smaller estates. Would Capability Brown have approved? In the democratic United States, a growing middle class owned property, too, and Downing, from a middle-class background himself, set out to downsize the English principles. How should Americans who owned less land—he recommended at least fifty acres, but consented to work with ten or twenty—"render their places tasteful and agreeable?" "We answer, *by attempting only the simple and natural*; and the unfailing way to secure this, is by employing as leading features only trees and grass." A few flowers, but no more. The utmost

A DOWNING IDEAL
In his
A Treatise on the Theory and Practice of Landscape Gardening
1859

axiom for turning a smaller landholding into Nature—and into all the meanings that Nature connoted—was to keep it free of ornament. You had to be very careful. "An humble cottage with sculptured vases" "would be in bad taste." Never "overload . . . with sculpturesque or artificial forms," he urged. The most "[tasteless lawns] in the United States" had "a mixed jumble of . . . ornaments and decorations." In his small-estate lawn strategy, Downing preached restraint and naturalness above all else. He generally referred to them as "taste." One could safely add a few rocks.

Taste: in the early 1800s, the American middle class had become obsessed with it. What *is* taste? It is hard to define, when one thinks about it. We can have taste in clothes, wine, furniture, art, décor. One generally has taste in things that one purchases, and the concept emerged with a vengeance as spreading wealth and new technologies for mass production equipped the growing numbers of urban middle-class consumers with the resources and tools to decorate and accessorize. Taste, you could say, is a style of consumerism. It is also a statement of identity, and it's exactly in the early 1800s that consumerism and American identity became inextricable. To some degree, taste was an upper-class injunction of restraint that advised the new consumers not to presume to be truly wealthy: it could be a fence that elites erected when class borders were threatened. And yet, the middle class rapidly made Taste their own, and counterdeployed it to reject the showy un-American excesses of the rich. In the United States, the middle classes often have had the upper hand on social authority. If you consumed tastefully, you advertised that you had abundant resources to buy things—unlike the working classes—but that you exercised a middle-class American virtue of restraint and the admirable market-economy ethic of self-control. "Taste" defended middle-class borders in both directions.

Yet taste was supposed to be a universally superior aesthetic. Is good taste supposed to be a middle-class style of consumerism? No, good taste just *is* (which is what can make it seem so hard to define). *Attempt only the simple and natural:*

it should not surprise us that tastemakers appealed en masse to Nature—the source of absolute social authority and a bedrock of American identity and of simplicity—to legitimate their aesthetic. American middle-class consumers converted the countermodern definition of Nature—a vision that erases people's economic ties to nature—into Taste's most essential accomplice. Andrew Jackson Downing, as much as anyone else, launched, defined and set into motion the canons of American taste. And why not? American consumers announced their identity on their most publicly visible possessions. Just as essential, they did so where Nature was closest at hand. And lawns swiftly became a chief battleground for ideas about taste, aesthetics, class, and how to be American.

In the United States, the yard-art wars, which European potentates had long waged among themselves, took on an excitable class dimension. The lawn battles intensified exactly as fast as the outward spread of suburbs. After the Civil War, a second Downing student, Frederick Law Olmsted—the legendary architect, of Central Park and the Boston Fens, who fiercely promulgated parks and lawns as refuges from the industrial cities and their social tensions—downsized the principles of Nature from smaller estates to largish lawns. He fueled a conversion of the countermodern definition of Nature into the rolling, tree-dotted, upper-middle-class neighborhood. But more and more people were leaving the cities. In the 1880s, as more modest middle-class suburbs proliferated, Frank Jesup Scott, another Downing student, downsized the Nature aesthetic even further to medium-sized lawns. In

The Art of Beautifying Home Grounds of Small Extent, a do-it-yourself manual, Scott advised the brand-new landowners to "endeavor to create an atmosphere of refinement." "Avoid spotting your lawn with . . . plaster or marble images of any kind, or those lilliputian caricatures." "There is nothing," he warned, "of which people . . . are so intolerant." Here, the rules of Taste and Nature left space for a tree or two, grass and a few flowers close to the door. If that sounds familiar, it remains the archetypal vision for the middle-class suburban front lawn. Scott's manual, Michael Pollan has written in his wonderful essays on the American lawn, "probably . . . more than any other [book determined] the look of the suburban landscape in America." Trees, grass and a few flowers.

The homeowners, however, were getting restless. In the 1880s and 1890s, advances in mass-production techniques made cheaper lawn ornaments available in cast-iron, lead, stone and plaster. In the 1920s, consumers bought cast-aluminum creatures. In the 1930s, do-it-yourselfers made deer, rabbits and frogs out of cement, which was the Depression material of choice. Each new decade brought more suburbs, more lawns, even smaller lawns and cheaper ornaments. It was inevitable that many Americans would transgress the boundaries of Taste. The down-classing of lawn art was well under way.

1950s Inventions

These trends culminated (or bottomed out) after World War II, in the dual and veritable explosions of plastics and suburbs. The remarkable affluence of the postwar years, with the dramatic expansion of the middle class, fueled a wildfire conversion of farmland into new suburbs. In the 1950s, developers plowed an average of three thousand acres each day. Many lower-middle-class Americans, and even some working-class families, now earned enough to buy single-family houses. Ranches, split-levels, Cape Cods, Tudors, Colonial Revivals, Mediterraneans. It was the era of upward mobility, of undreamed-of new levels of consumerism, and of the Baby Boom—when my parents moved into a tiny house just outside the St. Louis city limits, traded up five years later, in 1960, the year I was born, and took me and my three brothers to a spacious and memorable four-bedroom French colonial farther out.

The plastics industries, energized by an array of new wartime technologies, set out to accessorize the ranches and split-levels inside and out. Nylon, rayon, vinyl, polyester, Saran, Lucite, Plexiglas, Saran, polyethylene. The new petroleum-based plastics could take any shape and be any color. The companies could make anything cheaply with them, and did: radios, Tupperware, Barbie Dolls, Hula Hoops, duck-shaped juice pitchers, "walnut" paneling, "leather" car interiors, polyester pants, vinyl wallpaper and Naugahyde lounge chairs. "Better Things Through Better Living Through Chemistry," the Du Pont jingle went. After 1946, Union Products, a new plastics factory in Leominster (an industrial town outside Boston) manufactured outdoor dogs, frogs, ducks and a two-dimensional flamingo that sold very well. In

126

126

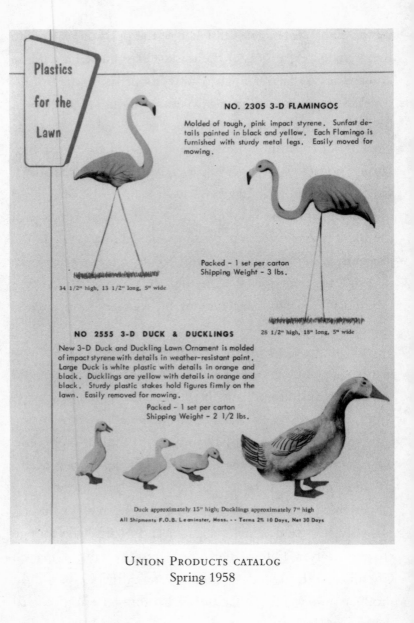

Plastics for the Lawn

NO. 2305 3-D FLAMINGOS

Molded of tough, pink impact styrene. Sunfast details painted in black and yellow. Each Flamingo is furnished with sturdy metal legs. Easily moved for mowing.

Packed – 1 set per carton
Shipping Weight – 3 lbs.

34 1/2" high, 13 1/2" long, 5" wide

28 1/2" high, 18" long, 5" wide

NO 2555 3-D DUCK & DUCKLINGS

New 3-D Duck and Duckling Lawn Ornament is molded of impact styrene with details in weather-resistant paint. Large Duck is white plastic with details in orange and black. Ducklings are yellow with details in orange and black. Sturdy plastic stakes hold figures firmly on the lawn. Easily removed for mowing.

Packed – 1 set per carton
Shipping Weight – 2 1/2 lbs.

Duck approximately 15" high; Ducklings approximately 7" high
All Shipments F.O.B. Leominster, Mass. - - Terms 2% 10 Days, Net 30 Days

UNION PRODUCTS CATALOG
Spring 1958

1956, the company hired Don Featherstone, a recent young art-school graduate, who for the sake of anatomical accuracy on a three-dimensional molded-polyethylene duck named Charlie the Duck—his first design creation—drew life studies on a live duck in his studio for six months. In 1957—when Wham-O introduced the Hula Hoop, and the peak year of the Baby Boom—Featherstone designed his second big project, a three-dimensional flamingo that sold even better than the company's flat version: he used photographs, since real flamingos were unavailable. Union Products marketed their wares at Sears, Woolworth's, Ben Franklin's and other variety and department stores. "Flamingo pink," the 1957 Sears catalog advertised. "Place in garden, lawn, to beautify landscape." "Lifelike." "Lovely." In the decades ahead the flamingo would only rarely outsell the ducks. But it would become far more famous.

The bird took up residence in working-class subdivisions. As you may suspect, not everyone bought the plastic lawn creatures. Middle-class suburbanites hewed fairly solidly to the aesthetics of Taste and the definitions of Nature. Lakewood, Park Forest, Springfield Garden, Glen Cove: even the names of many of these subdivisions define them as Nature's neighborhoods. For the newly affluent, the green lawns of Nature advertised the counterurban meanings of leisure, beauty and quiet that made these suburbs a refuge from the cities. And Nature was absolutely essential to Taste, and *its* well-established meanings of American virtue and economic independence. *How Good Is Your Taste?*, *Good Taste Costs No*

More. In the 1950s, a fast-growing literature and a brace of new home and garden magazines urged the new middle-class consumers to adhere closely to the canons of Taste. Avoid artifice, embrace understatement, stay natural. One can say that the sizable houses in these suburbs, such as the one in which I was raised, attested to social status and moderate wealth—and the green lawns of Nature stated an ethic of restraint. And on lawns that ranged in size from small-medium to medium-large, Taste mandated the near-total "trees, grass, a few flowers" ban on artifice. Any signs of human presence, such as swingsets, gardens and barbecue pits, were consigned to the backyard: my parents concealed our own side-lot garden with a rustic iron fence. An absence of humans remains a signature feature of the middle-class suburban front lawn. A second trademark of these lawns, of course, is that they require great investments of money and labor and a vast herbicide industry to maintain. As an ideal of all-Nature, the lawn is just a fickle square of one or two European grass species. And like a Capability Brown masterpiece, the lawn, as a no-artifice zone of Nature, actively hides much of the abundant human artifice that homeowners use to create it.

In working-class subdivisions, where lawn size ranged from small to large postage stamp, if you wanted to hew to the Nature aesthetic, you'd have to downsize to grass and perhaps a tulip. To achieve a convincing bastion of Nature, though, you had to have more space. To be tasteful, too, one really needed more room in which to act restrained. A plain green lawn in front of a large house stated "affluent, but tasteful." But a little swatch of lawn in front of a small house in a working-class neighborhood said "inexpensive, and can't afford more." Below a certain level of wealth, Taste ceases to work, which is not surprising, since Taste had emerged as a middle-class statement of identity. The counterurban definition of Nature, too, could be hostile. Nature as a refuge from what? From urban stress and noise, but also from the very social groups who lived in the neighborhoods closer to the cities.

Avoid artifice and stay understated? Working-class consumers generally embraced a different style. On average, they favored bolder strategies to landscape their pieces of the American dream. They emphasized rather than underplayed their presence and spending power, and made the most of limited means. They found ample space for human artifice. Many planted their lawns with squirrels, frogs, lighthouses, toadstools, flamingos and windmills. In Catholic neighborhoods, the plastic creatures became a logical extension, too, of the religious figures that immigrants in the cities had planted in their porches and window boxes. The new working-class suburbs now regularly made room for both genres, as families set flamingos next to Madonnas in half-sunken bathtub shrines. As second- and third-generation Catholics moved to middle-class enclaves farther out, however, many would reject their parents' lawn displays with embarrassment, or at least move their own to the backyard. What would Frank Jesup Scott have written? Sears did a brisk business in pink flamingos. The Union Products creature was not understated. It was not Nature. And in the 1950s, the plastic birds only cost $2.76 a pair.

The flamingo splashed into the market in the fifties as an especially bold and emphatic statement. The bird staked two major claims to boldness. First, it was a flamingo. Since the 1930s, Americans had been flocking south to Florida for vacations and traveling back home with flamingo souvenirs. In the 1910s and 1920s, entrepreneurs had dredged Miami Beach out of the swamps as a winter resort for the rich and had made the first grand hotel, the Flamingo, synonymous with the wealth and pizazz of south Florida. After a 1926 hurricane leveled Millionaire's Row, developers built hundreds of more modest resort hotels, in an anomalous building boom in the heart of the Depression, to cater to new train lines and an eager middle class. In South Beach, especially, architects built in the playful Art Deco style, replete with pinks, bright colors and flamingo motifs. The flamingo also symbolized Hialeah Park, the elegant and sophisticated racetrack that boasted private boxes for the Vanderbilts and Kennedys and had a stately landscape of lakes, palms and tropical gardens. In 1932, for opening day, the owners imported a flock of real flamingos, which promptly flew back to Cuba. The next season, a new flock with clipped wings made the infield lake at the site of the prestigious Flamingo Stakes their permanent habitat.

All of which was a little ironic, since flamingos had been hunted to extinction in south Florida in the late 1800s, for plumes and meat. But no matter. In the 1950s, the new interstates also drew working-class tourists to south Florida—and back in New Jersey, flamingo postcards, mugs, lamps and shower curtains testified to these vacations. The plastic bird from Union Products inscribed a suburban lawn emphatically with the same cachet of leisure, wealth and extravagance. The flamingo acquired an extra fillip of boldness, too, from the direction of Las Vegas, the flamboyant oasis of instant riches that the gangster Benjamin "Bugsy" Siegel had conjured from the desert in 1946. Siegel had launched his resort with a grand Flamingo Hotel, which boasted a neon flamingo sign, and imported live flamingos for opening day. His garish creation (he came from working-class Brooklyn) looks like a parody of extravagance. Anyone who has seen Las Vegas knows that a flamingo stands out in a desert far more boldly even than on a suburban green lawn. In the 1950s, namesake Flamingo hotels, restaurants and lounges cropped up across the country like semiotic sprouts.

And the pink flamingo was pink—a second and commensurate claim to boldness. In the 1950s the plastics industries marketed a vast array of consumer items in flashy colors, with pinks in the vanguard. The popular bright new colors, as Tom Wolfe described them, were "the new electrochemical pastels of the Florida littoral: tangerine, broiling magenta, livid pink, incarnadine, fuschia demure, Congo ruby, methyl green." The hues were forward-looking and not old-fashioned: they were for a generation raised in the Depression who were ready boldly to celebrate their new affluence. The new plastics seemed boldest, and most futuristic and high-tech, in colors you didn't often see in nature. The plastics and bright colors were not-Nature in a *good* way. Washing machines, cars and kitchen counters proliferated in passion pink, sunset pink, and Bermuda pink. As the historian Karal Ann Marling has written, the "sassy pinks" were "the hottest color of the decade." Even many middle-class suburbanites who stayed faithful to aesthetics of Taste and Nature on their lawns indulged a flashier style in their kitchens—as *Life* and *House Beautiful* droned on about the dangers of tasteless excess. Yet according to 1959 surveys in Vance Packard's *The Status Seekers,* working-class consumers on average favored brighter colors. Bugsy Siegel filled the Flamingo's hotel rooms in Vegas with bright-pink leather furniture. Elvis, as Marling has written, bought his first pink Cadillac after he signed his first recording contract in 1956: the working-class singer "was bound for glory in a fleet of Cadillacs and wanted the whole world to sit up and take notice." After all, why call the birds "pink flamingos"—as if they could be blue or green? The pink flamingo is a hotter pink than a real flamingo. On a green lawn, it is bold. Among even the pinkest of real pink flowers and real pink birds it is emphatic. It sticks out. Having put two of them in my mother's English shade garden, I can tell you this is true.

Historically, flamingos have always stood out. There are five species of real flamingos, which gather and feed in large flocks on algae and invertebrates in saline and alkaline shallow lakes and lagoons, in a range of mostly warm and generally inhospitable habitats around the world. The people who have lived near and around these places have without exception singled out the bright, big birds as special. Early Christians associated the flamingo with the red Phoenix. In ancient Egypt, it symbolized the sun god Ra. In Mexico and the Caribbean, the bird remains a major motif in art, dance and literature. Like other obvious and unusual creatures— such as lions, grizzly bears and passenger pigeons—flamingos have taken on heavy doses of human myth and symbol. But in the 1950s, people made the American flamingo meaningful for the very fact that it stood out. As with pigeon ballotines and terns on hats, the meanings of the plastic birds said a little about real flamingos—which latitudes they lived in and what color they were—but not much. Americans reproduced the likeness of a subtropical flamingo species in New England, and set the birds out across temperate latitudes onto an inland sea of grass.

Boundary Violations

It was bound to get noticed. As pink flamingos spread across the nation, they ran afoul very quickly of the arbiters of culture. And in the debates on lawn art, so far no one had developed a sense of humor. Art critics launched the most direct attacks. In *Kitsch: The World of Bad Taste*, Gillo Dorfles identified the new lawn-and-garden creatures as the "archetypal

image" of fast-spreading bad taste. Like many anti-kitsch critics, Dorfles took his cue from Clement Greenberg, who in a
1939 credo had defined and excoriated kitsch as "the debased
. . . simulacra of genuine Culture," in "the midst of the decay
of our present society." Greenberg had warned that kitsch
"[drew] its life blood" from real Culture, and Dorfles now
lamented that the "vampire kitsch" had evolved into "one of
the crucial problems in the history of art and aesthetics."

The art critics were just one set of postwar intellectuals
who engaged in attacks on American mass culture in the
1950s and 1960s. Critics had assailed the mass-produced arts
for many decades, but the evils were multiplying as fast as
plastics, and from Right and Left the new Jeremiahs fulmi-
nated against mass art, fiction and movies—and were on the
verge of uniting against the nascent sins of television. "Mass
culture is . . . a cancerous growth on High Culture," the influential critic Dwight Macdonald charged in 1953. It was a
"spreading ooze," and many like-minded intellectuals feared
the same: "Mass culture threatens . . . to cretinize our taste." It
was cheap and tasteless. The highbrow critics defended the
mandate of Taste with a tenacity that betrayed the swiftness of
its erosion. They showed even greater angst, however, for the
state of *reality*. Mass culture, Macdonald feared, "voids . . . the
deep realities," and "substitute[s] for the . . . originality . . . of
real life." Greenberg had attacked kitsch as "vicarious experience and faked sensations" and "the epitome of all that is spu-
rious in the life of our times." Dorfles agreed: it "killed all
ability to distinguish between art and life."

Reality: in the 1950s, it emerged as a central trope in dialogues on American society. Just as Taste was fortified by Nature and a countermodern sensibility, you can say that Reality—which, like Taste, defies exact definitions and easy explanations—expressed a set of rising worries about replication and the modern mediation of experience. Many Americans pitted Reality against whatever seemed ephemeral—as more enduring, more absolute, more unique. *Un*-Reality, you could say, was human artifice run amok. What more logical authority to appeal to than Nature? Like Downing and all the tastemakers, the new defenders of Reality drafted the idea of Nature—a bastion of anti-Artifice and an absolute source of human authority—as an essential ally. If a lawn flamingo previously had not been tasteful or restrained, now it was un-*real*; in both cases, it was anti-Nature. Fifties critics used the unerasable boundary between Nature and Artifice to define the border between Real and not-Real—and used it to set human standards in the midst of rapid changes in the ways Americans were both producing and consuming culture. In fact, Nature can seem even closer to Reality than to Taste. In the toolbox of useful ideas with which to judge and navigate modern life, the idea of Nature as anti-Artifice had received a promotion. And plastic lawn creatures—gnomes, flamingos, pietàs, Saint Francises and Donald Ducks—emerged as a nadir of the un-Real. As well as being fake, false, nonunique and ungenuine, they transgressed Reality publicly and brazenly, on the actual site of Nature itself. In the early 1960s, Union Products issued a new line of lawn mice: they sold very well, but

soon would be superseded by new ladybugs and beehives.
Macdonald was pessimistic about mass culture: "We will be
lucky if it doesn't get worse."

At the same time, mass tourism came under attack as the
dire proliferation of ersatz experience. Like aesthetic standards,
social boundaries were also in flux. And south Florida and Las
Vegas—where working-class Americans presumed to luxury
and extravagance at Caesar's Palace, Flamingo hotels and cheap
French provincial motels with parterre gardens—merited special attention (from Tom Wolfe, among others) as centers for
kitsch and tastelessness and as black holes of the fake and ungenuine. In the geography of un-Reality in the fifties and sixties, the suburbs attracted a battalion of critics, too. In the
influential 1956 tract *The Organization Man,* William Whyte
argued against postwar suburbs as homogeneous, cultureless
and void of the very individualism that so many Americans
had moved there to pursue. Suburbs were mass housing for
mass consumers. A *Fortune* editor, Whyte sparked a rash of
laments—"The Suburban Problem," "Trouble in Suburbia,"
"Suburbia: Lost Paradise?"—that bemoaned the consequences
of "mass experience" for a Real Self. "Little Boxes / made of
ticky-tacky / little boxes / all the same," as the 1963 song goes.
And nothing symbolized the un-Real suburbs better or more
visibly than the regulation lawn.

The American lawn suffered a separate rash of attacks, as
well, from a very different set of advocates of Reality. In the
1960s, Americans in the natural-lawn and organic-gardening
movements rejected the lawn—very usefully—as an alien

planting of nonnative species that required dangerous herbicides and a lawn-care industry led by ChemLawn and Tech-
niturf to maintain. The new eco-advocates charged that the
lawns of Nature in fact were bastions of toxicity. But if they
rejected lawns as ecologically disastrous, they also rejected
them as "lifeless [and] artificial": the lawn was anti-Nature. In
other words, natural-lawn promoters and ChemLawn clients
adhered to the same definition of Nature as a force of anti-
Artifice and a countermodern stronghold (" 'people
refuges,' " an *Organic Gardening* author wrote, "where we can
escape occasionally and knit the ravelled edges of our spirits
into place"), yet defined the lawn as either Nature *or* Artifice. And the antilawn camp pitted the gaining trope of Reality against the traditional canons of Taste—all fortified by
Nature. The eco-advocates promoted more natural planting
strategies, from the use of native grasses and a moratorium on
mowing to wildflower gardens, wetlands, organic vegetable
gardens, and burn-your-own prairies—"great pasture for the
hard-pressed human soul." The conflicts grew heated. "Are
you or have you ever been," a prosecuting attorney in Wisconsin asked one suburbanite whose grass had exceeded the
legal twelve-inch limit in Sun Shadows West subdivision, "a
member of any of those groups interested in preserving all
types of plants?" As Taste battled Reality in the courts—and
all sides battled Artifice—at least one natural-lawn practitioner vowed she would fill her yard, if she were forced to
mow the grass, with bathtub Madonna shrines, toilet-bowl
flower planters, and a lot of plastic pink flamingos.

"How to Quit Mowing Your Lawn Without Going to Jail"
Article in *Family Handyman magazine*
1979

By the mid-1960s, these battalions of postwar critics all had raised direct or indirect objections to lawn flamingos. Each vaunted different beliefs. Gillo Dorfles, Tom Wolfe and the home-prairie advocates weren't exactly bowling buddies. But all—and all were affluent—expressed deep concerns about American postwar society. All appealed to Nature as a countermodern source of authority to determine what is and is not Real. In the midst of an economic boom, each of these critics empowered a definition of Nature that both tells us little about nature and erases people's useful connections to it. And all rejected plastic lawn ornaments as one of the clearest transgressions of Reality and Nature. By 1970, even Sears had withdrawn the Union Products flamingos from its catalog, and replaced them with fountains and with fiberglass waterfalls "with uneven layering . . . that resembles the natural, rugged beauty of authentic slate."

Artificiality, mass conformity, false experience. These were fast emerging as the targets of the 1960s counterculture as well. The baby boomers in the expanded middle classes had grown up in the affluent new suburbs, with the pink washing machines and trimmed green lawns, and as they came of age, famously began to reject much of it. They rejected Taste and elitist standards, too, but you could say that my generation took many of the intelligentsia's critiques of postwar and modern American society and made them the basis of an entire middle-class generational *identity*. And the rebel demographic who made "Get Real" one of our most famous slogans adapted Reality to criticize a wide range of social, economic and political policies—and appealed, with the weight of historical logic behind us, to Nature as the absolute counterforce. We used Reality and Nature interchangeably, and made Nature less a supporting authority and more a reigning ideal than ever before. Some baby boomers joined back-to-the-land movements and went right to the source, following the advice of writers, such as Gary Snyder, who prescribed a simpler and more natural life as the antidote to capitalist high-tech consumer society. Among the rest of us, many went camping and backpacking. But as a generation, whether we went *to* Nature or not, so many of us used it as a metaphor: as an idea, Nature had always said far more about people than nature. In *The Greening of America*, the best-selling generational manifesto, Charles Reich commended blue jeans as a rejection of the "artificial look of the affluent society." As he reviewed, in order, the problems of corruption, hypocrisy, war, uncontrolled technology, the decline of democracy and liberty, the artificiality of work and culture, the absence of community and the loss of self, he championed the counterculture's mission to replace "the false culture that goes with false consciousness" with a new "culture that rejects the substitution phenomenon . . . wherein artificiality replaces the natural." The Revolution, as the historian Robert Gottlieb has remarked, would definitely be "an Earth Happening." We took the authority of Nature for ourselves and converted the definition of Nature as anti-Artifice—a vision that ignores the use of nature as economic resources—into a major supporting beam in middle-class baby-boomer identity.

Along with the postwar critics, the baby boomers armed themselves with Reality and Nature and converged on the ersatz and artificial. And in the fifties, sixties and early seventies, all the forces hostile to Artifice pounced on one target with unanimous and utmost scorn: PLASTIC. The uses and manufacture of plastics continued to soar. But plastic crashed from a metaphoric peak, as "better things through better living through chemistry," to "everything gone wrong with the nation's soul." As Joan Didion remarked, America's "most publicized self-doubts [were] Vietnam, Saran Wrap, diet pills, [and] the Bomb." Clement Greenberg had derided "plastic artists." Dorfles hailed a colleague's analysis of "the Plastic Parthenon" of mass culture. Little houses "made of ticky-tacky"—well, the suburbs were definitely plastic. A new natural-landscaping firm in Washington, D.C., set out to "[do] away with that evergreen plastic look." Snyder wrote poems against "plastic spoons, plywood veneer, PVC pipe, vinyl seat covers." Reich hailed blue jeans as a strike against "the neon colors and plastic," and a New Left manifesto excoriated the "white honkie culture . . . handed to us on a plastic platter." And in 1968, when an affluent white honkie suburbanite put his arm around Dustin Hoffman in *The Graduate* and said—"I just want to say one word to you. Just one word . . . PLASTICS"—the line captured perfectly the disaffections of an entire generation of middle-class baby boomers. Although Americans had tended to define plastic as not-Nature since the early twentieth century, they had most often described it as an improvement on or miraculous freedom from nature. In the 1960s, plastic became the supreme violation of Reality and Nature by the evils of Artifice. It had evolved into a kind of vile metonym.

What could be more plastic than the pink flamingo? What was more artificial than a bright-hot-pink plastic flamingo (in 1968, Sears sold the birds for $3.69 a pair) that stuck out like a UFO on a suburban lime-green lawn in Iowa or New Jersey? When, exactly, it became the very definition of anti-Nature—the lawn art of lawn art, the gewgaw among all gewgaws, the concrete actualization of the terrible sins of Artifice—is hard to say. But it's safe to say that by 1972, when John Waters's movie *Pink Flamingos* opened with a shot of plastic flamingos outside the trailer of a 300-pound woman played by the transvestite actor Divine—who vies successfully for the national title of Filthiest Person Alive by eating dog feces and murdering her competitors for the benefit of tabloid and TV reporters—it clearly had happened.

A Life of Irony

And that's when people began to laugh. Divine's character Babs Johnson has bleach-blonde hair and wears garish makeup and print housedresses. She drives a '58 Cadillac, urinates on suburban lawns, and has sex with her son, who himself has sex with a dead chicken. Waters advertised the movie as an "exercise in poor taste," and "liked the understatement." He enjoyed the reviews, too: *Variety* panned the movie as "one of the most vile, stupid and repulsive films ever made," and the *New York Times* critic Vincent Canby wrote that it "carries its audience back through puberty to the cradle and faulty toilet training." "It's like getting a standing ovation," Waters explained, "if someone vomits watching one of my films." The underground press loved *Pink Flamingos*, and crowned Waters the Prince of Puke.

Waters had grown up in an upper-middle-class suburb in Baltimore. And what more fun and satisfying way for rebel baby boomers to reject their parents' middle-class beliefs than to assault the collective faith in Taste—and to use a blatant symbol of Artifice and anti-Nature? Still, if our parents' generation embraced Taste, Waters's cohort adhered to the trope of Reality; and the plastic flamingo, as an exaggeration

DIVINE
in *Pink Flamingos*

of Artifice, at once made a statement about the extreme un-Reality of modern American society. Waters and his cronies were like the comic wing of the counterculture and the New Left—and a reaction to self-seriousness. They, too, defined American society as plastic and un-Real, but Artifice could be fun, couldn't it? Their ironic celebration of Artifice presupposed the critique. In sum, the boomers excoriated Nature as the accomplice of Taste, and at once emphasized Nature as Reality's chief deputy. "We were united," Waters has said of himself and Divine, "by four things: anger, pot, defiance, and a sense of humor." In Waters's 1977 movie, *Desperate Living*, which features nudism, cannibalism, a sex change and female wrestling, the heroine yells, "Look at those disgusting trees stealing my oxygen! . . . ALL NATURAL FORESTS SHOULD BE TURNED INTO HOUSING DEVELOPMENTS! I WANT CEMENT COVERING EVERY BLADE OF GRASS IN THE NATION!" To "understand bad taste," Waters has written, "one has to have very good taste." It was the middle-class baby boomers, who had been well-schooled in the canons of Taste and Nature, and who themselves guarded the Nature-Artifice boundary, who adopted the bird, converted it into a tool for rebellion and started it on a second, ironic life.

Elsewhere, in the 1960s art world, pop artists also brazenly celebrated the extremes of Artifice. Led by Andy Warhol most notoriously, they actively sought out the cheap, the ersatz, the mass-produced, the plastic, the not-Real. Warhol's grids of identical Campbell's soup cans, Brillo boxes, Elvises and Mona Lisas deliberately tapped the deepest fears of the standard bearers and kitsch haters. "I am for the art of cheap plaster and enamel," Claes Oldenburg declaimed in an early-sixties manifesto. "I am for art you can pick your nose with or stub your toes on," "for the majestic art of dog-turds," "for Kool-art, 7-UP art, Pepsi-art . . . Ex-lax art . . . Meat-o-rama art." Warhol christened his 1966 disco the Plastic Inevitable. Just as Waters transgressed the boundaries of Taste by embracing Artifice, the pop artists mocked Nature and embraced Artifice to transgress the established boundaries of Taste and Art. And like Waters, they commented on mass culture, and exaggerated Artifice, in terms that at once celebrated and critiqued them. As Oldenburg wrote, "I am for an art that embroils itself with the everyday crap & still comes out on top."

The uses and meanings of the pink flamingo had forked into new territory. Gay men, too, adopted the plastic lawn bird. Waters planted his movies firmly in the camp sensibility of the 1960s and 1970s, in which transvestism and drag queens have played a major and visible part. Gay men waged arguably the most creative celebration of the extremes of Artifice. And the most transgressive—since for what mainstream social standard have postwar Americans appealed to the absolute authority of Nature more vehemently than heterosexuality? What more provocative way to transgress sexual norms than by the violation of Nature? As Susan Sontag wrote in a groundbreaking essay, "Nothing in nature can be campy. . . . the essence of Camp is its love of the unnatural . . . of artifice and exaggeration." Camp devotees played kitsch, and the most despised detritus of mass culture, to the hilt. Versailles emerged as a camp Eden. Drag queens donned a preponderance of pink and plastic. And the pink flamingo settled in to enjoy a secure berth in the symbolic arsenal of the gay and camp subcultures.

The tastemakers soldiered on. In the early 1970s, a new spree of manuals—such as *Good Taste: How to Have It, How to Buy*

It—urged suburbanites to keep their lawns simple and natural. Union Products issued a new pig in a three-piece suit that sold well. They also marketed a "flamingo deluxe," with more natural, yellow legs, but it didn't sell. Who would prefer it? Not the working-class fans, who liked their lawn birds flashy; nor the tasteful middle-class homeowners; nor especially the baby boomer fans, who deployed the bird as a statement of Artifice and anti-Nature. In the late 1970s, pink flamingos began to accompany middle-class baby boomers on spring skiing trips, and to vanish into the hands of thieves under cover of night. Having become an established symbol—a marker of the transgression of the unmovable boundary of Nature—the bird became a useful thing to have around if you were doing anything outrageous, rebellious, oxymoronic, inappropriate or transgressive. It became an effective way to post a sign: Something Subversive Happening Here. What did the pink flamingo have to do with real flamingos—any of the five species that feed in flocks on alkaline and saltwater coasts? Increasingly even less. It had a lot to do, however, with definitions of Nature: their resonant meaningfulness, limits of revelation and well-proven usefulness for navigating the cultural, social and economic moguls of the postwar era. The baby boomers didn't invent the bird. But as with television, we were born with it and grew up with it. And we appropriated it for ourselves. Through the 1970s, we used the pink flamingo as a ubiquitous signpost for crossing the various, overlapping boundaries of class, taste, propriety, art, sexuality and Nature.

And then, the uses and meanings of the pink flamingo became highly complex. In 1984, the popular new cop show *Miami Vice* splashed a glitzy vision of Miami, and real flamingos in the opening credits, across American TV screens. Plastic flamingo sales boomed. In 1986, a year before the bird's thirtieth birthday, Union Products sold more flamingos than Charlie the Ducks for the first time. The flamingo reclaimed its original fifties cachet of flashiness but with a new constituency of higher-income fans. Soon you could order the plastic lawn birds through a *Rolling Stone* ad, or from the flamingo specialty store Cat's Pyjamas, where the same box of two cost two dollars more than a pair for $7.95 at Kmart.

The 1980s had arrived. As the sixties rebels streamed into their thirties and moved as adults into professions in the economic mainstream, the thirty-something yuppies famously liked to remain, on average, social critics and cultural rebels. As the early-1960s Port Huron manifesto for the New Left had begun, "We are people of this generation, bred in at least modest comfort . . . looking uncomfortably to the world we inherit"—and in the Reagan 1980s, we began uncomfortably to inherit the world in more than modest comfort. As we gained adult legitimacy, so did our desires and pet peeves. The crossing of boundaries, that had in the sixties and seventies been so transgressive, remained a badge of identity, but was now safer, and was very often a matter of style. The flamingos at poolside and on condo porches were like blue jeans in boardrooms and Jeeps in Upper West Side garages— or the Don Johnson combination, in *Miami Vice*, of a white

Armani suit with a two-day beard and no socks—except that as an established signpost for boundary transgression, the flamingo was a veritable billboard for the new legitimacy of not selling out. As the Cat's Pyjamas catalog advertised, just above a listing for a pink-flamingo vinyl doormat: "On every page, you'll find just what you need to ruin your neighborhood." You could even say that the social-rebel style mimicked Taste, which so many of our parents adhered to, as an approach to American consumerism—that it let us enjoy our wealth and status and consume a great many things, but with an agreed-upon sense of virtue and even aesthetic restraint. The well-off baby boomers were not tasteful consumers necessarily, but we were cool.

In the 1980s, many of us began to use flamingos to cross boundaries of all sorts. Americans traveled with the birds across the borders of states and nations. Like Eudora, many flamingos went hiking, skiing and snowmobiling into the wildest reaches of the Rocky Mountains, the Sierras, Alaska and the snowed-in shores of Hudson Bay. We bought flamingos as birthday, housewarming and moving presents. The birds showed up as wedding decorations, and we used them instead of reindeer in Christmas lawn tableaux—and as the bird's creator Don Featherstone has pointed out, "I've never seen a wedding cake with a *duck* on it." They got drafted as croquet wickets at bring-your-own-Jell-O lawn parties, thrown by the sort of people who do not throw lawn parties. In sum, after the flamingo had become a baby-boomer signpost for boundary transgressions—having evolved in the

1950s, 1960s and early 1970s into the metonymy of Artifice and anti-Nature—in the 1980s, we logically began to use it, in an unorchestrated rash of gestures coast to coast, as a marker for crossing into new places, times, eras, stages of life and even into the most sacrosanct reaches of Nature itself. We used the bird as a generalized boundary crosser, not just as a boundary transgressor. At the same time, the truly transgressive crossings had become less dangerous than they once were. Thieves, for example, still snatched the ornaments at night, and a great many police-station evidence rooms held flamingos waiting to be identified and retrieved, but the owners of the birds now posted mock reward notices and met ransom demands with play money and pink champagne. In the early 1970s, by contrast, such thefts had shared the same reception and nocturnal defiance as Leftist missions to repaint black lawn jockeys with African liberation colors.

The boundaries of art, too, had become easier and less dangerous to transgress. The steady border traffic after the pop artists inevitably had to wear them down, as more and more artists flocked to pop-culture topics and used cheap mass-produced materials. By the 1980s, kitsch exhibits appeared in art galleries, while historic-preservation groups campaigned to save and restore Art Deco centers such as South Beach. In 1983, the artist Christo—who had run an orange nylon curtain across a canyon in Colorado—wrapped eleven islands off the coast of Miami with bands of hot-pink polypropylene plastic. What did the floating tutus mean? The project could be a self-conscious transgression from high art to mass culture which, like Warhol's soup cans, maintained the boundaries by commenting on them. It also could be evidence of the erosion of these same borders. Inevitably it made a statement (what, exactly?) about Nature and Artifice in modern American society. Of course, the pink flamingo made exactly the same sorts of statements, for less than ten dollars and without the aid of a fleet of boats. Young artists in the 1980s built pink flamingo installations, and featured the birds in photography shows on lawn ornaments. In 1987, the governor of Massachusetts formally proclaimed the state's indigenous pink flamingo an essential contribution to American folk art. The metonymy of Artifice, the worst and kitschiest example of mass-produced fake wannabe art, actually had been crowned Art. The bird's ascendance reigns as cogent evidence of the shake-up of the hegemony of highbrow aesthetics—of both the increase in border crossings and the breakdown of the borders themselves.

Still, the pink flamingo graduated to Art as an alembic of Artifice. It gained its new legitimacy not so much on its own aesthetic merits, but from the ascendance of baby boomers in the art world—and to the centrality of Artifice to their collective identity. The idea of Artifice, in turn, had evolved, as if from Adam's rib, from definitions of Nature. In the 1980s, Artifice as anti-Nature consolidated its firm place in the adult baby boomers' identity by at least two routes, and continued to fuel the flamingo's enduring power as a meaningful object. First, the thirty-somethings began to wax nostalgic en masse about the 1950s. The pink flamingo effectively called up a collective childhood past: the innocence and optimism, and exuberant Artifice, of the era of passion-pink washing machines and grassy new suburbs. Pink flamingos manufactured in the fifties and sixties began to appear (with Art Deco bric-a-brac) in antique stores—even though these fifty-dollar birds had been manufactured from essentially the same mold as the new ones at Kmart. But the 1950s children had been 1960s rebels, too. We'd used the authority of Nature to rage against the plastic artificiality of postwar society, and we'd embraced the extremes of Artifice both to rebel against Taste and to emphasize American society as un-Real—but also to show that the un-Reality of American society could be fun to play in. In the 1980s, many middle-class baby boomers would exude a cool, ironic, half-affectionate, half-mocking stance toward TV, lawn ornaments and the rest of what Dwight Macdonald had labeled the "spreading ooze." Some of us worried and wrung our hands about mass culture. Some of us enjoyed it. Many of us did a little of both. Regardless, whether in the comic or tragic vein, the Get Real generation continued to rely on the definitions of Nature and Artifice (or anti-Nature) to define the modern postwar era and their place in it.

The retail landscape was changing fast to tap into the yuppies' convictions and desires. Ironically, or conveniently, as we fortified a definition of Nature as a Place Apart—that erases people's *uses* of nature as economic resources—we were consolidating our own economic affluence and power. And many new companies sailed into two major nerve centers of our identity: Nature and Artifice. One set of companies—

Forever Flamingo, Do Wah Diddy, Sarsaparilla Deco Designs—satisfied the nostalgic embrace of 1950s Artifice. A
second set marketed the Waters-style, ironic embrace of the
extremes of Artifice: Cat's Pyjamas, Poor Taste, the Pink
Flamingo Boutique and Archie McPhee's Toy Store and
Espresso Tiki Hut—"outfitters of popular culture," with velvet tapestries, plastic executives, Pez and a $5.95 Gumby-like
two-child 1950s Bend-A-Family. All these stores either specialized in pink flamingos or featured them prominently. In
the Nature camp, The Nature Company, which had founded
the nature-store genre a decade earlier, spread nationally after
1983. Here, the pink flamingo was non grata. These were
anti-Artifice zones. The Nature Company, Natural Wonders,
The Natural Selection and zoo gift shops—so many of
which were remodeled in the 1980s to mimic this genre—
sold nothing that Do Wah Diddy, Archie McPhee's and Poor
Taste did. The St. Louis zoo gift shop sold flamingo pins, a
polyester flamingo named "Laverne," and a music box that
had two revolving flamingos and played "The Way We Were."
But a plastic pink flamingo on the shelves—the very emblem
of Artifice—would have cast suspicion on the Nature of
everything else.

By the late 1980s, the flamingo had acquired a great measure of legitimacy and marketability. Lawn ornament fads
came and went—Granny Fannies and fuzzy lawn sheep in
1987–1988 and a lawn mice revival in 1989–1990—but the
flamingo had outlasted all trendiness. *USA Today*, *People
Weekly* and a raft of local newspapers ran features on the

PLASTIC FRIED CHICKEN
in Archie McPhee's catalog, 1992

bird's surge in popularity. In 1987, fans nationally—some in new clubs such as the Flamingo Fanciers of America and the International Society for the Preservation of Pink Lawn Flamingos—celebrated its thirtieth birthday. John Waters, on the other hand, who made *Polyester* and *Hairspray* in the 1980s, in rebellion gave away every flamingo he had ever collected—even as the mayor of Baltimore proclaimed February 7, 1985, John Waters Day. At Union Products, Don Featherstone was promoted to Vice President. He signed with an agent and moved into a large home in Fitchburg, with his wife and with their poodle Bourgeois. And in 1987, he made the first major alteration to his original mold: he inscribed his autograph on the bird's flank, to distinguish his design from copies by two other companies. "We're trying," he explained, "to protect its image as the original." From that

DON FEATHERSTONE

point on, Kmart shoppers could check to be sure that they were purchasing the real and legitimate symbol of inauthenticity and artificiality.

And so the fifties children entered the 1990s—a decade in which we have been obsessed with boundaries, and in which the Internet seems to question even the boundaries of time and space. As multiculturalism became a watchword, affluent white Americans rifled cultural traditions worldwide as a sort

JOHN WATERS

of global rummage sale for new food, clothes, music and religion. Culture Wars waged fiercely in the universities, where newly tenured baby boomers elevated African folk tales, Pearl Jam and yard art to the same cultural legitimacy as Shakespeare, Rodin and Beethoven—albeit in an arcane language, that like the border crossings of Waters and Warhol challenges boundaries and at once maintains them. Meanwhile, sexual borders became roiled in their own set of battles, in the arts, the courts, the universities and the military. In 1997, the comic Ellen Degeneres's coming-out drew the same media scrutiny as a small war.

It's not surprising that pink flamingos flew off the shelves in the 1990s—even as concrete "fashion geese" reigned as the new rage in lawn ornaments that you actually put on your lawn. We continued to travel with flamingos—you didn't do that with Charlie the Duck or a concrete goose wearing a dress—and a pair even showed up next to Cape Kennedy just before a rocket launch. We use the birds, in old ways and new, to mark the whizzing traffic across borders—intact, blurred, safe, dangerous, social, cultural, national, aesthetic, spatial, temporal, sexual, planetary. A 1993 segment of the PBS show *Travels* showed a pink flamingo in tow on an American's canoe expedition from London to Scotland ("and he's traveling really light," a friend marveled to me). A yard-art specialist, Felder Rushing, takes a flamingo named Empress on his travels, and photographs her "to mark where I've been." Campers post the birds outside their tents at National Forest campsites. The birds mark birthdays, holidays and moving days: to celebrate a birthday, you can now hire the company Flamingo Surprise to plant thirty- or forty-something flamingos on the person's lawn the night before. Shocking Gray, a gay-products company, sells flamingo boxer shorts, and Pink Flamingo Publications markets novels about "women who thrive on hot and sometimes kinky sexual escapades." An avant-garde theater troupe in St. Louis has posted the birds outside on performance nights. The late 1980s and early 1990s have seen a flurry of crime novels—*Flamingo*, *Neon Flamingo*, *A Morning for Flamingos*—that send outsider heroes into a seedy underworld in the South. And my own fast-growing collection of flamingos? It's not purposeful, having been mostly bestowed on me by friends and relatives—except a special pair that Featherstone autographed when I interviewed him, and a small stuffed bird that serves as my Clio. Still, I'm a baby boomer raised in an affluent suburb—a keeper of the object—and at once a onetime academic and self-identified "nature person." So perhaps the birds have marked my forays into a subject that does not appear on the surface to be either very scholarly or natural—tame border traffic, really, compared to a "pink flamingo relay" at the 1994 Gay Games in New York, which featured a combination swim race and costume pageant. A few years before that, a TV commercial for SoHo Natural sodas went right to the point (as TV ads so often do) and compared a picture of a real flamingo— "*Natural*"—to a plastic one—"*Artificial*."

In the 1990s, affluent baby boomers entered their forties and fifties to achieve new heights of status and power, as professionals and as consumers. The border crossings and the definition of Artifice as anti-Nature—both at the center of their collective identity—advanced past legitimacy to power and dominance. The pink flamingo swept into its more middle-aged years of glory and reward. The Annals of Improbable Research awarded Don Featherstone the 1996 IgNobel Award in Art at Harvard. The Smithsonian Archives of American Gardens has begun to consider whether to add a flamingo to their statuary collection. And in 1997, a new Internet site on pink flamingos, "On Stagnant Pond"—a counter-Walden of anti-Nature—swiftly garnered a raft of awards. In the art scene, lawn ornaments moved from galleries into museums. Tulsa's Philbrook Art Museum, housed in an Italian Renaissance-style villa, posted a plastic flamingo in a pot outside a 1996 exhibit on Marilyn Monroe and Elvis; and in 1998, the Museum of Contemporary Art in Los Angeles began to sell the bird for $19 a pair in their bookstore. As pop culture got analyzed, catalogued and preserved, and baby-boomer nostalgia for fities pop culture and Artifice turned hagiographic—the last years of the millennium have seen Pez conventions, hundredth-anniversary celebrations of Jell-O, and a new National Plastics Center and Museum in Leominster—the pink flamingo has reigned inevitably as patron saint. It is a featured entry in the 1990 *Encyclopedia of Bad Taste* and the 1991 *Whole Pop Catalog*.

In 1996, Featherstone bought and became president of Union Products. In 1997, the bird's fortieth birthday met with national hoopla, and Featherstone traveled to flamingo-signings around the country. The date coincided with the twenty-fifth anniversary of *Pink Flamingos*, and the Sundance Film Festival—itself a rebel upstart turned 1990s mainstream powerhouse—commemorated the event with a special showing, as Fine Line rereleased the movie nationally, with extra footage that included Waters' justification for killing a chicken—"Well, I eat chicken and I know the chicken didn't land on my plate from a heart attack. I think we made the

chicken's life better. It got to be in a movie"—and to glowing reviews. "They *hated* [it]. I have the clippings!" Waters re-
called amid a rash of interviews and at least one (in *People*)
with his steadfast parents: "We're very proud of John, but we
just don't see any point in subjecting ourselves to that film."
Some reviewers, however, lost sight of all irony, and of the
movie's emetic and rebellious role in the annals of postwar
culture: "With all the plastic product around," the *Entertainment Weekly* reviewer enthused, "[this film is] a *nutritiously* entertaining event."

In 1995, when Princeton University was faced with a
dorm-room shortage, they rented trailers to house the extra
students, who promptly planted pink flamingos outside. The
boundaries of class and culture that these birds marked
haven't exactly crumbled into dust. And to locate the enduring boundaries of Taste, one only has to look for it in its
home-court bastion of lawn and garden design. Few well-to-
do baby boomers put flamingos on their *front* lawns, or even
in the back; rather, we tend to put them in our mothers'
yards, and keep our own inside. In the 1990s, the ever more
affluent, mid-life homeowners have spurred a renaissance in
upscale garden ornaments, which have included eighteenth-
century English antiques: the catalogs for Earthmade, Gardener's Supply and other upscale outlets feature $299 rustic
copper herons, $179 Classic Fiberglass urns in cast-iron or
"classic stone," and even a $24.95 stone shark ("Eats pink
flamingos for breakfast!") Still, the dialogues of Taste and aesthetics have come such a long way since Capability Brown

AS SANTA'S REINDEER

ATOP MT. WASHINGTON
(highest point in northeast U.S.)
THE WEATHER STATION

and Andrew Jackson Downing. These sets of boundaries, like so many others, may be recognizable. But they are still under intense negotiation.

All except one, lone boundary—between Nature and Artifice. In three decades, the baby boomers have challenged and broken down boundaries of every kind. And as we have done so, we have consistently made the sharp divide between Na-

In Aspen

On the Internet

ture and not-Nature more visible and powerful, and left it standing. And this is the last secret, so far, of the pink flamingo, and of its enduring meaningfulness. In an age of ever more fluid and negotiable boundaries, an effective boundary marker itself has to mark a boundary that one defines as less negotiable, and as more rigid and absolute. Nature and Artifice. The pink flamingo still works so beautifully precisely because it marks the ur-boundary that we have used so consistently to mark and challenge the boundaries of aesthetics, Taste, class, Reality, sexuality and a diverse host of others. The countermodern definition of Nature—as an artifice-free Place Apart—has remained remarkably unchallenged. We have asked, What is Art—and can it be a pink flamingo? What is good taste and what is bad taste—and should we care? By what standards, if any, should we evaluate works of literature, music, TV and film? What is "normal" sexuality? How do we have to redefine time and space in the new age of the Internet? *But has anyone ever asked whether a pink flamingo is nature?* If a few of us have called the plastic creature Art, who has called it Nature? And for all of us who have questioned the nature of Art or Taste or sexuality or cultural differences or moral right and wrong or even Reality, how many of us have asked what *nature* is?

Nature and Artifice Revisited

What does a pink flamingo mean? You can think of the bird, first, as an extreme post–World War II descendant of a pigeon ballotine or a tern on a woman's hat—a modern object with which many Americans have made a wild bird species deeply meaningful, but which says far more about people than about the bird itself. We've used the plastic replica of a nonnative bird species to wage lawn wars, class wars and culture wars, and to engage in heated arguments about aesthetics, taste, sexuality, how to be American and the moral complexities of grass. Deep within modern American cities, our nature totems have acquired their own separate realities, their own strange lives. And yet, you can also read in a pink flamingo the

very *definition* of Nature. John Waters, pop artists, anti-kitsch critics, drag queens, natural-lawn advocates and especially my generation of boundary crossers: whether they have adapted the flamingo to defy Taste, buttress Reality or cross sexual borders, they have all brandished the bird as a statement of anti-Nature. At the core of each of these flamingos lies the compelling, modern definition of Nature as anti-Artifice, not-human, and countermodern.

The power of this definition of Nature has been enduring. Its endurance has been remarkable. And if the affluent baby boomers hardly invented it, we have put it to our own uses. We have made it work very hard. Of course, this definition of Nature *also* tells us far more about ourselves than about nonhuman nature. So many well-to-do baby boomers have used Nature, since the 1960s, to navigate the hallmark features of late-twentieth-century life—its confusions and fluidity, its inequities and excesses—and to judge and critique, to order and set standards, to have something that stays put and doesn't change so fast. But a Nature Out There says powerfully little about the ways people *use* nature every day. (Think of Andrew Jackson Downing's staff, mowing the lawns of Nature with "invisible hands" under the moonlight.) Long-distance economic networks make it easy to lose track of nature—but Nature as a Place Apart actively erases our connections. In an era of unrelenting economic expansion, my generation and class have wielded a definition of nature that sidesteps our complicity in the aggressive and unsustainable uses of natural resources—and have made it ever more powerful as our economic power has come into its own. In sum, an extraordinary nexus of desire and power drives the late-twentieth-century definitions of Nature and Artifice. And shopping malls and TV sets turn out to be unusually good places to plumb them.

What *can* a pink flamingo mean? If you visit the Union Products factory—a brick and concrete compound on an industrial route—you see outsized cardboard Mobil and Phillips 66 boxes that contain the raw ingredients of plastic flamingos: polyethylene crystals flecked with pink petroleum-based dye. Using a large tube, workers suck the crystals from the boxes into metal molds, which they heat to create sets of two birds. Other workers paint the bills, with black and yellow petroleum-based paints, and cut lengths of rolled steel, made from iron and other ores, for the legs. The plastic pink flamingo is literally real and wholly natural. It is the nature that has been mined, harvested, heated and shipped. It is the nature we lose track of: newspapers, computers, Armani suits, art museums, breakfast and chicken. Like a lawn, and even a National Forest or designated wilderness area, it is nature mixed with artifice. The countermodern definition of Nature as anti-Artifice has always erased the human artifice in our bastions of Nature—and the definition of Artifice as anti-Nature has in every case erased the nature used to manufacture it. Would you believe that the history of the pink flamingo has a moral? The symbol of Artifice is actually nature incarnate.

An "unnatural link to the natural world"—as Terry Tempest Williams has branded the plastic flamingo. But I prefer the judgment passed by the garden writer Allen Lacy, who has observed that "every garden tempts us to live within [the] illusion . . . that it is something natural, not the creation of artifice." "The plastic flamingo . . . remind[s] us what gardens are: not the gifts of nature to deserving human beings but the products of human beings cooperating with the natural order to create utility and delight." Signposts everywhere, in the venues of nature and culture. Flamingos on lawns, in movie theaters, on ski slopes, in the hands of kidnappers, in art galleries, on the shores of Hudson Bay and in TV commercials. We have read the signs, uprooted them and reinvented them. Yet the pink flamingos seem to me much like the Jell-O at the bring-your-own-Jell-O lawn parties. The more variations we come up with, the more the plastic birds insist on their essential nature. As for Don Featherstone, he has pondered the history and stardom of his creation with some wistfulness: "I really like how my flamingo looks. . . . But I can't help but wonder, why not my duck?" He adds, "My duck is anatomically correct, you know."

I suspect that in that last observation exactly lies the answer.

4
LOOKING FOR NATURE
AT THE MALL
A FIELD GUIDE TO
THE NATURE COMPANY

Entry

I don't recall the exact mall where I first encountered The Nature Company. It was around 1989, in the St. Louis Union Station or perhaps the Bridgewater Commons in central New Jersey. Say it was a Saturday afternoon, and I was searching for the exit after three hours of shopping. I do remember that I stopped in my tracks, after which I slowly toured the entire store and bought something—but I do not remember what it was. "Customers often exclaim, 'Wow!'" The Nature Company's press release begins, and that accurately describes my reaction.

The history of the pink flamingo chronicles the baby boomers' attachments to a powerful definition of Nature as a nonhuman Place Apart. But if you want to see the uses, desires and convenience of these definitions powerfully at work in the 1980s and 1990s, there are few better places to go than your nearest nature store. Since the early 1980s, the retail genre's meteoric success has paralleled exactly the well-off baby boomers' emergence as the consumer group with the most spending power. And it is exactly the yuppies—or "affluent middle-aged," as *Forbes* has ventured more sensitively—who have been enjoying these encounters with nature at the mall.

Why? The Nature Company pioneered the concept, and amid a spree of 1980s-zeitgeist enterprises, such as Sharper Image and The Banana Republic, has dominated the expanding subfield of companies—The Natural Selection, The Ecology House, Nature's Own Imagination and the company's most serious competitor, Natural Wonders—that specialize in geodes, bug T-shirts, bird sculptures and glow-in-the-dark stars. The Nature Company itself was founded in Berkeley in 1973 by a young couple, Tom and Priscilla Wrubel, who had met in the late 1960s in the Peace Corps. They gambled that a store "devoted to the observation, understanding and appreciation of the natural world" might fill a useful niche for a "population taking to the wilderness in record numbers," and for a generation of new parents, like themselves, who wanted to introduce children to the joys of nature. By 1983, they had four stores in the Bay Area. Seeking expansion capital, they sold their enterprise to the parent CML Group, which specialized in companies that might track the baby boomers' wealth into the 1990s, and which also has owned NordicTrack and Smith & Hawken—or in the not-so-sensitive words of *Business Week*, "a package of yuppie goodies unlike anybody else's." By 1994, The Nature Company ran 124 stores in the United States, 3 in Canada, 12 in Japan, and 7 in Australia. At the end of 1993, they posted net sales of $162 million. The baby boomers who set out hiking and backpacking in a generational drove in the 1960s clearly had taken to the malls as well.

Not without skepticism, however. "People come in and say, 'Ahhh!'" the Company's marketing director has said. But "wow" better describes my own reaction. It's subtler, more ambivalent. In 1989, a *New York Times* columnist wrote a glowing report after a first visit, to the Bridgewater Commons store, yet asked what is perhaps *the* nagging question:

"Why, on earth, weren't the people in the store outside experiencing [nature] instead of . . . indoors buying it?" The Nature *Company*? In the Mall of America? The very name and habitat can provoke a post-1960s nature lover's deepest antimaterialist suspicions. I, too, have marveled at the wondrous array of bird feeders, kites, telescopes, fossils and jewelry, and at the trademark bins of wind-up dinosaurs, rubber animal noses and cow-moo noise boxes. As a birder and hiker, I have lingered by the shelves of videos and natural history books. "I bought a beautiful pair of gardening shears there," a friend explained, "but I feel somehow manipulated. It feels inauthentic"—but she loves the wildlife ties her brother gives her husband for Christmas. "It feels fake," another friend says—but she had just bought a spectacular geode there. If The Nature Company beckons irresistibly, to more than a few of its patrons it also feels vaguely troubling. And the real revelations of eighties nature stores, I'm convinced, and the persistent troubles with our definitions of Nature, rest squarely in that contradiction.

By the mid-1990s, The Nature Company's fortunes had started to slide, in part because its huge success spurred nature and nonnature stores alike to copy its innovations in design and wares. In 1996, CML sold the company to Discovery Communications, which would focus more squarely on adventure than nature. And the boomers' children have emerged to rival their parents as a powerful consumer demographic. But from 1983 to 1993—the very decade in which the baby boomers' social and economic power soared to match our desires—The Nature Company evolved to be an unusually powerful retail magnet for my generation and class. I myself have made frequent trips since my first visit—wherever it was. What has The Nature Company been selling us, exactly? Why have they sited most of their stores in upscale malls, within bowling distance of Emporio Armani? Why do people say "wow": why have many of us harbored such deep suspicions, and yet made The Nature Company a first stop for holiday shopping? And most of all, why has my adult generation of well-to-do baby boomers been looking for nature at the mall? Have we expected to find it there? And will we?

Natural Selection

What has The Nature Company been selling? Images of nature, pieces of nature, and tools for going out into nature. By 1994, the company was marketing over twelve thousand products. They have sold bird T-shirts, wind chimes, paperweights, bird feeders, wildflower seeds, field guides, videos, note cards, CDs, herb teas, bat shelters, rain gauges, field hats, Swiss army knives, Rainforest Crunch, plastic periscopes, amethyst geodes, stuffed tigers, Zuni fetishes, petrified wood, rock polishers, dinosaur everything, star charts and galaxy boxer shorts. At first glance, it seems that anything that has to do with the natural world must be here. But The Nature Company is not a biome. It is on average 2,900 square feet of retail space—a very small space for all of nature—and what lives here must sell. The company has, from the start, hewed to strict principles of natural selection. And the principles hew to the resonant, countermodern definition of Nature that the pink flamingo's history charts so well.

To see the definition clearly, it is easier to begin with what the company will *not* sell. What has it classified as not-Nature? The Nature Company refuses to market "trophy" items, which require the killing of animals: no butterflies, seashells or furs. No mounted heads. Under the Wrubels' regime, the company avoided products that anthropomorphize animals. The popular children's book *Goodnight Moon* is still non grata, since the bunny wears pajamas and sleeps in a bed. Anthropomorphizers, as a species, were also unwelcome: you could discover almost no human images on the posters, and (until the Discovery takeover) very few human voices on the CDs. And no Enya, though often requested. Domestic animals have been in short supply. The company has selected nonhuman, wilder and unused forms of nature. When asked to sum up their inventory, Nature Company personnel have used the terms "authenticity," "uniqueness" and "quality." Also "whimsy"—but only authentic whimsy. The toy animals here do not smile or wag their tails. The dolphins and cicadas on the keychains have been accurate replicas. The bat puppets look like real bats, the piggy banks like real pigs and the angelfish bathtub toys like real angelfish. The wind-up dinosaurs in the stores' "ning-ning" bins (the Wrubels' children coined the term) still come in bright colors "in line with new scientific thought," and the inflatable emperor penguins are anatomically correct. Nature Company products have been humorous, but not kitschy, cliché or sentimental. They are inexpensive, but not cheap. You see real rocks, plastic grasshoppers, dolphin keychains and stone bird sculptures—but no I ❤ dolphins bumperstickers, plastic pink flamingos, real grasshoppers or plastic rocks.

Among all the items, the products that limn the definitions of Nature here most visibly are the ones that do not, if you think about it, look like nature as a separate place, or summon it to you or send you out into it. For example, The Nature Company has marketed handmade paper lamps and Amish oak-hickory rockers. And why Zuni fetishes? The company has enjoyed a brisk business in Native American crafts, and, until the CML sale, the few human voices on the CDs were ethnic or indigenous. "Each product," says the company's press kit, ". . . introduces customers to an aspect of the natural world"—so how do the Australian wool throw blankets connect you to nature? They don't, at least not directly. Zulu baskets satisfy the entrance criteria not because they are nature, but because like the brightly colored wind-up dinosaurs, they are "authentic" or "unique": many of us tend to invest rocks and Zulu handcrafts with the same meanings. Each item here, the company states more accurately in a handout for employees, "[relates] in some magical way to . . . natural phenomena." *Viento de los Andes*, a CD of Andean folk music, got in by meaningful association, since to so many baby boomers, both nature and indigenous cultures connote authenticity and simplicity in a modern era. And why ask for Enya, a New Age

Irish singer, in a nature store? The piggy bank has to look like a real pig, but more important, it comes with "layers and layers of associations," including "French farmyards," "childhood dreams" and "the good old days." The Nature Company has billed itself as your direct connection to the natural world. But the stores connect us not so much to what nature is as to what Nature *means:* they tap the powerful, meaningful routes by which we use Nature to define who we are, and with which we have navigated late-twentieth-century American life.

At The Nature Company, you can really put Nature to work. If the stores have sold over twelve thousand products, they have hawked a small and well-chosen set of outsized meanings. The *Glacier Bay* CD invites shoppers to "escape" to one of the "Last Great Places"; and in 1994, you could buy a trip to "Alaska: the Last Great Adventure," as advertised in the catalog:

> People in towns . . . dream of serene sanctuaries far
> away from fax machines. . . . This is where you pull out
> of the fast lane and change the course of your revved-
> up life. . . . Please see the order form.

You can buy walking sticks, vests and backpacks here, too, to enjoy nonhuman Nature as Wilderness—a distant and untamed realm, a solitary refuge from the modern city, which is ideally as unpeopled (and as devoid of cows and cats) as The Nature Company's poster collection. Nature as Adventure is vivified in the subgenre of books (the book section has anchored the stores as a kind of philosophy section) that the head book buyer in 1987 classified as "tales of personal adventure in a wild land." *Wolf: Spirit of the Wild. Forgotten Edens: Experiencing the Earth's Wild Places.* A canvas hat from the Sierra Club John Muir collection will "give me the Simple Life." The Zuni fetishes, Zulu baskets and African jewelry associate Nature nearly interchangeably with indigenous peoples. The throw blankets "might have come from the cedar chest of your great-grandmother." And the whole inventory constitutes a monument to an understanding of Nature as a place for Leisure: the Nature Company Cap is "for days off . . . afoot and lighthearted down an open road." Leisure, Adventure, Simplicity, Uniqueness, Authenticity, the Primitive, the Past, the Autochthonous, Tranquility, Exoticism, Wildness, Freedom. Here you can use the definition of Nature as a Place Apart to define, critique or counteract the urbanism, anonymity, commercialism, technological control, complexity, white-collar work, artifice and alienations of the postwar era. What is for sale here is exactly the established definition of Nature that well-to-do baby boomers adapted for themselves in the 1960s, and marshaled as a chief weapon to critique what troubled them about American society. On the first page of *Walden,* Thoreau opposed Nature to "civilized life"—and you can buy the essay here in a pocket size edition for hikers.

Nature is available for purchase above all as what is Real: what is enduring, nonreplicated, non-mass culture, Authentic, non-Artificial and absolute. The amethyst pieces "vary according to natural structure." The Polish folk-art candles are "one-of-a-kind handmade." The Get Real generation have always used Nature to combat their postwar anxieties about mass culture and high-tech society.

> Jet has been fashioned into beads and amulets for 5,000 years and Native Americans have fashioned turquoise into . . . jewelry for centuries. Now Chilean artists combine the gems to create a . . . handmade necklace, bracelet and pair of earrings which follow the natural curve of the throat, wrist and ear. . . . Bracelet $95.00

> Our Dakota Earth Mailbox is a piece of history, made of reclaimed barnwood . . . to look like a rustic, wind-weathered birdhouse. Each one-of-a-kind piece . . . re-calls a way of life amid hard Great Plains winters. . . . $49.95

The fossils, "sculpted by nature . . . more than 350 million years ago," and "quarried and polished by Moroccan crafts-people," are "handfinished." "Our Nature Company Recordings" in the Last Great Places series, the company assured us in a 1994 catalog, "blend the elemental harmonies of music and the earth." Nature Company products, Priscilla Wrubel stated in the Fall 1994 catalog, are "tools"—and "human hands have guided tools since the Ice Age."

Of course, while baby boomers in the 1960s adapted the idea of Nature as a Place Apart to combat artifice, conformity and anonymity, in the 1980s—as we became affluent professionals and consumers—we began to use Nature less as a tool for battling the System than to get some temporary relief from it. CML's stated mission was to "enhance people's health, understanding of the natural world, and sense of well-being." Or in the slightly different words of an investment-analysis firm, CML marketed "products for stress relief." At The Nature Company, the "yuppie leisure market," in *Business Week*'s words, could enjoy Nature as a key therapeutic resource for what has become a virtual obsession with stress relief:

> Pachelbel Canon in D Blended with the Eternal Sound of the Sea—Creates a tranquil atmosphere for quiet meditation. . . . CD $16.98.

The *Cloud Forest* CD, in the 1994 catalog, "weave[s] a spell of peace." If you sited the birdbath fountain indoors, "the sound of running water [had] a calming, beautiful effect." And *Tranquility*, a video "moodtape" of sunrises, clouds and "peaceful ocean waves," "perfect for relaxing, entertaining, love-making" and designed to create a "soothing and harmonious atmosphere," was an especially safe bet to sell well. Of course, the yuppies have searched for stress relief, and harvested Nature for a psychic yield, not just to escape the system but to act more effectively within it. "Clearly," the investment-analysis firm remarked with enthusiasm, "anything which reduces stress increases time and energy, which are always valuable commodities."

Reality, stress relief, self-improvement and emotional healing: these had more generally emerged in force as chief New Age goals in the 1980s. The explosive New Age movement is multifaceted, but on average the pursuits have tended to exalt a search for a more Authentic self and more Authentic experience in a modern society that seems to fail to offer it. The well-off baby boomers had always advertised themselves as the Real generation. But New Age philosophies have tended to reorient the quest for Reality away from society and the self—that is, from changing both one's head and the system—toward the Self *in* Society. And New Age adherents have recruited the countermodern definition of Nature as an essential and authoritative tool. The Nature Company's mission statement says: "Authenticity and knowledge are balanced with sufficient humor to give our customers an experience which makes them *feel good* about themselves and the world in which they live [emphasis added]." At The Nature Company, you can construct an authentic, Real Self in an un-Real society. The whale and eagle calls on the *Glacier Bay* CD "create moods and emotions within us." Environmental Sounds CDs "will open your mind and awaken your heart." Nature is the source of Real emotion, Real thinking, Real feeling. To appreciate Nature here is to be a more Real person. It is to be a *better* person and the right *sort* of person.

Who can use Nature as a route to the Real? The use of Nature to define a certain kind of person recalls the fifties suburban lawn owners, and the English landowners who lounged in Natural postures in their own vast and Natural landscapes.

The Nature Company brand of Nature appreciation can work best if you have the means to shop here, and to travel to Glacier Bay and other far wildernesses on your vacation. Like others before us, affluent baby boomers have tended to invest a lot of human social authority in our encounters with nature. We graft meanings onto nature to make sense out of modern middle-class life, but also define ourselves by what we think nature means. What better resource, then, to use to educate the baby boomers' children? Nature is also the source of Real values. The company's large, highly publicized kids' section usefully teaches children about the nonhuman natural world—but you can also use it to teach them how be the right sort of person, and how to join the human company of the Real. As the Company's Summer 1994 catalog assures us, "Kids are the original naturalists."

If The Nature Company's trademark sense of humor, or "whimsy," caters to the baby boomers' evolving parental desires, it also appeals directly to a consumer generation who once vowed notoriously, in an enduring gesture of self-identity, to remain forever young. "Pretend it's for the kids," the company advertised its butterfly raise-and-release kit. Spy Scope: "if the kid in you isn't quite a serious grown-up yet." Rubber noses, wild-animal cookies, *Scaly & Slimy*, *Everyone Poops*, gecko ties, bird-droppings T-shirts, UnpredictaBalls! Whimsy is a tricky meaning here. Laughter in the American tradition of Nature has been notably scarce—which is why John Waters could use anti-Nature so easily to get laughs. Not too many jokes in Thoreau: Nature and Reality must not be trivialized, so The Nature Company walks a fine line here. But the 1960s children of Nature have also always been the ironic lovers of Artifice—the keepers of the pink flamingo. Whether partial to Nature or Artifice, we've committed to a boundary between the two. As a source of laughs, the angelfish bathtub toys that look like real angelfish encourage the children of baby boomers to be at once Real children and initiates into Artifice. Kites, bubble kits, bat puppets and paint-a-snakes encourage the parents to remain ironic, young and playful, and to stay trustworthy past the age of thirty.

The store sounds like fun. And it is. And The Nature Company has both catered and served as monument to the no-Artifice definition of Nature as a key to the identity of my generation and class. Why, then, have some of us felt so uneasy? Why have the stores sparked ambivalence? I finger everything in the ning-ning bins, but maintain a cool reserve. Why have the stores felt "fake," "inauthentic" or "manipulative" to at least some of its patrons?

To begin with, The Nature Company has not sold nature. It has not sold forests, deserts and wetlands. It has sold meanings. And in the pool of changing, countermodern meanings, the most powerful and overarching has always been that Nature is *not* a changing set of human meanings. Nature, unlike everything else, is unchanging. It is absolute. It is stable, secure, tangible, rocklike, self-evident, definable, Real. Of course, we know that nature means certain things to us, such as "solitude" and "authenticity." But the meanings seem universal, indelible and unchanging: they're indigenous to the rocks and trees themselves. And shouldn't the meanings of Nature be for everyone?

But if you take the complete set of meanings and stack and shelve them together in one room, they can start to look like a stack of meanings. The definitions of Nature may inhere deeply in a plastic pink flamingo, but they are harder to see in the plastic bird. And in your garden or on a camping trip, where you are surrounded by what is undeniably tangible and real about nature, the countermodern definition of Nature feels securely unconstructed. It is safer, really, to shop for your gardening tools at the hardware store: my friend testified that if she had bought her pruning shears at Ace Hardware, it would not have felt like an "inauthentic" experience, nor would she have felt "manipulated." But here, when you are surrounded by thousands of "nature-oriented" products that "relate in some magical way" to nature, definitions of Nature begin to look a lot like definitions. And in this upscale venue, just down the hall from Neiman Marcus and Victoria's Secret, *whose* meanings these are becomes an almost palpable question. Of course, few of us have walked into The Nature Company, looked around, and said "Aha, so the meaning of nature is not so self-evident, universal, or absolute after all." Rather, the response, I think, has often been closer to "wow." Nature stores have invited us in, but have planted the vague uneasiness that the meaningful Nature that we look for here, as an unchangeable Place Apart, is not necessarily what nature *is*—and that the Nature here actually says less about nature than about ourselves.

The meanings of a pigeon ballotine, a tern on a hat, and a plastic flamingo betray the same disconnections. But at a nature store, the disconnections and the constructedness of Nature—generally more safely hidden—all threaten to surface. The Nature Company and the nature-store clones that followed have engaged in a tricky and very ambitious pursuit. They have marketed a commodity—middle- to upper-class meanings of nature—to a class of consumers who nourish serious doubts that the product exists. The Nature Company has tapped flawlessly into the market for anatomically correct inflatable penguins. The pioneer nature store has been an excellent place to go to encounter what Nature has meant to "affluent middle-aged" Americans in the 1980s and into the 1990s. But this retail genre inevitably has bred a degree of mistrust among its target clientele.

Habitat

Yet in the 1980s, backed by CML capital, The Nature Company set out to expand into shopping malls, of all places—and their competitors followed suit. Why sell Nature or anti-Artifice at a site that is famous as a black hole for Artifice? Why hawk Authenticity at a locale whose reputation for genericness is so notorious that we call every mall on the continent "the mall"? And why the glitziest sites and the mega-malls? It is not difficult to predict where to find a Nature Company. In Denver, the Cherry Creek Mall. In St. Louis, the Galleria and Union Station. In Los Angeles, the Century City Shopping Center and the Beverly Center in Beverly Hills. In Orange County, South Coast Plaza. The Mall of America has one.

The logic lies surely in how malls work, and in the intricacies of the *mall's* particular worlds of meaning—and how these worlds have intertwined with the meanings of Nature. Shopping malls: Americans have called them "gardens of delight," "worlds of artifice" and "palaces of consumption." And since the 1950s, when the first enclosed centers began to dot the suburban landscape, they've been targets of derision, or at least ambivalence. Between 1957 and the mid-1970s, developers built fourteen thousand shopping malls to cater to the postwar affluence and the expanding suburban populations. With large open spaces and deliberately modern in design, most of these malls looked essentially like broad indoor avenues, with a few plants, that connected the "magnet" department stores at either end. In 1979, Joan Didion branded them "toy garden cities in which no one lives but everyone consumes." Malls have been accused, before and since, of being identityless, un-Real, devoid of character and, along with TV, a major culprit in the postwar homogenization of American culture. With interstate highways, they have homogenized the American landscape. Lost along the corridors of chain-outlet shoe stores, you could be anywhere. The mall, as Frank Lloyd Wright has said about the postwar sprawl generally, is every place and no place.

In the 1980s, mall developers hired architects cross-country to outfit these installations with more individuality. The new designers gave face-lifts to most of the larger malls built in the sixties and seventies, injected the new eighties mega-malls with more character, and designed the malls to be more upscale on average—and these are exactly the malls The Nature Company moved into. Many malls now look like European villages or Mexican haciendas. The corridor spaces are more mazelike, irregular and niched. The designers favored tropical settings, especially—in no small part because plants such as figs and rhododendrons grow well in climate-controlled indoor spaces. In other words, the ungeneric malls of the 1980s, like the Foot Locker stores, are essentially replicants. They simulate and connote other places. (The Los Angeles malls tend to simulate Los Angeles, a city notorious as both a simulation of place and an outsize shopping mall.) The Italian piazza and Caribbean courtyard are places out of place. Architects have gathered together the *meanings* of more Real-seeming places than suburbs and malls, mixing and matching as if the globe were a giant salad bar. And the replicants say less about the real places than about what consumers want them to mean. The 1992 Mall of America, Minneapolis's mall for the twenty-first century, contains within its ninety-six acres an "East Broadway" avenue, a mock European railway station, a seven-acre theme park with a Minnesota woodland motif, and the Rainforest Cafe, with live animals, waterfalls, fog and a "star-filled" sky.

The Nature Company has been a one-store global assemblage itself: it sells posters, videos and calendars of Alaska, Tanzania and the Galapagos. And most of the nature here is simulated: the plastic whales and sculpted giraffes, the inflatable penguins, the spiders on the T-shirts. The Nature Company markets nature out of place. You can buy African malachite earrings patterned on Indonesian designs. Here you can connect to the world's wild things close to home, because the company has installed similar assemblages in malls in thirty-four states and two Canadian provinces, in Australia, and in the giant malls in Japan's underground railway stations. The stores at South Coast Plaza (store no. 7), the St. Louis Galleria (no. 60) and the Century City Shopping Center (no. 21) stock the same *Virtual Nature* videos and inflatable globes. On a 1994 visit to the store at the breezy Century City center in Los Angeles, where The Nature Company faces Rand-McNally, a "map and travel store," I could choose to eat at the Market food court next door, at Bueno Bueno, Gulen's Mediterranean Cuisine, DeMartino's Pizzeria, Raja, La Crepe or Kisho An. On the store's other flank sat El Portal Luggage, two doors down from Toys International and within sight of the United Colors of Benetton. The "now playing" CD combined Western instrumental forms with Baka Pygmy music from the border of Congo and Cameroon. I sifted through the zebra- and panda-footprint stamps, but bought the polar bear.

The Nature Company makes sense here. If I harbor doubts about the mall as a suitable habitat, The Nature

THE NATION'S MALLS

THE FASHION CENTRE
Pentagon City, Arlington, VA

BRIDGEWATER COMMONS
Bridgewater, NJ

OWINGS MILLS TOWN CENTER
Owings Mills, MD

Company feels intuitively well-sited. Why? Since the late-nineteenth-century adventures (and misadventures) with bird hats and wild pigeons, Americans' encounters with wild nature have become as thoroughly disconnected from place, but also as intensively simulated, as malls themselves. Economic globalization and explosive postwar advances in manufacturing and communications technologies, have made my generation's adventures more consistently long distance, and far more mediated. Even postwar nature lovers—who hike and camp, and make vacation pilgrimages to wild places—encounter wild nature more often in the everyday urban and suburban haunts of living rooms, shopping malls, magazines and TVs. Most of our daily encounters with nature transpire quite separately from real pieces of nature rooted in specific places. We have become globe coasters all. *Where* have we been looking for nature most often since the 1980s? Not in the "where" where we generally think of nature as being. It is not surprising that one of the more successful Nature Company stores, while not in a mall, has been in the Pittsburgh Airport.

Just as with the pink flamingo, we've used Nature Company totems to tell meaningful stories about where we live and who we are—as all humans do in their encounters with nature—but these totems often tell us markedly little about the pieces of nature. And yet, The Nature Company's stated mission is to connect us to nature—not disconnect us. And to be sure, postmodern globe coasting works both ways. The products teach their owners potentially a great deal about distant places and animals. The toy plastic whale in the Ocean Authentics Collection, for example, can convey information about the blue whale, and about the circumpolar oceans the species inhabits. What it basically does, however, is to bring a miniature, essentially accurate image of a whale into one's life. What one does with it is up to its new owner. To a child in suburban Chicago, the palm-size whale might look like an endangered blue whale, the largest animal that ever lived. And it might look like Jonah, Shamu, Monstro, the hero in *Free Willy* or a friend or enemy of a Mighty Morphin Power Ranger. The distance from the Pacific makes the whale unusually open to interpretation.

And if The Nature Company connects us less to nature itself than to what Nature *means*, the modern unmoored-ness of meanings has not been flatly undesirable. As always, modern complexities of geography and economics conveniently encourage a consumer's desire to make a piece of nature—or Nature itself—mean whatever one wants it to. Far from the ocean, the plastic whale reduces more readily to a motif, a feeling, an association, a meaning. The company's best-selling *Glacier Bay* CD comes with a booklet that reads:"ALASKA— ...a superlative for ... unbounded wilderness"—or as the catalog blurb reads, "Escape to Glacier Bay's arctic cathedrals." The CD is "for relaxation," one sales clerk told me—so I bought it. The music has a New Age dreamlike quality. It's a quiet, flowing mélange of flute, cello, whales, eagles and waves, that sounds not unlike the flute, cello, frogs, wrens and flowing water on the Costa Rica *Cloud Forest* CD. It's self-advertised mood music, in which the humpback whale makes a cameo appearance. From a boat in the Bay itself, would Alaska be relaxing? Isn't the far North notorious as mosquito country? I have been to a rain forest: in Peru, at least, the jungle is not relaxing. It requires alertness; it has mildew. In suburban somewhere, however, after a stressful day at work, in counterpoint to noise, enclosure and schedules—even if one reads the notes on natural history in the booklets—Glacier Bay and a Central American rain forest easily reduce to meaningful abstractions such as Wilderness, Relaxation and Tranquility: the call of the humpback whale promotes human peace of mind. Distant landscapes and wild animals become ever more shadowy realities. And what better place to sell these abstractions of Nature and the Last Places than in the placeless vacuum of the mall?

And yet, Place—along with Reality and an Absolute Force— is among the most powerful in the set of meanings that the affluent baby boomers have invested in Nature. Place has been one of The Nature Company's most appealing commodities. "The Last Great Places": Nature counters the pervasive, troubling placelessness of modern (and postmodern) life that the mall so definitively represents. In this fast-paced, ever-changing world, we count on nature not only to stay constant in meaning but to stay put.

Just as collecting the many meanings of Nature into one store can plant the suspicion that Nature *is* a set of meanings, does this assemblage of the world's places suggest the actual rootlessness of our encounters with nature? Again, the store nearly unmasks our definitions as definitions. Again, "*wow.*" The Nature Company connects me to Nature and Place, but it can also instill a sneaking sensation of detachment. You can *almost* see the contradiction—that the ways I *think* I connect to nature are the ways I *want* to connect to nature but are not the ways I actually *do*.

At the nature store, the meetings of the worlds of meaning in the Mall and Nature get more ironic and complex. The mall architects in the 1980s, of course, had converted the sixties and seventies malls into Mexican haciendas and New England fishing villages exactly to assuage countermodern angst about malls and the meltdown of Place. Not surprisingly, they added liberal new quantities of Nature. Skylights, greenery, fountains: the St. Louis Galleria's "garden court" has topiary bird mobiles and a fountain that is eight stores long. The face-lifts were designed precisely to attract the baby boomers—the new chief commanders of disposable income—who objected to the generic, placeless aura of the malls they grew up on. Build a fountain, they will come: mall developers installed Nature like a sign to the affluent thirtysomethings, saying this place is a Real Place, and it's for you.

The Nature Company took the design strategy to its logical extreme. The dark-hued slate-block entrance, and the stream flowing through an open window display: the exterior quickly became famous for its ability to immobilize shoppers, as if they had stumbled onto a landmark in a maze.

Into the early 1990s, especially before the designers of malls and other stores caught up with them, the store stood out. It looked like a distinctive Place. Inside, in contrast to the open and brightly lit interiors of its neighbors, The Nature Company looked more like sun and shadows, and not cluttered but intricately niched. The Wrubels deliberately set out to replicate a "dappled forest." And browsing here feels a bit akin to taking a nature walk in that forest. The company's strategists have instructed store managers to set products low on the shelves, out of their boxes, inviting shoppers to touch, experience. Videos attract browsers to stop and watch. Open the mineral drawers, turn the posters, put a quarter in the Rainforest Meter, read a book on the couch in the book nook, all to the accompaniment of Baka Pygmy music or bird tweets: the stores have promoted a mall version of a Thoreauvian outing. In the 1980s mall, the store felt like a sylvan refuge—a quiet glade amid the bright lights and echoes. To anyone at all anxious about malls, it could feel like a relief. "I suppose I should state," the *New York Times* columnist claimed his countermall bona fides as he reported on his surprisingly enjoyable first run-in with The Nature Company at the sprawling Bridgewater Commons, "that shopping bores me and malls make me yearn for the relative tranquillity of a dentist's chair." The Nature Company has attracted nature lovers precisely by inhabiting a notoriously placeless site.

The upscale mall boasts at least one more advantage as a logical home for nature stores. As Tom Wrubel has pointed

THE CHERRY CREEK MALL STORE
in Denver

out (in a 1986 interview for the *San Francisco Chronicle*), "There's nothing we sell here that [people] really need." The *Tranquility* moodtape may be meaningful, but it's been an optional item in most people's lives. And the upscale mall itself specializes in the strategic marketing of things we don't really need. It can be hard to find something you *do* need. Why, for example, in the vast acreage of the mall, is it so difficult to find a bar of Dial soap? The motives behind mall design lie in the answers to questions so many of us have asked. Why are there so few entrances? Where is the one map? Why is it so hard to find the restrooms? Why can't I ever remember which floor The Gap is on? And why can't any of us remember where we parked the car? Nearly every square inch of the mall, from the locations of stores to the curves in the

Sign for nature-based
combination-museum-zoo-and-theme-park
at Ontario Mills mall, Ontario, CA

hallways, hews to a science the shopping-center industry has been refining since the 1950s, in which "discourage direct navigation" reigns as the supreme law. It has been statistically proven that the longer we stay, the more we buy. Hence, no Dial. No drugstores, Safeway, or dry cleaners: necessities encourage beeline, goal-oriented, quick-exit shopping. "It's a hard place to run in to for a pair of stockings," as a friend of Joan Didion's remarked. The upscale mall draws in shoppers (or "invitees," as the trade literature refers to us) through a few well-spaced entrances and keeps us rambling around inside—the current average mall visit is three hours—to stimulate the 45 percent of total purchases in the mall that we make on impulse. After one's first run-in with The Nature Company, like any other store it can be difficult to relocate. In the mall, looking for nature can become a very literal search.

For a company that markets moodtapes and plastic polar bears—who intentionally sets out to find these?—the mall therefore is an optimal site. The architecture of malls has careened more than a few invitees through the company's doors. Inside the store itself, if you careen into the field hats while searching for the Rainforest Crunch, you may be tempted to buy one. Have patience, though. You will find the candy eventually, next to a telescope, though en route you may decide to buy a wildflower T-shirt and a wind-up dinosaur. The company has deployed mall-design savvy. Even the catalog has no index, and has been organized as much by color as by item. The search for items can be an outdoor adventure. Friends report that although they played with the toys and watched the videos, they didn't buy much—except for fish magnets, and a geode and the wind chimes. The design is so successfully antimall that patrons might not even notice when they have purchased something unnecessary.

Yet, the same patrons feel somehow "manipulated." But has The Nature Company manipulated us more objectionably than The Gap or The Banana Republic? It should not surprise us that the company speaks two languages: the language of Nature, Reality and Place, and the language of profits. It has to. The mall has sales-per-square-foot requirements for its tenants. The store can *feel* more manipulative, I think—because it hawks Nature, not jeans. If the very meanings the company markets can make me uneasy about what nature the company sells, and how and where we really connect to nature, I am a little suspicious that they sell it at all.

The main reason, after all, that we've been looking for nature in the mall is that the mall is the place where you buy things. And it's the buying and selling, I'm convinced, that engenders the greatest uneasiness. Why have we been looking for nature with our credit cards? After the *New York Times* columnist left the Bridgewater Commons, and while searching for his car in the parking lot, he experienced a troubling set of second thoughts—but not because he had forgotten the computer paper he had driven to the mall to buy or because "we bought something we didn't need and didn't mind a bit." Rather, he voiced a deep anxiety that many of the company's affluent clientele have shared: "Is it possible that people in our culture have become so estranged from nature that their only avenue to it is consumerism?"

Ecology

Americans spend a tremendous amount of time buying things. The ways we use a world of *consumerism,* to make meanings and to navigate modern life, are what makes the malls work. Shopping ranks second only to TV-watching as a leisure-time pursuit—but not every American watches TV. Even those of us who aren't thrilled about shopping still make frequent shopping trips, and have filled our homes, offices and cars with necessities, luxuries, gadgets, equipment, art, décor and knickknacks. We fill our lives with an abundance of *things*. In the early 1800s, when Taste emerged so forcefully as a route to middle-class identity, Americans used an ever-expanding cornucopia of consumer items to define themselves. After 1900, as the national economy grew increasingly dependent on consumer spending, buying things evolved into an ever more important way of moving through the world. And in the affluent post–World War II era, the baby boomers grew up more instinctively consumeristic than any prior generation. In the global-market, high-tech late twentieth century, Americans make only a tiny percentage of the items we personally use—and in an urban society of comparative anonymity, we use the things we buy to create ourselves. The clothes, the sound systems, the books, computers, cars and bumperstickers: we use these not only as key tools to work and to have fun, but also to act, think and communicate. Gifts, too—and one could argue that an upscale mall is an outsize gift arcade—have become essential and abundant fuel for social relationships. We give gifts to mark important events, to reward and motivate, to tell stories about the places we travel. And shopping itself can be as much a social outing as a quest for goods. Buying something is at once an economic act, a social act and an act of creativity and imagination. And it's been shown that many Americans prefer shopping to sex.

Baby boomers have approached the natural world, like everything else, intuitively as consumers. It is perfectly logical—even inevitable—to articulate a vision of nature, to learn about nature, to share our enthusiasms through the common arts of shopping for things, buying them, using and displaying them and giving them to others. The bird feeder imports Nature into one's life. We make the Yosemite calendar a daily utterance about what Nature means: Majesty, Solitude, Adventure, Escape. The ready-to-install waterfall marks the owner as the kind of Real person who knows and values what Nature means. A Saturday-afternoon browse through geodes, bat puppets and rain forest posters can be a value-forming experience, and fun, too—and with a friend or partner, an affirmation of shared values. On a birthday, an inflatable emperor penguin—in 1994, The Nature Company's best-selling inflatable—binds an adult gift giver to a child, fosters shared meanings, purveys values about people and animals and places from one person to another. Within the economic logic and routes to meaning in the late-twentieth-century United States, The Nature Company has been an excellent place to reiterate, enjoy and share one's commitments to nature. It has made perfect sense to connect to nature on a trip to the mega-mall.

If a run-in with The Nature Company sets one's consumer instincts into motion, the store can also trigger a nature lover's anticonsumer instincts. Many of us use Nature, too, to define who we are and to navigate the world. Nature means a countermodern Force, an antidote to modern life—and critics and enthusiasts alike have so often pegged consumerism as the economic and cultural lifeblood of modern American society. Simple, primitive and Natural, Nature is a palliative for modern materialism. Like the *Times* columnist, many Nature Company patrons define Nature as something we should experience rather than consume, and the whole store flashes NATURE like a neon warning sign. "Thoreau was right," the company has advertised their Survival Tool, which has twelve tools in one: "Simplify, simplify." Doesn't that feel contradictory? If I define myself using the things I buy, I define myself also by what I think Nature means. At The Nature Company, I am an anticonsumer consumer.

Again, "wow," in all its ambivalent glory. The definition of Nature that The Nature Company sells tells me Nature is separate from consumerism. And the store telegraphs that an essential way I connect to nature, and make it meaningful, is via consumerism. The Nature Company is nothing if not self-contradictory and ironic. And no ironies get more complicated here than those swirling around consumerism. The company has countered anticonsumer instincts—"It looks so mercantile," Tom Wrubel said during a 1986 interview, as he took down a "cash only" sign in the San Jose store—in ways that are both well-intentioned and very strategic. Essentially, The Nature Company has positioned the store as a site for *better* consumerism. To begin with, it emphasizes "quality" consumer products—lifelike bronze frogs for $995, for example, rather than plastic lawn creatures—with a rhetoric that echoes Taste, and urges consumers to exercise restraint on quality, if not on quantity. The company makes concerted efforts, too—and publicizes them avidly—to sell recycled products, such as luminaria, "waste not" stationery and flying-animals wrapping paper. Riding the crest of Green Consumerism in the 1980s, The Nature Company has divided acts of consumption into good and bad. A customer can put a

quarter in the Rainforest Meter and send her money off to a worthy cause. You can buy home recycling kits and books about tropical deforestation. A percentage of profits goes to the Nature Conservancy. Here, you can consume to preserve nature.

At the same time, in the Mall of America or South Coast Plaza—a monument to overconsumption—it can be hard not to conceive of shopping as a quantity more than a quality experience. If there are hundreds of ways to shop for a better world, do we shop too much? And this, I'll venture, points to the most stubborn irony, and to the most troubling and deeply buried source for "wow." Every "nature-oriented" product—recycled, nonrecycled, "quality," nature-preserving, Nature Conservancy-supporting—has literally been manufactured *from* nature. An inflatable plastic penguin constitutes approximately the same natural resources and energy as the utterly non-grata plastic pink flamingo. Who thinks about that? Looking for the meanings of Glacier Bay from my living room, I so readily lose track of real facts about the actual Arctic landscape—yet doubly ironic, its oil might be in my stereo system, or in the CD itself. Who thinks of the whale calls on the *Glacier Bay* CD as Petroleum more than Freedom? Has The Nature Company connected people to nature? Absolutely: perhaps too much. And it would be impossible not to find nature at the mall: Nature provides the raw materials the malls are made from. Here, the definition of Nature as a Place Apart—as separate from modern consumerism—not only tells us little about what nature is and where we actually connect to it. It also actively *hides* our connections, as the definition always has done. And can I really be a better consumer if I fail to identify my connections to nature?

The mall itself historically has been designed to disguise all these connections, natural and economic, to the world outside. Architects and managers deliberately sequester all traces of producing, sending and receiving: for example, they relegate business offices to the basement, and truck in goods in the early morning hours before the invitees arrive to shop. They have actively set out to erase connections—to encourage us to focus on the meanings we make, but not on our complicity in the economic networks through which people convert nature and human labor into the stuff and sustenance of everyday lives. As Leah Hager Cohen has written about our modern brand of fetishism: "The notion of connections seems charming, but not quite real." Retail stores, too, set out to create slices of magic that bear few traces of where products came from, other than "made in China," of how they got to suburban Chicago, or where your money will go after you trade it for a shirt. "Gardens of delight," "palaces of consumption." The Nature Company calls its stores a "magical space." The back rooms, however, are windowless spaces of steel and concrete stacked with boxes floor to ceiling. And while the nature store may be Oz, like the mall it is also a flow chart.

As the company has detailed its own workings in an informational sheet for the sales staff: "Although the public would hardly be aware of it, there is, in fact, an order to the magic in the form of eight professionally managed buying departments." The Nature Company has sold products from Brazil, China, Zaire, Portugal, Chile and the Philippines, among other countries. All the products are shipped to a distribution center in Kentucky, which in 1994 was reshipping them to 146 stores in 4 countries. Profits from these products have gone far too many places to map, but among other places: the eight buying departments; 850 sales employees (in 1994); a vice president of real estate development; a director of public relations, image and special events; a company naturalist; mall managers and leasing agents; advertising agencies; the CEO and the president of CML, who earned $1.38 million and $1.37 million, respectively, in fiscal year 1993; and among CML's stockholders, Reader's Digest, the Ford Foundation, my former phone company US West, and the Bank of Tokyo, IBM and GE.

"Commodity consumption," the historian Jean-Christophe Agnew has written, has not "enhanced our appreciation of the remote consequences of our acts or . . . clarified our responsibilities for them." During my research visits, I spent $180.18 at The Nature Company—mostly on gifts. The *Glacier Bay* CD (recorded in San Francisco, with notes printed in Canada), a polar bear stamp (made in China) and other items connect me to the working conditions and everyday lives of people worldwide who mine, plant, assemble and transport the company's materials and products. A hummingbird feeder on my back porch connects me to the CML Group chairman, who in the 1980s delved into his $1 million-plus salary to contribute to his friend George Bush's political campaigns. These items also connect me to nature— to the abundant pieces of nature worldwide that The Nature Company's operations touch on, and that stockholder companies mine with the profits. To shop at The Nature Company has been to plug into the flows of energy and resources, economic power and influence that have defined the American capitalist economy in the 1980s and 1990s. And one of the touchstones of this economy has been the ravenous global consumption of natural resources. Like any successful company, The Nature Company has expanded as rapidly as possible. In 1992, *Fortune* named CML one of the best hundred growth stocks—one of seven to make the list two years in a row—and *Money* named it one of the seven best growth buys. Perhaps the perfect metaphor for The Nature Company is a famous outdoor sculpture by Isamu Noguchi at South Coast Plaza, called "California Scenario"—a strikingly serene landscape of rock and cactus and water. If you turn around, you see its perfect reflection in the thirty-story glass walls of the Great Western Bank.

And who controls the bulk of this economic activity? The class of shoppers the stores have drawn—*whose* meaningful

Nature the company has marketed—are exactly the affluent baby boomers who, coming into their economic power in the 1980s, now own and invest substantial capital and reap the material benefits. CML's target consumers, in the words of *Business Week*, are the "folks [with] lots of money to spend and a seemingly irrepressible urge to spend it": we have come to control, according to a 1988 *Forbes* profile of CML, "a great deal of the economy's discretionary income." If Americans in the late twentieth century are globe coasters all, the globe has increasingly belonged to my generation of higher-income baby boomers not only figuratively but literally. The *Glacier Bay* CD channels serenity into my leisure hours, and channels profits from Alaskan oil mining into my portfolio. As Susan Davis has concluded, of her own visits to Sea World, the kind of person who has appreciated Nature is likely to be the kind of person who has consumed more nature than most.

The very people who have used an idea of a Nature Out There to define who we are, and to navigate the hallmarks and confusions of postwar American life, are also the people who use nature the most. And evasions are themselves a way of navigating. We've used Nature to circumvent our own complicity in the serious modern problems we critique. And here, at last, are the ur-ironies that lie at the heart both of the new nature stores and of the affluent baby boomers' encounters with nature since the 1980s. The Nature Company has marketed twelve thousand products that, on one hand, have sustained an American middle- to upper-class definition of Nature that mitigates the materialism and artifice of modern capitalist society—and at the same time, have sustained, through the creation of artifice, the capitalist overconsumption of resources that underpins American middle- to upper-class life. The Nature Company constitutes a store-size contradiction between how we want to connect to nature and how we actually do, and between what we want Nature to be and what nature actually is. It is also a store-size monument to the convenience, however willful or half-conscious, of these contradictions.

Exit

It's exactly these contradictions that prompt me to say "wow." As the well-off baby boomers have acquired more economic power, the contradictions have become more powerful. And The Nature Company is a rare place where these contradictions *almost* speak to us. When I hike or cross-country ski, or go to the park or tend my garden, these ironies tend not to chase after me. But in a nature store, they practically catch up. I feel ambivalent about what nature these stores are hawking—and where they do it and whether they should do it at all—but mostly I am uneasy about myself, and my own attraction. I fear that my meanings for nature, all on sale here, contradict the actual whats, wheres and hows of my connections to the natural world. At the heart of my ambivalent "wow" lies not so much the nature store itself, but a vague, uneasy suspicion that the store is a logical place for me to be.

And I think "wow," as a one-word analysis, sums up my uneasiness about The Nature Company more effectively than "contradiction." "Wow" projects more of the desire, confusion, utter meaning and depth of feeling that *drive* the contradictions. "Wow" betrays a certain confusion of intention. It suggests a murkiness of desires. What do I really want? How do I really *want* to connect to nature? The contradictions make me uneasy because they threaten the definitions of Nature as a Place Apart that are so powerfully meaningful to me. But they are disturbing also because I *want* to connect to wild nature, and to understand it, and to not destroy it. I want to counter—not strengthen or indulge—my own complicity in economic excesses, in social inequities and in ecological devastations. Yet how much? Am I willing to yield these meanings? Do I really want to see humans and cows and cats on the posters here? Do I want my definitions of nature to help me track the routes by which I convert nature to useful artifice? In the early 1990s, The Nature Company itself installed "field stations" in some of its stores, and stocked them with maps and guides for nearby wild areas— but would shoppers want to see maps for where the water comes from and where the garbage goes? In the 1990s, I think, there are few better routes in American culture to examine these desires and intentions than through television.

Practical decisions about nature stores remain. Is The Nature Company really "a gracious balance between commerce and environmental consciousness"? Should I be using the sounds of Glacier Bay to relax? And should I buy the inflatable penguin for my nephew on his birthday? These turn out to be extraordinarily wide-ranging, conflicted questions. In the 1990s, the marketing of Nature continues to expand. Nature's Jewelry, The Natural Selection, Forever Green, Into the Woods, The Last Best Place, NorthStyle, Coldwater Creek, the Rainforest Company, Serengeti, the Endangered Species Store. American Wilderness Zoo and Aquariums are now appearing in malls cross-country. In 1996, the Mall of America posted a large sign: OCEAN UNDER CONSTRUCTION. The definition of Nature as a Place Apart seems only to continue to grow more compelling. The contradictions have gotten stronger. The questions get more expansive.

5

ROADRUNNERS CAN'T READ
⌒ THE GREENING OF TELEVISION ⌒
IN THE 1990S

Blow up your TV . . . Go to the country . . . Plant a little garden,
eat a lot of peaches
— *John Prine, "Spanish Pipedream"*

Where the pavement ends, the world begins
— *Ford Explorer commercial*

Ha-ha-ha-HA-ha, ha-ha-ha-HA-ha
— *Woody Woodpecker*

Not all woodpeckers, it turns out, look just like Woody, with
red crested heads and blue hands. And roadrunners don't say
"beep beep" —but they actually do run on roads. To navigate
between reality and unreality on TV can be a perilous un-
dertaking. What do I *really* want the nonhuman natural
world—and my connections to it—to be? In pursuit of such

powerful desires, I have taken a brief, and not always safe, eco-trip through TV nature.

TV demands attention here. It is a storytelling medium, a vaunted engine of popular meanings. More Americans have TV sets than indoor plumbing. We watch an average four hours daily—though this is a hotly debated statistic that varies from two to eight—and in 1996, over 93 percent of *TV Guide* readers said they wouldn't give up TV forever for

half a million dollars. Also, since the late 1980s, the proliferation of wild nature on TV amounts to a virtual green revolution. *Nature*, *Wild America* and other nature shows have
evolved into flagship programs on PBS. The major networks
air nature specials—*When Animals Attack, Terrors of the Deep,
World's Most Dangerous Animals III*—to boost ratings during
"sweeps" months. *Dr. Quinn, Medicine Woman* and *Northern
Exposure* revived the TV outdoor western. Perfume commercials look like a Sierra Club wilderness calendar. The mountains on the newest Volvo ads can "save your soul."
Cablevision's Fish Channel broadcasts swimming fish from 6
A.M. to 8 P.M. The fish in the Bayliner boat commercial "play
together in the water" "24 hours a day." And the new Nissan
Pathfinder ads look remarkably like a *National Geographic* series on the Serengeti. And so much of this nature caters to,
and is created by, the Nature/Artifice generation of affluent
thirty- and forty-somethings.

What does all the Nature mean? Everyone worries about
TV's meanings, from Congress to the sociologist Jean Baudrillard to my brother Joe to Murphy Brown. You can easily
spend two to eight hours daily reading anti-TV polemics
such as *The Evil Eye* and *The Plug-In Drug*—also *Abandoned
in the Wasteland, Unplugging the Plug-In Drug, Down the Tube,
Bonfire of the Humanities* and "Why Watch It Anyway?" In a
1995 *New York Times* poll on popular culture American viewers found almost nothing positive to say about their reigning
leisure-time activity. In the postwar era, wringing one's hands
about television has been a parallel pastime to watching it.

Baudrillard has opposed TV to the really real world, and if the many critiques of TV share a heart or center, I think he captures it. You can distill much of the anti-TV furor to two connected fears: that TV distorts the Real World, and that TV can remake the Real World in its own image. Since the 1950s, Americans from Left and Right have defined TV as a major enemy of *Reality*—the postwar trope with which so many of us have powerfully expressed our angst about mass culture, mass behavior, mediatedness, alienations and disconnections in modern society. We've blamed TV for everything gone wrong in the real, off-TV world: breakdown of family, corruption of the political process, the rise of illiteracy, rampant consumerism, juvenile violence, teenage promiscuity and Americans' weight problems.

Very few critics have tuned in to TV nature, and not surprisingly, the consensus so far is unmistakably grim. As an Absolute Force, after all, Nature is Reality's mainstay. As a Place, Nature is where Reality lives. The most influential critic has likely been the persuasive writer and environmentalist Bill McKibben, who in his 1992 book *The Age of Missing Information* contrasts two "24-hour" ventures: he went camping for a night in the Adirondacks; and he spent four months watching videotapes of every TV program broadcast in 24 hours on the 93-channel Fairfax, Virginia cable system—after which he co-founded TV-Free America, which sponsors National TV Turn-Off Week. Television, he concluded, when he finally turned the set off, "worries me because it alters perception." McKibben devotes a full chapter of anxieties to the unrealities of nature shows: "Trying to understand 'nature' from watching [them] is as tough as trying to understand 'life' from watching *Dynasty*." While real lions mostly sleep, for example, on TV they rip apart wildebeest after wildebeest, when they are not having sex. The shows speed up nature's pace, and show us charismatic creatures rather than biological systems. The programs, Charles Siebert agrees in a 1993 *Harper's* essay "The Artifice of the Natural," are "extravagant animal opera." Like McKibben, critics of TV nature tend to focus on nature shows, and to attack the Reality problem with categorical angst. As Ron Powers states in *Audubon,* in an essay that *celebrates* the Audubon Society specials, TV "alters, distorts, oversimplifies, even colonizes the fields of reality it sets out to portray."

NEW THEORY ON WHY DINOSAURS BECAME EXTINCT

McCARTHY/AMARILLO GLOBE-NEWS/CREATORS SYNDICATE

My own methods as a TV-nature critic are less heroic. I simply taped the nature-drenched TV I watch—nature shows, but also commercials and a few 1990s prime-time dramas—and afterward considered it more deliberately. To the question, Does TV distort reality? I bring less anti-TV zeal than a kind of sanguine ambivalence. That is perhaps, in part, because I am in fact a TV watcher—who clocks in under the national average but not by much. Less subjectively, I suspect, first, that the problem with TV nature lies as much in critics' expectations of what nature *should* mean— in the powerful vision of Nature as Reality and anti-Artifice—as in the inarguable fact that TV nature is not real nature. What follows is not a reckoning with *TV*: we have engaged in TV criticism galore, and are familiar with the pitfalls and dangers. Rather, I am interested in the powerful meanings of *Nature,* and what one learns about them by watching TV. While McKibben and like-minded critics exalt Nature as our salvation from the sins of TV, I have been trying to persuade you that Nature entails more than a few sins of its own. And both the seductive power of Nature and the desires of forty-somethings look especially clear on TV.

Also, it's imperative to ask *how* people watch TV—and at least some TV analysts agree. We're not, exactly, like the zombies in an *Earthworm Jim* episode, in which the cartoon worm superhero wards off an invasion of evil furniture that makes people sit down, watch TV and take it literally. We can't be, or the story wouldn't be funny. So many of the meanings on television—whether in comedy, drama or commercials—rest precisely in the *gap* between the real and the unreal, and in viewers' skills at knowing the difference. And how many of us grew up honing these skills every day? A common view of TV as something that is constructed stands in stark contrast to a powerful definition of Nature as absolutely unconstructed: when you put Nature on TV, things can only get interesting. When Wile E. Coyote posts the sign "School—Slow Down," the Roadrunner posts the sign "Roadrunners Can't Read." E.R. physicians are not uniformly handsome and punctual. NYPD detectives don't lead weekly crisis lives. Woodpeckers don't have blue hands. Jerry Seinfeld sings the praises of American Express for money. Real lions mostly sleep. If I buy a Nissan Pathfinder, I won't drive it to Africa. Not all viewers watch with the same admixture of belief and disbelief. On average, though, we can read, as many people would argue, the "Roadrunners Can't Read" signs.

Yet, watching TV is never an exact art or science. While as a child, I knew that woodpeckers never install elevators to get to their tree holes, until I finally saw a real woodpecker, when I was thirteen, I assumed they all had red crested heads. And real roadrunners do run on roads—which I'd pegged as a comic device. TV producers are hardly in the business of sorting these things out precisely for us. But more important, if we may easily spot TV unrealities, we still may invest hopes, dreams and very real emotional or intellectual energy in them. Think of a child who knows that Michelangelo, the Ninja Mutant Turtle, is not real, but cares about and mimics all the moves of her favorite Saturday-morning superhero. We may recognize the fictions, yet willingly agree to believe in them. The pleasures of TV, like the meanings, lie in navigating back and forth—and it is our *desires* that so often create the bridge. Of course, some say the greatest pleasures and desires lie in having both at once. The child wants to be like her Ninja Turtle, but most of all she wants to reap the double rewards of being both the mutant superhero *and* herself. TV allows us to enjoy the real and the unreal at the same time.

And it's exactly in this nebulous terrain, I'm convinced, that most of the dangers and pleasures of a TV eco-trip ultimately lie. As *Newsweek* TV critic Meg Greenfield has written, "There is a great disposition in this country not to trust us TV junkies with our junk." The germane questions about TV nature and its meaningfulness are not only whether and how TV producers distort real nature, but also, Can we tell the difference? And do we always want to?

Nature has its own song. And so few of us ever take the time to listen to its notes.

—*Dr. Quinn, Medicine Woman*

There's a sorta evil out there . . . something very strange in these old woods. Call it what you want, a darkness, a presence . . .

—*Twin Peaks*

I've never listened to trees before, all right? . . . Do they speak English? Esperanto? What?

—*Northern Exposure*

The first years of the 1990s brought three popular and well-publicized prime-time TV dramas that featured wild outdoors settings in the American West: *Dr. Quinn, Medicine Woman, Twin Peaks* and *Northern Exposure*. The success and meanings of these shows all pivoted significantly on the meanings in the abundant images of mountains, forests and birds. When *Dr. Quinn*, the most recent, premiered in 1993, the critics derided it as "treacle," "frontier hooey," "hackneyed folderol" and "in a word . . . square." The CBS show would never attract a big high-income audience. Yet it became an instant runaway success, and singlehandedly salvaged the family drama, the frontier western and the Saturday-night viewership for network television.

In the pilot episode, Dr. Michaela Quinn packs up her 1860s medical practice and moves to Colorado Springs. En route, she performs emergency surgery and watches the U.S. cavalry tangle with the Cheyennes. Soon after her arrival, Dr.

Mike has befriended the town prostitute, an Indian medicine man, and the handsome and laconic mountain man Byron Sully, whose closest companion is a wolf. *Dr. Quinn* was a stock TV western—and used the stock codes of nearly all TV westerns since *Gunsmoke, Wagon Train* and *Have Gun Will Travel* ruled the waves in the late 1950s and early 1960s. The TV genre has adapted a cheerier, more domesticated version of the stock codes used in film westerns. This Colorado Springs is the paradigmatic frontier town, where heroes struggle triumphantly with their allies and detractors for the moral soul of America at the western edge of civilization. *Dr. Quinn* championed pluck and individualism, family values and neighborly behavior in even doses. The show made a few nods to the 1990s. The good guys, Mike and Sully—who will marry, though he will be detained by Custer on their wedding day—have great hair. And a woman M.D., after all, fights for racial justice, gun control and a cleaner environment in the Old West. Still, as a weekly showcase for Right and Wrong, the show was essentially *Bonanza,* with a politically correct twist.

No meaningful codes in westerns are more integral to the genre than those of Nature. The show's producers deployed them here in abundance. The title sequence shows us panoramic shots of the mountains, Dr. Mike galloping through the canyons on horseback and Sully in a broad meadow as he hurls a hatchet. And the writers stocked each episode with at least two or three full scenes in a rugged outdoor setting. In a TV western, we know, Nature is far more

DR. MIKE IN THE MOUNTAINS

than scenery. In these emphatic vehicles for the dialogue on American identity, the wild landscape has been an active, powerful presence: westerns have served as a major vehicle for the countermodern definition of Nature as a Place Out There, an absolute authority for human actions and values. Most of the pivotal events in *Dr. Quinn* take place outside. How does Mike celebrate her thirtieth birthday? She climbs Pike's Peak. Where will she and Sully have to deliver their baby? Away from civilization, in the mountain wilderness. The plots just about write themselves. It is Nature that encourages Mike's free spirit and strength of character. It is exactly Sully's intimacy with Nature—and lifelong distance from cities and civilization—that renders him so intuitive and wise. Nature is a timeless, Authentic and peculiarly American

On the *Dr. Quinn, Medicine Woman* set

force. When Mike and Sully gallop across the landscape together, the Natural wind makes their hair fly: Nature, you could say half seriously, is the protagonists' Original and Absolute Blow Drier. Out there at the edge of modern life, Nature invests the heroes' human pursuits with Absolute Truth.

The nature we see in *Dr. Quinn* is not exactly "real" nature. To begin with, the Colorado mountains are not in Colorado. The show was filmed outside Los Angeles at Paramount Ranch—a longtime film set, where *Gunfight at the OK Corral* was shot. For the rugged mountain scenes, the cast and crew shuttled to Malibu Creek State Park, an erstwhile Fox Studios backlot, where Butch and Sundance jumped off the cliff in *Butch Cassidy and the Sundance Kid*. The Rockies here are at the wrong altitude and in the wrong biome, and grow Pacific Coast tree species. Sully's wolf is actually a malamute. Like all TV shows, *Dr. Quinn* was constructed from a great many disparate pieces, and the Nature here is a collection of mountains, forests, birds, valleys and sunsets that a large production staff filmed, edited, spliced, reedited, overdubbed. They purchased images from suppliers of stock footage. Like all TV, nature has a budget; and location filming is expensive, compared to shooting on controlled indoor sets. The details can be ersatz. The nature shots are highly goal-oriented. Nature here is not so much a set of specific

WGBH Film and Resource center ad in *Variety,* 1994

places or evolutionary details but rather an essential and Absolute Force. It is a well thought out, meticulous, efficient construction of a mythic set of abstract meanings.

Did we know it? Can viewers tell that nature here is a constructed set of meanings? You might not have pondered whether Pike's Peak is actually Malibu, or asked which stock-footage company supplied the shots of the bald eagles. But yes, basically. Most of us who watch TV, or movies, are conversant in westerns and their standard codes. I do not expect Colorado necessarily to be in Colorado. I understand that what's most important about the mountains, valleys and sunsets is not exactly where they are, but what they mean. Not that, if you think about it, there's much difference between what Nature means on a TV western and how it's so often defined off TV. Here, Nature means a Place Apart and an absolute source of authority. Off TV, many of us say that's what nature *is*. I've been arguing that Nature Out There— whether an absolute authority for landscape gardens, Taste, American identity, baby-boomer rebellion or New Age Reality—is not in fact what nature is. How many of us would say that the saintly, perfectly respected Dr. Mike is the same as a real woman in the Old West, and that the meanings of femininity that Dr. Mike represents are the Absolute definition of who a woman really is? Or that Sully's hunk-of-the-1990s masculinity is the same as for any real man? If we are self-conscious about the uses of television to create meaning—and know that *television* is constructed—we tend to show far less self-awareness about the uses and meanings of Nature.

Yet in the context of TV and a familiar western narrative, the Nature on *Dr. Quinn* still looks like a device. In 1998, CBS canceled the series for lagging ratings and an unprofitable shortage of hipness: the show failed to draw the urban, higher-income viewers whom advertisers sought. But before that, CBS dubbed the powerhouse Saturday night lineup "America's Night of Television," for which *Dr. Quinn* served as both lead-off and essential anchor in the show's salad days. Investing heavily in outdoor locations, the network reaped a payoff that was less aesthetic than certifiably mythical.

> *There's . . . evil . . . in these old woods. . . . It's been out there for as long as anyone can remember.*
> —Sheriff Harry Truman, *Twin Peaks*

Twin Peaks, by contrast, had a surfeit of hipness—and got canceled for it. This show, too, sported a transplanted eastern hero, FBI Agent Cooper, who when he arrives in the small western town of Twin Peaks marvels at the mountain views. He detects a fresh "hint of Douglas fir needles in the air" and pronounces the coffee at the Double R diner "damn fine." He takes up whittling. Sent to investigate the murder of the town's high-school prom queen, Agent Cooper effuses the enthusiasm of a young eastern urbanite raised on equal mythic doses of the Frontier West and the small-town Simple Life.

Twin Peaks premiered in 1990, and ran less than a year. But in that time, "Who killed Laura Palmer?" became a national refrain, and the show mobilized a small deconstructing army, who have dissected *Twin Peaks*' debts to a range of TV genres—soap opera, detective series, TV gothic and true-crime drama. The actual intent of David Lynch, the show's famous co-creator, is likely to remain forever enigmatic. Yet the show worked wonderfully as a western, too, which was equipped with all the standard codes of landscape and Nature. The *Twin Peaks* title sequence opens on a songbird, and moves on to the Cascade Mountains, a 270-foot waterfall and a lake. And Lynch and his production staff wired the episodes in abundance with mountain panoramas, rushing water, hooting owls and full moons. These TV mountains, however, bound a town awash in evil and perversity. The sheriff is handsome and laconic, and the Indian deputy, vaguely wise, but the prostitute is in high school, the town doctor is a lunatic psychiatrist, and the loner living up in the mountains is a paranoid middle-aged woman who enjoys a log as her closest companion. The owls turn out to be satanic incarnations. By the end, the town's resident homicidal spirit, BOB, seems even to have taken possession of the heroic Agent Cooper himself.

It's perfect. After skewering suburbia in his 1986 movie *Blue Velvet*, Lynch created a TV show that skewers the Good Life in small-town America. What better device than to locate it in the West, and to invest it with the familiar codes of Nature—as an absolute authority—so central to American identity myths? While Dr. Mike would fight for the rights of single working mothers in the Rockies, Agent Cooper tracks sexually hyperactive teenagers across a rugged Cascades landscape of fresh murder scenes. Nature on both shows was an essential Force. But *Twin Peaks* was anti-*Bonanza*. You could read Nature here either as Absolutely Evil—the owls are possessed, and the lush Northwest landscape evokes a western

Nature run amok—or as a standard landscape of Truth, inhabited by BOB, the Log Lady and a dwarf in Cooper's dream instead of Ben, Hoss and Little Joe. Either way, the images of wild nature invest the evil goings-on in Twin Peaks with Absolute Truth. Who killed Laura Palmer? Each week, the answer grew more perverse. In this western-American TV town, the ultimate truth is that the Truth is all lies.

In *Twin Peaks*, too, Nature is less a set of ecological facts than a mythic narrative power tool. As in *Dr. Quinn*, it is meticulously constructed. In fact, the owl hoots in *Twin Peaks* do not match the species in the owl shots, and the 270-foot waterfall actually lies just below a hydroelectric plant. The real details are unimportant. Did viewers see the differences? Did they see Nature as a constructed set of meanings? Many may not even explicitly have identified *Twin Peaks* as a western. Yet here, too, one readily registers the meanings and conventions of a TV genre that to many of us is as culturally instinctive as apple pie. Here, too, Nature means a Place Apart and a force for Truth. Here, too, the meanings of Nature also match the powerful off-TV definition of what nature really is.

And just in case you missed it, a media blitz showcased the real location of *Twin Peaks*—the town of North Bend, in Washington's Snoqualmie Valley—as essentially the West and real Nature that the show inverts. The real Twin Peaks, you could read, was "a small town, classically so," with "immutable rhythms." Agent Cooper would have loved it: the locals were so paramodern that many chose to go to softball

SNOQUALMIE VALLEY - THE REAL TWIN PEAKS!

SOLD AT THE ALPINE BLOSSOM AND GIFT SHOPPE
North Bend

games rather than watch a weird show like *Twin Peaks*. Of course, the media portrayed the valley itself as Nature's bastion. At the Salish Lodge, the real Great Northern Hotel in "the snow-capped Cascades," mist rose from the mountains by the "majestic" falls, "forming magical clouds [below] in the valley." In fact, the Snoqualmie Valley is an easy half-hour drive from Seattle—whether or not the pie at the Mar-T Café (the real Double R diner) has a crust that "melts in your mouth like a butter cookie." Failing to mention the six-lane interstate, factory-outlet mall and new Nintendo warehouse complex, journalists provided the show's fans with a cultural primer on the meanings and definitions of the West and Nature—on *and* off TV.

As TV watchers, however, *Twin Peaks* viewers were already an unusually savvy lot. Along with *Northern Exposure,* Lynch's show crested a decade of "quality television"—a kudo that critics invented to describe *Hill Street Blues* in the early 1980s, and that went on to grace such well-heeled late-1980s shows as *The Wonder Years, thirtysomething* and *Murphy Brown.* "Quality TV" has attracted a range of definitions but tends to stick to shows that cater to an upscale, TV-suspicious demographic. In its first years, some called it yuppie-style TV. "Quality TV" has targeted viewers with consumer dollars, cultural pretensions and a lifetime of TV-watching experience, and has tended to look very different from the TV on which we baby boomers honed our vast TV-watching skill. It has targeted the Get Real generation—the keepers of the pink flamingo—who in the 1960s hijacked the trope of Reality (and deputized Nature) to critique postwar society as un-Real, but also to play ironically with un-Reality and Artifice to rebel against cultural standards. Like Waters and Warhol, we've observed the boundary between Nature and Artifice—and used it to mark the boundary between reality and un-Reality—in a lasting stroke of self-identity, to both enjoy and critique mass culture, to be at once above it and part of it. What could be more un-Real than television—defined as the very soul of American society and mass culture? As TV watchers, many of us particularly like to watch TV that points out the un-Reality of TV. Some "quality" shows, such as *Murphy Brown,* have satirized TV: "Everything is art," an art critic says in one episode, "everything except

Before TV, two world wars.
After TV, zero.

abc

television. Television is crap." Like *NYPD Blue*, these shows can look self-consciously Realistic, or at least explicit. Or like *Moonlighting*, they can flaunt their own un-Reality. Essentially, "quality" shows are un-TV TV. The trend has culminated most recently in ABC's TV Is Good campaign— "8 hours a day, that's all we ask," "Don't worry, you've got billions of brain cells" and "It's a beautiful day. What are you doing outside?" —which prompted an NBC comedy writer on NBC to send off faxes that subvert the parodies themselves: "Museums cause cancer. We mean it. You will die."

By 1990, when *Twin Peaks* arrived, it was so un-TV it verged on anti-TV. It featured nonlinear plot lines that the writers refused to resolve, and made no pretensions to reality, underlying belief, obvious intent or redeeming social value.

Now here was a show, ABC executives gambled, that the coveted baby boomer demographic could believe in. In a brash un-TV move, the network even announced they would air the *Twin Peaks* pilot with no commercials—but they backed down, and Cadillac advertised on it. TV critics—at this point mostly baby boomers—reviewed the show like a Second Coming. "Like nothing else on television." "Unprecedented." "The series that will change TV." In the end, of course, *Twin Peaks* took the un-TV trend too far, even for the yuppie demographic, and when ABC canceled it the show became literally un-TV. In 1993, though, the art-film cable channel Bravo rebroadcast *Twin Peaks* to launch a new series: "TV Too Good for TV." And soon, David Letterman, TV's crown prince of TV-savvy hip, would be lobbing potshots with the critics at *Dr. Quinn, Medicine Woman*—a show that, while it drew a more average-income demographic, was panned as "unapologetically artless and affirming," and garnered an Emmy Award in 1996 for individual achievement in hairstyling.

In sum, *Twin Peaks* viewers specifically prided themselves on knowing their way around a TV screen. Self-awareness about mass culture—and about the constructedness of TV—lies near the core of their self-identity. As a class and generation, we had always cultivated a well-developed sense of irony, and could tell Reality from un-Reality—well enough to know the TV Nature on the show was constructed and un-Real, and many set out to find the Real Thing. The show's fans (and many nonfans, too) trooped into the

magically cloudy Snoqualmie Valley, where they docked at
the Salish Lodge for $165 a night, by the majestic Sno-
qualmie Falls. They hiked to the top of Mt. Si for scenic
views of the snow-capped Cascades. Many came for week-
ends from Seattle—a famous cyber-center and coffee-bar
mecca, on the cutting edge of urban yuppie makeovers. Not
all observers of the Nature–Artifice definitions have wanted
to go *to* Nature—just as not all of us have enjoyed Artifice
and wanted to watch TV (McKibben, for example). Still,
many of us have. We have taken refuge from the un-Real
World—for which TV, as McKibben avows, is both central
fact and potent metaphor—in the Real World of Nature. On
TV, Nature is a construction. Off TV, it is unassailable. In
other words, if TV viewers recognized the Nature on *Twin
Peaks* as a stock TV device—and a construction of an *idea* of
Reality—many at once headed out into essentially the same
definition of Nature off TV.

Of course, a weekend trip to "Twin Peaks country" let you
enjoy both Reality *and* un-Reality. When you sat on the
deck of the Salish Lodge, a.k.a. the Great Northern Hotel,
you could enjoy un-Reality at its TV extreme and Reality at
its most off-TV basic. You enjoyed Nature and Artifice at
once. You could have the amenities of modern life that your
affluence allowed and a countermodern critique, too. You
could have it all—and like the Nature–Artifice definitions,
wanting to have it all has been a persistent trademark of the
affluent baby boomers' identity.

Is that right?

> —Town mayor in *Northern Exposure*,
> when told that a friend who was killed
> by a falling space satellite has returned as a dog

We're real and they're not.

> —*Northern Exposure* producer Matthew Nodella,
> on comparisons to *Twin Peaks*

Northern Exposure premiered in the summer of 1990, several months after *Twin Peaks* and on the crest of the "quality TV" trend. It became an instant hit. The producers targeted the same demographic, but avoided the aggressions of *Twin Peaks* and got much more of it. In this pilot episode, too, a sophisticated young big-city Easterner lands in a small mountain town near the Pacific Coast. Here it is Joel Fleischman, a newly minted doctor from New York City, who arrives to practice in one-street Cicely, Alaska, as repayment to the state for medical-school scholarships.

Unlike Agent Cooper, Joel is not the West-loving sort. He dreads Cicely as an uncivilized anti-New York, "beyond the end of nowhere." What he fails to anticipate, however, and finds most horrifying, is that the town and its inhabitants are anti-*rational*. *Northern Exposure*'s producers flaunted un-Reality with consummate un-TV skill. In the show's first season, a young man in Cicely is smashed by a falling space satellite. In the second season he returns as a dog. The show's characters have visions. They dream their neighbors' dreams, and converse with ghosts, trees, sandhill cranes, ancient spirit

The Northern Exposure Set

Making Cicely windy

Making Cicely snowy

guides and men who fly. At one point, they build a medieval-style catapult with which they launch a piano. The cast of locals here—who conduct and register these events with a matter-of-factness that startles Joel as surely as the miner's ghost who haunts his cabin—include an ex-con radio deejay who spouts Jung and Kierkegaard, and an Indian teen with a vast knowledge of popular culture. Joel's female nemesis, the bush pilot Maggie O'Connell, hails from Grosse Pointe. Her last four boyfriends all have died in unpredictable ways—fell asleep and froze on a glacier, drove his Volvo by accident onto a missile range, something unspecified with potato salad—before the satellite kills her fifth. The loner up in the mountains, an unshaven barefoot misanthrope, is a superb gourmet chef. "Dogs are dogs. People are people. That's it. End of story," Joel informs them all—but as always, his Enlightenment reason enjoys the impact of one warm exhale in an Alaskan blizzard.

In the history of prime-time TV dramas, *Northern Exposure* certainly has been the greenest. The production staff undertook unusual efforts to wire Cicely with an unprecedented abundance of snowy peaks, deep forests, crystal-clean mountain rivers, hawks, owls, moose, bears, moonrises and sunsets. Not in Alaska, of course. They filmed the outdoor scenes in and around Roslyn, Washington, in the Cascades—fifty miles east of the Snoqualmie Valley, and a more expensive choice, which required that they haul semitrailers weekly from Seattle over icy Snoqualmie Pass. In between snowstorms, the crew hauled in extra snow. The producers hired a tame moose for $5,000 per day. And we knew it, basically. "Alaska is a state of mind," the show's co-creator Joshua Brand remarked: "We used [it] more for what it represents than what it is." We knew that, too. Like *Twin Peaks* viewers, if you were conversant in TV westerns, you could readily register the TV Nature here as an Essential Force. You could read the meanings. And just in case, the media blitz on this show, too—in *TV Guide, People,* fan books, the *New York Times*—read like a crib sheet on the meanings of Nature and the West. Roslyn, population 875—a "picturesque town" in a "majestic, greenwood-covered" mountain landscape—had a main street "out of an Old West daguerreotype," the state's oldest tavern, and a bank that was said to have been robbed by Butch Cassidy and the Sundance Kid in 1892.

What does all the Nature as Essential Force do on the show? Nature here is not only richly abundant but also unusually proactive. The midnight sun activates Fleischman's libido. A river icejam makes the white people act out of character. The northern lights bring important visitors to Cicely. An owl watches from a tree as the satellite smashes to earth. But these events simply remind you that every strange event here happens by Force of Nature. As in any proper TV western town, the wild landscape infuses the goings-on with absolute Truth—and Cicely's berth on the Last Frontier gives its truths an extra fillip. But here in the far TV Arctic, the central Truth is that the truths of the world are mysterious, and that people behave irrationally and unpredictably in their grip. On *Dr. Quinn,* Mike enjoys the Natural Truths of virtue. Agent

Cooper learns the Truths of evil. But Fleischman is tutored in the absolutes of relativity. Truth is relative. Reality is a state of mind. And Cicely's locals understand these Truths as instinctively and well as they can navigate the mountain landscape itself. It's an irony-rich postmodern parable, but also a straight western narrative, which uses Nature in the standard meaningful ways. *Northern Exposure* was a critics' darling and won a score of Emmys—in 1992, more than any other show. For a few bright years, the show wore the un-TV crown. And nature images, I think, worked a great deal of the magic for the show's target upscale baby-boomer demographic. As a stock device in a TV western, Nature here frames a 1990s universe that is self-consciously un-Real, that is an outsize "Roadrunners Can't Read" sign. Nature thereby assures me of my TV savvy and my general suspicions of modern TV-centric life, and it ratifies my hip, ironic, boundary-challenging, postmodern take on the iffy state of Reality.

But all these mountains made the show safe for baby boomers in *two* ways. *Northern Exposure* also featured more images of wild nature than any western or drama show in TV history. As fans and TV critics remarked, the show *looked* different. It looked more Natural. If it used stock TV Nature, it also looked like real off-TV Nature. To an audience who defines Nature as the mainstay of Reality, the show looked, as viewers remarked, more *real* than the rest of the prime-time schedule. Nature made *Northern Exposure* un-TV by making it both un-Real and ultra-Real. And in contrast to *Twin Peaks,* you could say there was something real-seeming and believably poignant about the absurd goings-on. At the least, *Northern Exposure* made relativism, its central allegory, something you could believe in. At the most, when Fleischman argues "categorically, and . . . as a scientist . . . no dog can come back to earth and be Rick," you believe—at least for this hour, on this night, in this universe—that the dog is Rick.

As with *Twin Peaks*, I won't make dire claims as to the producers' intent. But if you want the affluent Nature–Artifice generation to believe in your TV world, what more effective strategy to use than Nature? As a bastion of the Absolute, Nature circumnavigates irony. As anti-Artifice, it is the opposite of TV. Nature—the last, unconstructable, unassailable ur-Reality in a modern world of Artifice—can equip TV producers with a unique power to muck around with the TV-watching skills and confident self-awareness of a key demographic. Nature disarms our self-awareness about the differences between the realities on and off TV: it is one of the few and best remaining strategies against our TV-watching defenses. This, I think, is the major meaningful force that has driven the TV greening trend in the 1990s. In middle age, the affluent baby boomers have become the dominant writers and producers of TV, and at once the audience that advertisers covet most. Of course, *Northern Exposure* gives you Nature *and* Artifice. You get Nature as the ultimate Reality, but you also get the un-Realities of TV. You get an absolute Force and Place, and you get a postmodern relativist universe. You get Nature—but the real power of the definition of Nature as a Place Apart lies not in Nature itself, but in the *boundary* it draws between Nature and not-Nature. It is the boundary that allows us to have all we want.

It's just a TV show. But like all TV, it can work in complex ways. "There was something so pleasurable about watching *Northern Exposure,*" as a baby-boomer friend has explained, and I have to agree. Nature and Artifice. Un-Reality and Reality. Here, Nature means the enjoyment of two worlds at once—just as at the Salish Lodge, except that you never had to leave your house. The self-awareness about TV, and the suspense of one's disbelief. The liberating unrootedness of a postmodern world, but the yearning for an ultimate Reality. The enjoyment of mass culture, and the simultaneous desire to be above it. The amenities of an affluent American lifestyle, and the Simplicity of Nature. The real pleasures of Nature, like the real pleasures of watching TV, lie in desiring and having two things at once—not an amalgam or reckoning of two worlds, but rather both, simultaneously, at once. But the uses, and double pleasures, of Nature are far better hidden.

> *An automotive designer looks at the shapes of nature . . . [for a] design that is honest and natural . . . an ancient . . . notion of what is beautiful. It's called Infiniti.*

> *KitchenAid ranges mirror nature in surprising ways. With even warmth, a strength that endures, a mystery that unfolds, the fire of creation.*

Commercials, too, hand double pleasures to us. But contrary to *Northern Exposure*, which did it gently, TV ads do it with the force of a sledgehammer. Gravity cologne: "a force of Nature." Chevy Tahoe: "Get into the heart of the Wilderness." Cover Girl: "for the ultimate Natural look." The Volvo All-Wheel-Drive Cross Country: to "save your soul." The greening of commercials in the 1990s has been dramatic. Advertisers deploy mountains, deserts, birds, bears, oceans and sunsets to hawk soda, jeans, makeup, beer, refrigerators, cleaning fluids, credit cards, herbicides, cereal, satellite dishes and shoes—and the marketing of cars and perfume on TV now appears to *require* Nature's semiotic powers. And like *Twin Peaks* and *Northern Exposure*, most of these ads target the adult upscale demographic that dominates the consumer base.

What does Nature mean? And what do the ads give us, exactly? A Jeep Eagle drives you right up a mountain stream: it will take you *to* Nature. Bally Total Fitness machines are *in* Nature—planted and ready for use in an uninhabited desert. Many products are *like* Nature, as in a Vanilla Fields perfume ad in which a hummingbird hovers by a flower: "Only Nature could inspire so perfect a fragrance." The Pledge ad deploys a peacock and flowers: "Natural beauty is not created, it is revealed." Clinique Turnaround Cream: "Do for your face what the ocean does for the shore." (Really?) Some products are made *out of* Nature: Tampax, "100 percent cotton, for 100 percent natural protection." Some products *become* Nature: a brown desert dune in a Nissan Maxima ad morphs into a tan leather seat. A canyon sunrise turns to a pilot light in a KitchenAid range. Clairol Natural Instincts:

"At last, there's a hair color born of the Earth." Jeeps, Acura Coupes and Duracell batteries erupt right out of the earth itself. Award-winning Infiniti ads feature flocks of geese, breaking waves and pure blue skies, but no cars at all.

As a genre, TV commercials dispense meanings to us with the slickness and delivery of a gumball machine. While a prime-time drama runs about forty-five minutes (minus commercial breaks), a commercial airs for exactly fifteen, thirty or sixty seconds. TV ads can cost millions of dollars, take months to create and cost $200,000 to run in a single prime-time spot. The producers of TV ads traffic in meanings that are obvious, powerful, highly efficient, assiduously crafted and a heavy investment. So many of these creations connote, swiftly and efficiently, the same countermodern meanings that The Nature Company sells so successfully: Freedom, Adventure, Leisure, Tranquility, anti-Materialism, Simplicity, Place, the Past. Above all, Nature is Reality, an absolute source of authority. The supermodels who wander like Israelites in the wilderness landscapes of TV perfume ads become Really, more Naturally feminine. The well-toned men with whom they rendezvous on tops of mountains and under the sea become Really more masculine. As a consumer—just as at The Nature Company— one can use these products to construct and maintain a Real Self. Bally Total Fitness: "Escape to Reality." Nature in TV commercials is "ancient," "timeless" and "enduring." The batteries and 4-wheel-drive trucks that erupt from the earth are half industrial product, half evolutionary creation. Brut Actif Blue: "the essence of man." The Infiniti-turned-flock-of-geese is "a design that is honest and Natural, an ancient notion of what is beautiful."

The intentions seem clearer here. Advertisers, one can say, use Nature as a terrific un-TV strategy, to reach out to consumers with large quantities of TV-watching savvy, countermodern angst and disposable income. In the nineties, ad producers have amassed an impressive arsenal of anti-Artifice and un-TV maneuvers: black-and-white photography, handheld cameras, depictions of a less modern Past, ads that parody and comment on the constructedness of TV ads. But again what more effective strategy than Nature? As the new, in-the-wilds ad for Isuzu Amigo asks: "There are people who believe the world is radically different than how it appears on television—Would you like to be one of them?" Ad agencies can deploy images of wild nature to dissociate their clients' industrialized wares from what is manufactured, Artificial, corporate, materialistic, changeable and un-Real, and from the hard sell that TV ads themselves represent. "In a world of constant change," as the Prudential ad says, "there's only one certainty"—THE ROCK. The ads associate products with the Real World off TV. And make no mistake, Nature here is the Real World. Bally: "Escape to Reality." Ford Explorer: "Where the pavement ends . . . the world begins." Mercury Sable: "Imagine having the world at your fingertips." EasySpirit shoes: "Inside there's a walking shoe . . . Outside there's a whole world." In these commercials, as in so many others, Reality and the Whole World look exactly like pristine wilderness preserves.

Does the strategy work? Do the target upscale baby boomers see the Nature here as the Real, off-TV World of Nature or as a set of meanings? And does Nature on TV ads circumnavigate our self-awareness about the constructedness of TV? Well, yes and no. On one hand, how can you *not* see the uses of Nature? To begin with, the Nature here is entirely uprooted from actual place and habitat. Where is that canyon supposed to be, exactly? The "stress rate among fish" obviously is not zero. Also, the products so often have little to do with mountains, deserts and oceans. At The Nature Company, at least (where one can *almost* see Nature as a set of meanings), geodes, hiking sticks and bird T-shirts seem securely more Nature-identified than cars, mascara, shoes and credit cards. If I can exercise my TV-watching skills on TV westerns—and know half-consciously that the Alaskan wilds on *Northern Exposure* are "a state of mind"—the constructedness of Nature on TV commercials is hard to miss. "Arizona [is] not just a state of the union," the Arizona Jeans ad just tells us outright—"It's a state of mind." Finally, how could the TV-savvy baby boomers, of all TV-watchers, be fooled by the hard sell? I know I'll drive my Toyota more often in downtown traffic than to the edge of a remote mountain precipice. Actif Blue and Vanilla Fields are not really more Natural. Neither is a Jeep a Dionysian creation. If there is anywhere where we can see the Real World of Nature as a constructed set of meanings, it is here.

And yet, the seductions of this definition of Nature are enormous. If I can see the meanings (and ad agencies must

GREENING OF TV ADS

TOYOTA PREVIA

KitchenAid ranges

NISSAN INFINITI

TIMBERLINE COLOGNE

Toyota 4-Runner

Nissan Pathfinder

Nike

Stetson Sierra cologne

expect me to), these ads still work their magic. The seductions are the same, both on TV and off—and few inventions in American culture play up the seductions with more neon and bright lights than TV commercials. Just look at what you get here: Isuzu Rodeos, TVs, fitness machines, perfumes, batteries, furniture polish, electric ranges, satellite dishes, running shoes, and all the industrially manufactured products that sustain an upscale, resource-intensive American lifestyle. You also get Nature as a Place Apart. Nature is a refuge from the serious social, ecological and emotional *costs* of this lifestyle. In a TV ad, an Isuzu Rodeo takes you *to* this Nature, but the Rodeo is never nature itself. You get nature as resources, and Nature as Meaning—and the absolute boundary we draw between wild Nature and modern Artifice erases the connections. The commercial fails to tell us that an Isuzu Rodeo, like each of these products, requires the use of a great quantity of real nature to manufacture, and just like all sport-utility vehicles is an unrepentant gas guzzler. In the TV ad, I can use the Rodeo to go to the mall, to take refuge in Nature or to haul home the countermodern meanings of Nature from a mountain range—but I never have to carve up the mountains themselves.

As the old Doublemint gum jingle goes, double your pleasure, double your fun. What do I really want? I suspect, two different things. Ravenous resource use—and restraints on rampant materialism. I want both. Each is a very real desire. My desire for ecological sustainability is not necessarily a mask for my desire to consume. It is not necessarily insincere.

I honestly want both. The strict boundary between Nature and Artifice—and the definition of Nature as a Place Apart, with which we draw it—allows me to enjoy both, without compromise, at once. I want the pleasures of mass culture— and I want to say it is something un-Real that I am above. I want social equality and multicultural differences—and I want the absolute authority of Nature for human social power and values. I want to assail every boundary—and I want one Absolute boundary that will never budge. I want, too, the rewards of self-awareness and irony—and I want a refuge from constant skepticism. This vision of Nature testifies to well-meaning intentions, and real anxieties, and real desires to grapple with the defining problems of postwar modern life. But it betrays a competitively stronger refusal to grapple with the costs of modern life, by those who have the economic resources to best enjoy the benefits. The well-off baby boomers have been notorious for wanting to have it all. And our Nature–Artifice boundary appoints contradictory desires to two separate places, and erases the connections. It avoids reckoning.

In the Volvo ad, the contradictions in our desires become more visible than any other place I can think of. Yet what could be a more powerful, blinding desire than wanting to have it all? *Does* the obvious constructedness of meanings here prod us to challenge the off-TV meanings of Nature? When I have asked my friends and colleagues about these cars-suffused-in-nature ads, I have fielded a lot of outrage. How can they use Nature to sell big trucks? How can they hawk Nature so shamelessly? A Volvo ad does not necessarily challenge the off-TV vision of Nature as a Place Apart. It's an illegitimate habitat. The ad is slanderous. In sum, you can say that TV commercials showcase the meanings and con-structedness and seductions and contradictions of Nature so boldly and shamelessly as to render them unusually, and very usefully, visible. There are cultural inventions in which the trickiest fallacies in our most ingrained myths and habits of thinking rise close to the surface—and jog our self-aware-ness—and TV commercials are potentially one of them. *And* you can say that TV commercials are one of the most inces-sant, skillfully constructed and enthusiastically financed cul-tural vehicles for a reigning definition of Nature—whose abundant and seductive pleasures reside powerfully in anxi-ety, convenience, denial and desire.

> *As a means of defense, zebra often congregate in herds, placing their young . . . in the center of the pack. In a group, their dizzying array of stripes blends together, making it exceptionally difficult for preda-tors to single out what would otherwise be an easy meal.*
> —Nissan Pathfinder commercial

Why? When baby boomers like me encounter Nature on TV, why does our self-awareness—and trademark penchant for questions—dive underwater? My surpassing desires can safeguard the contradictions in Nature from my love of ques-tions. But so can the very definition itself. And that brings me back, finally, to the most scrutinized and criticized TV nature—nature shows—and why I have been harping more on the definitions of Nature than the dangers of TV.

Nature shows are the one genre in which TV producers do not show us nature images first and foremost as meanings. They televise nature *as* nature, and identify most of the animals and places. And yet the nature on popular shows such as *Nature*, *Wild America*, and *The Natural World* looks remarkably like the Nature on so much of the rest of TV. The title and promotion sequences are montages of wild landscapes and animals from all parts of the globe. Like a nightly parade of commercials, the sequences collapse all wild nature into Nature with a capital N. Here, too, Nature is hardly ever urban. It is practically unpeopled. Scientists do appear occasionally (not too rarely with sport-utility vehicles), as do indigenous people—who more often have vacated the landscape and left only a strange surfeit of flute music behind—and the narrators, if we see them, typically show up only to begin and end the shows, to say, essentially, "Let's go out there now" and "Great trip, wasn't it?" On TV nature shows, humans visit and discover nature, but rarely use or change it.

"We'll take you there," PBS assures us. "We give you the whole wide world." Where the pavement ends, the world begins. The programs do show us extraordinary places. They teach us about remarkable creatures. Of all my tapes, I enjoyed these the most. *Wild Wings*, *Birds of Peace*, *Patagonia: Life at the End of the Earth*, *Great Owl of the Mountains*. The shows acquaint us with the earth's biological diversity, and argue environmental conservation to large audiences. But just like westerns and TV ads, they also define Nature consistently as a Real World Apart from modern everyday life. "An empty land," in *Flight of the Condor*, *Nature*'s spectacular and groundbreaking series on the Andes—"as still as if it were the beginning of time." Nature is unchanging, timeless, Absolute: "The ageless cycle of the Antarctic"; "ancient birds, as old as the Andes themselves." "A strength that endures . . . the fire of creation": the James Earl Jones-style voice telling us what Nature is in a KitchenAid commercial could be George

ADVERTISEMENT IN
St. Louis Post-Dispatch
TV Guide

Page, the narrator of *Nature*, inviting us to the Sahara. If you surf at random onto the Discovery Channel, as I did one evening, "the peace of Eden hovers over this small herd of antelope" might be akin to the first sentence you hear, too.

If you think about it, the signature nature-show style—so easily recognizable—consists of a well-established brace of techniques that all reinforce the definition of Nature as a Place Apart. In fact, if Nature is quintessentially not modern, then how can it be TV, the very soul of Artifice and mass culture? The genre's style is one of the earliest and best-entrenched un-TV traditions. While the rest of TV abhors silence, here silences are common and quiet is the norm. Panoramic footage is endemic, on a small screen that favors close-ups. If many of us object that TV defines the triviality of mass culture, here the grave, solemn tone is unmistakable. The shows are defining staples of PBS too, which assiduously broadcasts counter-TV: "Some of the garbage on TV today is definitely worth watching," runs a Sesame Street ad with Oscar in a trashcan. Even for PBS, the pace is slow: the inevitable switch to slow motion for the trademark predator-prey chases renders these life-and-death events more suspenseful (will the cheetah catch the antelope? the hawk the rabbit?) but also converts the fastest footage in these programs to the slowest. As the rest of TV has sped up, spurred in part by the 1980s rapid-fire style of MTV, the un-TV quietude of nature shows has become more entrenched. Since the 1950s, in fact, when Walt Disney's pioneering, highly anthropomorphic shows established the genre as popular, nature filmmakers steadily and deliberately have made nature shows more real and naturalistic. The quiet, human-free *Flight of the Condor* in 1982 was a landmark that documentarians widely copied. They have made the shows spectacularly, and often gratifyingly, more real. But they've also made them more un-TV and more Real. They've refined a set of techniques to televise a vision of what we *want* real nature to be: slow, quiet, remote, untouched by humans and unassailably Real.

Do we know it? Can viewers see the constructions of TV Nature *here*? Not necessarily. And this points directly to a final source of power for the definition of Nature as a Place Apart. Sure, I don't need terrific TV-watching skills to theorize that a lion's life on the African savanna is not, in fact, a continuous orgy of sex and violence, or that TV is not the most conducive medium with which to show me that lions sleep twenty hours a day. I can see that an on-TV lion is not the same as an off-TV lion. But the constructedness of the big picture here, of Nature as the Real World? On TV westerns and ads, Nature *looks* like this set of meanings—a Place Apart and Absolute Force—more than a set of ecological facts. But while I readily suspected that *Dr. Quinn's* Colorado Springs isn't in Colorado, why was I so surprised to learn that George Page's host sequences in *Flight of the Condor,* on the Andes, were filmed in the mountains of southern California (not far from Paramount Ranch)? On *Dr. Quinn, Northern Exposure,* and an Isuzu Rodeo ad, Nature as an Absolute Force authenticates Dr. Mike's moral values, the utter saneness of catapulting a piano skyward, and reasons to buy a sport-utility vehicle. Here, Nature—the same shots of snow-capped mountains—authenticates the definition of Nature itself. George Page tells us what nature *is*—"an empty land," like "the beginning of time"—and the very images of wild nature he shows us verify that it's all true. The producers of *Northern Exposure* and TV ads can use Nature, as the Real World, to circumnavigate viewers' self-awareness about the constructedness of TV. But Nature is sort of our Achilles heel not just of TV skepticism, but of self-awareness *generally.* On *and* off TV, Nature—as the Last Absolute—circumnavigates self-awareness about how we construct the meanings of *Nature.* It at once powerfully torpedoes the potential to define nature as something else.

Why does my self-awareness dive underground? In part, because of the magnitude and abundance of my desires. But the definition of Nature is also powerfully self-authenticating. The definition has built-in defenses against questions. And if commercials are potentially the genre of TV Nature in which contradictory desires swim closest to view—and allow for questions—the contradictions here seem more like bottom-feeders in the Pacific. Hence a new, 1990s style of commercial. "As a means of defense, zebra often congregate in herds": in 1996, Nissan's seven-part campaign for their premier sport-utility vehicle, the Pathfinder, which chronicles a safari on the African savanna, took the greening trend in TV ads to its logical extreme. "The world's last remaining paradise," a narrator invited us into the quintessential nature-show landscape—"where animals still run wild, as Nature always intended." Like recent ads for American Express and Visa, which also mimic the look and sound of nature shows, these ads don't fool us, exactly. But they cadge a little authority from another brand of TV altogether, in which the Truth and Reality of nature images are unquestioned.

Well, not entirely unquestioned. The critics of TV nature have targeted nature shows in particular. But what do they say are the dangers? The nature here, they object, is entirely different from real nature. McKibben, for example, charges that nature on TV is faster and too dramatic. He fears the impact on TV-watchers' off-TV encounters with nature: viewers will "wander the forest path and wonder . . . where are all the large ungulates and giant cats who are supposed to be alternately mating and killing each other?" My own experience is that kids—for whom the jeremiads fear most—are satisfied to see rocks and leaves. Also, I fear that McKibben's definition of "real nature" sounds remarkably close to a Ford Explorer commercial—Where the pavement ends, the world begins. Nature, he says in *Age of Missing Information,* "is the *real* real world, the one that was here before us"—A strength that endures, the fire of creation. "Nature shows are much more like cities," Charles Siebert has leveled a complaint in *Harper's*—"fast-paced, multi-storied, and artificially lit"—and in letters to the editor, a string of like-minded critics weighed in: the "quick and savage Africa" on TV misrepresents the "timeless pace of the savanna"—The peace of Eden hovers over this small herd of antelope. What are the dangers of TV nature? McKibben fears that it isn't *enough* like a Nature Apart. But I fear that his definition of Nature as the Real World isn't the real world at all—and that nature show producers and their critics actually agree on what nature *is.*

The detractors either have urged producers to make the shows more real, or have urged viewers to "Just Turn it Off." In pursuit of the first solution, nature filmmakers themselves have engaged for several decades in a heated debate on the increasingly tough standards of realism. The debate flared in the media most recently in 1996, with accusations against *Wild America*'s Marty Stouffer—who had, he admitted, planted prey animals close to hungry predators, and edited out cages from scenes he'd filmed in cages. "Jeers to messing with Mother Nature," *TV Guide* chided: "Nature films should be natural." Stouffer defended the scenes as "factual recreations," but executives at the Discovery Channel demurred to the *New York Times*: "We would rather have a guy stand in a creek in Alaska for three weeks waiting for a grizzly bear to catch a fish in its mouth than have somebody standing off camera throwing the fish." You would? Really? To demonstrate how a bear catches and eats salmon, why can't you toss a single salmon in its direction? The BBC assured readers that their producers, too, hew to strict guidelines: "You can't feed a vertebrate to a vertebrate." You can't? Why not? Questions such as these have been guaranteed to make tempers flare. But the controversy, I think, says far more about the powers of Nature than about the best uses and worst abuses of TV.

"Just Turn it Off": that's the solution that McKibben implies in *Age of Missing Information*. It's also TV-Free America's slogan—although their literature suggests it may have won by a hair over "Just blow it up." Blow up your TV and move to the country, as the famous John Prine song goes. TV, I agree, can be seductive. My own jeremiads about the dangers of TV Nature are not an apologia for TV: I confess, even, to being tempted by National TV Turn-Off Week. But so many of us enjoy a self-awareness about TV that we have so consistently and thoroughly failed to bring to our encounters with nature. As an Absolute Force, Nature circumnavigates questions. As a refuge from modern life, it is a *reprieve* from irony and self-awareness—and from the abundant, challenging, often confusing complexities of life in the late-twentieth

TV-FREE AMERICA!
THE ENVIRONMENTAL MOVEMENT OF THE MIND...

TVFA, WASHINGTON, D.C. (202) 887-0436

TV-FREE AMERICA BUMPERSTICKER

century. It is even a refuge, I'll argue, from its own contradictions—and like constant skepticism, the persistent experience of contradictions can be exhausting.

Also, as an engine of desire, TV is most seductive where our desires make us most vulnerable. And while the well-off baby boomers have always used the Nature–Artifice boundary to define who we are and to navigate the world around us, in the 1980s and 1990s, as we've literally inherited modern America, we've used the boundary to pursue everything we want. An uninhabited refuge, which we use intensively. Ecological restraint, and unlimited resources. Grave doubts about materialism, and consumption at will. Social equality and cultural relativism, and an Absolute Force with which to judge. The pleasures of mass culture, but cultural superiority. Pervasive skepticism, and the reassuring belief in something. And among these unreckoned, double desires, I want to trumpet my own self-awareness and irony—and I want Nature to be immune to questioning and irony. What dangers do TV-watchers encounter? What's seductive about my all-time favorite show *Northern Exposure*? Why worry about a half-minute of footage that shows a sport-utility vehicle in the Arctic? As Volvo's promotional literature says, their new Cross Country sportswagons "[demand] no compromise from those with lives that combine urban pursuits and country escapes." And what's really dangerous about so much of TV nature is that it showcases these evasive, contradictory, self-authenticating, extraordinarily powerful off-TV definitions of nature so beautifully.

> *Nature* is made possible by the financial support of viewers like you, your gas company, and the gas industry—who would like you to know that virtually all the gas used in North America comes from North America.
>
> – American Gas Industry plug on PBS

The definitions are rooted historically in American identity. They're rooted deeply in the geographic and economic disconnections of modern American life. And for my affluent postwar generation, at least, they're rooted in vast territories of desire. But nature has more human artifice in it than I've tended to think. And artifice has more nature. A table in my apartment living-room is made out of wood, glues, tools, human labor. The trails through Yellowstone are full of boots, backpacks, bottled water and polypropylene—and are accessible because of 1950s interstate highways. The park's design, management and boundaries: human creations all, they speak to 120 specific years of changing needs and demands of competing human groups. To make good decisions about sport-utility vehicles, tables, and national parks, we have to think clearly about how we've mixed nature and artifice in the past, and how we want to in the future. We have to think about how to consume nature, and restrain the use of resources at the same time. Ideally, we have to bring a healthy skepticism and a relativist's appreciation of different perspectives, *and* an eye—ecologically, morally, socially—for what's better, truer, more useful.

What is nonhuman nature? It can be beautiful, wondrous. It is a set of resources, which humans use to survive, build, play, fix, decorate and trade. It is a remarkably complicated network of ecological relationships, which it's imperative we respect, investigate, and understand. Nature is not a separate place. It is no more or less real than a plastic pink flamingo or an Isuzu Rodeo. It is not a more reliable or authoritative place to look for guides to human behavior. It is, you could say, a continuum, that ranges from the wildest pieces of nature to the most transformed.

Not least, the nonhuman natural world is a rich source for human meaning. What should nature *mean?*—is not for me to say. But to make nature exceptionally meaningful—and to use our everyday encounters to navigate the world and define who we are—is simply to be human. Wild pieces of nature will, and should, take on different meanings in different places and eras. But some meanings are better, truer, and more useful than others. In the late 1990s, when Americans connect to pieces of nature across great distances, and through vastly complex economic networks, it's so easy to lose track of our connections. So as we craft ideas of nature to navigate an increasingly complex era, and as we use them to tell us about ourselves, shouldn't we ask our meanings to help us identify rather than avoid a reckoning of all these connections among people and nature?

The real challenge is to tell the difference between TV Nature, as an absolute ur-Reality at the edge of modern life, and real nature, as something we can use and change, in all its forms in the late-twentieth century—Yellowstone, wildlife refuges, farms, city parks, sidelot gardens, suburban lawns, pink flamingos, dinner, TVs and Isuzu Rodeos. This is one of the soggiest TV-or-reality swamps of all, and it's very hard to navigate. Off TV, it's one of the soggiest and most challenging social, cultural, economic, and environmental swamps of all. Escape to Reality. Just Blow it Up. The suggestions sound akin to the claims of TV ads that a Volvo Cross Country can save your soul, and that fish lead stress-free lives. They all beg for a rejoinder that enjoys a similar ring, but draws, in the end, from a different well of desire: Get real.

NOTES

Introduction

For an expanded set of notes to the book see Jennifer Jaye Price, "Flight Maps: Encounters with Nature in Modern American Culture," Ph.D. diss., Yale Uni., 1998.

xvi Volvo ad campaign: Jean Halliday, "Volvo's V70 Intro Rides on $35 Mil in Ad Support" (September 1997), at http://www. adage.com.

xvii "birds have wings": "Letters," *Audubon* 95 (March–April 1993), 16.

    Calls: my most immediate influences include William Cronon, e.g., *Nature's Metropolis: Chicago and the Great West* (New York: W. W. Norton, 1991); Michael Pollan, *Second Nature: A Gardener's Education* (New York: Atlantic Monthly Press, 1991); Giovanna Di Chiro, "Nature as Community: The Convergence of Environmental and Social Justice," in *Uncommon Ground: Toward Reinventing Nature*, ed. William Cronon (New York: W. W. Norton, 1995), 298–320.

xviii 700 to 1: "Harper's Index," *Harper's Magazine* 284 (February 1992), 11.

Chapter 1

1 "I was suddenly": Alexander Wilson, *American Ornithology*, with a continuation by Charles Lucian Bonaparte, illustr. notes by William Jardine, vol. 2 (London: Whittaker, Treacher, and Arnot, 1832), 201–4.

3 "Some persons": John James Audubon, *Ornithological Biography*, vol. 1 (Edinburgh: Adam and Charles Black, 1849), 319–27; ibid., vol. 5, 552. "Too strange": W. Faux, *Memorable Days in America* (London: W. Simpkin and R. Marshall, 1823), 249. "Beyond the power": Dr. Gideon Lincecum, "The Nesting of Wild Pigeons," *American Sportsman* 4 (27 June 1874), 195.

On biology, see A. W. Schorger, *The Passenger Pigeon: Its Natural History and Extinction* (Norman: Uni. of Oklahoma Press, 1973); Duane E. Young, "Ecological Considerations in the Extinction of the Passenger Pigeon (*Ectopistes migratorius*), Heath Hen (*Tympanuchus cupido cupido*) and the Eskimo Curlew (*Numenius borealis*)," Ph.D. diss., Uni. of Michigan, 1953.

4 "They went": Edward T. Martin, "What Became of All the Pigeons?" *Outing* 64 (July 1914), 480. Sightings: G. C. Tremaine Ward, "The Passenger Pigeon," *Auk* 18 (April 1901), 192; W. B. Mershon, *The Passenger Pigeon* (New York: Outing Publishing, 1907), 174; Schorger, *Passenger Pigeon*, 211. Martha's story is in David Wilcove, "In Memory of Martha and Her Kind," *Audubon* 91 (September 1989), 52–55.

1874 nesting: L. M. Hartwick and W. H. Tuller, *Oceana County: Pioneers and Business Men of To-Day* (Pentwater, MI: Pentwater News Steam Print, 1890), 81; Mershon, *Passenger Pigeon*, 114.

Market hunting: see the rare firsthand account, H. Clay Merritt, *The Shadow of a Gun* (Chicago: F. T. Peterson, 1904). Railroads and markets: see William Cronon, *Nature's Metropolis: Chicago and the Great West* (New York: W. W. Norton, 1991).

Wildlife declines: I've relied on Peter Matthiessen, *Wildlife in America*, rev. ed. (New York: Viking, 1987); James A. Tober, *Who Owns the Wildlife? The Political Economy of Conservation in Nineteenth-Century America* (Westport, CT: Greenwood Press, 1981); Theodore Whaley Cart, "The Struggle for Wildlife Protection in the United States, 1870–1900: Attitudes and Events Leading to the Lacey Act," Ph.D. diss., University of North Carolina-Chapel Hill, 1971; Thomas R. Dunlap, *Saving America's Wildlife* (Princeton: Princeton Uni. Press, 1988). Bison: see esp. Andrew Isenberg, "Social and Environmental Causes and Consequences of the Destruction of the Bison," *Revue Française D'Études Américaines* no. 70 (October 1996), 15–27; Dan Flores, "Bison Ecology and Bison Diplomacy: The Southern Plains from 1800 to 1850," *Journal of American History* 78 (September 1991), 465–85.

"No other bird": John Muir, *The Story of My Boyhood and Youth* (Boston: Houghton Mifflin, 1913), 158.

"yet be hidden": Martin, "All the Pigeons," 480.

5 Monuments: Walter E. Scott, ed., *Silent Wings: A Memorial to the Passenger Pigeon* (Madison: Wisconsin Society for Ornithology, 1947), 3; George S. May, "The State Markers Program: A Progress Report," *Michigan History* 41 (1957), 209–15; "News," *Passenger Pigeon* 10 (January 1948), 29. Novels and children's books include Susan Dudley Morrison, *The Passenger Pigeon* (New York: Crestwood House, 1989); James Ralph Johnson, *The Last Passenger* (New York: Macmillan, 1956); Graham Coleman, *Passenger Pigeon* (Milwaukee: Gareth Stevens, 1996); Allan W. Eckert, *The Silent Sky: The Incredible Extinction of the Passenger Pigeon* (Boston: Little, Brown, 1965); Esther S. and Bernard L. Gordon, *Once There Was a Passenger Pigeon* (New York: Henry Z. Walck, 1976).

Aldo Leopold, *A Sand County Almanac* (London: Oxford Uni. Press, 1949), 109.

6 See Schorger for a review of the theories: *Passenger Pigeon*, 211–17. Among the few postmortem works by ecologists, see esp. David E. Blockstein and Harrison B. Tordoff, "Gone Forever: A Contemporary Look at the Extinction of the Passenger Pigeon," *American Birds* 39 (Winter 1985), 845–51; T. R. Halliday, "The Extinction of the Passenger Pigeon *Ectopistes Migratorius* and Its Relevance to Contemporary Conservation," *Biological Conservation* 17 (1980), 157–62; Wilcove, "In Memory of Martha," 54–55. Advantages of group living: see J. R. Krebs and N. B. Davies, *An Introduction to Behavioural Ecology*, 3d ed. (Oxford: Blackwell Scientific Publications, 1993), 120–26. Population thresholds: a review is Michael E. Gilpin and Michael E. Soulé, "Minimum Viable Populations: Processes of Species Extinction," in *Conservation Biology: The Science of Scarcity and Diversity*, ed. Michael E. Soulé (Sunderland, MA: Sinauer Associates, 1986), 19–34.

"God, what were": John Harold, "Passenger Pigeons," *Live at Max's* (Paramount Records, 1973).

8　Philadelphia: John F. Watson, *Annals of Philadelphia* (Philadelphia: Uriah Hunt, 1830), 240, 410. "Everyone takes": Schorger, *Passenger Pigeon*, 196–97. Toronto: ibid, 198.

9　"Here they come!" "hard gale": Audubon, *Ornithological Biography*, vol. 1, 324. Methods: Schorger, *Passenger Pigeon*, 167–98; Faux, *Memorable Days*, 249. Pigeon mania: e.g., J. Benwell, *An Englishman's Travels in America* (London: Binns and Goodwin, 1853), 72–75; Anne Grant, *Memoirs of an American Lady* (New York: Dodd, Mead 1901), 95; James Eldridge Quinlan, *History of Sullivan County* (Liberty, NY: W. T. Morgans, 1873), 508.

Pigeons in large-mast years: e.g., Morris Schaff, *Etna and Kirkersville* (Boston: Houghton, Mifflin, 1905), 107; Pehr Kalm, "A Description of the Wild Pigeons Which Visit the Southern English Colonies in North America, During Certain Years, in Incredible Multitudes," trans. S. M. Gronberger, repr. in *Auk* 28 (January 1911), 59. Beech and oak phenology: I've relied on *Seeds of Woody Plants in the United States*, Agricultural Handbook No. 450 (Washington, D.C.: Forest Service, U.S. Department of Agriculture, 1974).

"pigeon years": Isaac Weld, Jr., *Travels through the States of North America, and the Provinces of Upper and Lower Canada, during the Years 1795, 1796, and 1797*, vol. 2, 3d ed. (London: John Stockdale, 1800), 44.

Cooking pigeons: e.g., Maria Elisa Rundell, *American Domestic Cookery* (New York: Evert Duyckinck, 1823), 104–5, 112–15, 154, 156; *The Housewife's Guide*, rev. and corr. by M. McGetrick (New York: G. F. Bunce, 1834), 7, 28–29; Mrs. Child, *The American Frugal Housewife* (Boston: American Stationers' Co., 1836), 56.

Tiring of pigeons: Wilson, *American Ornithology*, 205; C. J. S. Bethune, "Recollections of the Passenger Pigeon," *Ottawa Naturalist* 16 (May 1902), 41.

10　Andrew Burnaby, *Travels Through the Middle Settlements in North America, in the Years 1759 and 1760*, 3d ed. (London: T. Payne, 1998), 101–2. "three feet": Rundell, *Domestic Cookery*, 156. Pot pie nostalgia: e.g., Margaret H. Mitchell, *The Passenger Pigeon in On-*

tario (Toronto: University of Toronto Press, 1935), 14; John Lewis Childs, "Personal Recollections of the Passenger Pigeon," *Warbler*, 2d ser., 1 (Third Quarter 1905), 72.

Analyses of attitudes as utilitarian place varying emphasis on capitalism, science and technology, nationalism, and Judeo-Christian thought: e.g., Kirkpatrick Sale, *The Conquest of Paradise: Christopher Columbus and the Columbian Legacy* (New York: Alfred A. Knopf, 1990); Roderick Nash, *Wilderness and the American Mind*, 3d ed. (New Haven: Yale Uni. Press, 1982), 31; and see Lynn White, Jr.'s influential "The Historical Roots of Our Ecologic Crisis," *Science* 155 (10 March 1967), 1203–7. On resource commodification, see Cronon, *Changes in the Land*.

Game markets: I've relied on Tober, *Who Owns the Wildlife?* 13, 17, 24–28. Early pigeon markets: e.g., Thomas F. De Voe, *The Market Assistant* (New York: Orange Judd, 1866), 175; William Douglass, *A Summary, Historical and Political, of the First Planting, Progressive Improvements, and Present State of the British Settlements in North America*, vol. 2 (London: R. and J. Dodsley, 1760), 218.

11 "abounding with deer": Tober, *Who Owns the Wildlife?* 3. Diet and abundance: see ibid., 3–13; Cronon, *Changes in the Land*, 22–25; Waverley Root and Richard de Rochemont, *Eating in America: A History* (New York: Ecco Press, 1981), 51–73.

"I have seen": William Wood, *New England's Prospect*, ed. Alden T. Vaughan (Amherst: Uni. of Massachusetts Press, 1977), 50.

12 "before the mouth": Thomas Morton, *New English Canaan*, ed. Charles Francis Adams (Boston: The Prince Society, 1883), 190.

Everyday meanings of animals: I've been influenced esp. by Clifford Geertz, *The Interpretation of Cultures* (New York: Basic Books, 1973), esp. 3–30; Mary Douglas, *Implicit Meanings: Essays in Anthropology* (London: Routledge & Paul, 1975), 27–46; Robert Darnton, *The Great Cat Massacre and Other Episodes in French Cultural History* (New York: Vintage Books, 1984); Harriet Ritvo, *The Animal Estate: The English and Other Creatures in the Victorian Age* (Cambridge: Harvard Uni. Press, 1987); Angus K. Gillespie and Jay Mechling, eds., *American Wildlife in Symbol and Story*

(Knoxville: Uni. of Tennessee Press, 1987). Meanings of hunting: I've found especially helpful Donna Haraway, *Primate Visions: Gender, Race, and Nature in the World of Modern Science* (New York: Routledge, 1989); Louis S. Warren, *The Hunter's Game: Poachers and Conservationists in Twentieth-Century America* (New Haven: Yale University Press, 1997); Stuart A. Marks, *Southern Hunting in Black and White: Nature, History, and Ritual in a Carolina Community* (Princeton: Princeton Uni. Press, 1991).

13 "thirty and forty": Schorger, *Passenger Pigeon*, 9.

Vermont: Samuel Peters, *A General History of Connecticut*, 2d ed. (London: J. Bew, 1782), 155; see also, e.g., Douglass, *British Settlements*, vol. 1, 126.

"quails that fell": Schorger, *Passenger Pigeon*, 8.

14 "a white pigeon": J. Curtin, "Seneca Fiction, Legends, and Myths," *Annual Report Bureau American Ethnology* 32 (1910–11), 694–95. Senecas and pigeons: I've used William N. Fenton and Merle H. Deardorff, "The Last Passenger Pigeon Hunts of the Cornplanter Senecas," *Journal Washington Academy Sciences* 33 (15 October 1943), 289–315 (the evidence comes from captivity narratives and 19th- and 20th-century oral histories). On other Native American groups, see also Schorger, *Passenger Pigeon*, esp. 133–40. Seneca history and ecology: William N. Fenton, "Northern Iroquoian Culture Patterns," Thomas S. Abler and Elisabeth Tooker, "Seneca," and James A. Tuck, "Northern Iroquoian Prehistory," in *Northeast*, ed. Bruce Trigger, vol. 15 of *Handbook of North American Indians*, ed. William C. Sturtevant (Washington, D.C.: Smithsonian Institution, 1978), 296–321, 505–17, 322.

14 Jones quotes: George H. Harris, "The Life of Horatio Jones," *Publications Buffalo Historical Society* 6 (1903), 449–51.

Festivities: Fenton and Deardorff, "Last Pigeon Hunts," 292; Sarah E. Gunn, "Sarah Whitmore's Captivity," *Publications Buffalo Historical Society* 6 (1903), 517–18.

16 "*young pigeons*": Curtin, "Seneca Fiction," 695.

"learned these songs": ibid., 666.

17 On Native Americans' approaches to the environment, which were diverse, but shared important features in contrast to Euro-American approaches—I've used Richard White and William Cronon,

"Ecological Change and Indian–White Relations," in *History of Indian-White Relations*, ed. Wilcomb E. Washburn, vol. 4 of *Handbook of North American Indians* (1988), esp. 417–21; Richard White, "Native Americans and the Environment," in *Scholars and the Indian Experience: Critical Reviews of Recent Writing in the Social Sciences*, ed. W. R. Swagerty (Bloomington: Indiana Uni. Press, 1984), 179–204; and for New England, Cronon, *Changes in the Land*.

18 Scarcity in the East: e.g., Kalm, "Description," 65.

Hudson River: Audubon, *Ornithological Biography*, vol. 1, 325. Newburgh and Coehecton: Quinlan, *Sullivan County*, 508–9. Chicago: E. Duis, *The Good Old Times in McLean County, Illinois* (Bloomington: Leader Publishing and Printing House, 1874), 234. St. Paul: Evadene Burris Swanson, "The Use and Conservation of Minnesota Game, 1850–1900," Ph.D. diss., Uni. of Minnesota, 1940, 133.

19 "Never in": *Milwaukee Sentinel*, 13 May 1871. "A stranger": "The Great Pigeon Roost," *Sparta Herald*, 2 May 1871. Sixteen tons: A. W. Schorger, "The Great Wisconsin Passenger Pigeon Nesting of 1871," in *Silent Wings*, 17.

Railroad lines: James P. Kaysen, comp., *The Railroads of Wisconsin 1827–1937* (Boston: Railway & Locomotive Historical Society, 1937), 20.

"Hardly a train": "Pigeons," *Wisconsin Mirror*, 6 May 1871.

Price quotes: *Milwaukee Sentinel*, April 27–May 18, 1871; early-1870s market columns in *American Agriculturist* and *Prairie Farmer*.

19–20 The nesting: *Wisconsin Mirror*, 6 May, 29 April 1871; "The Pigeons," *Sparta Herald*, 25 April 1871; "The Pigeon Trade," *Wisconsin State Register*, 6 May 1871; *Badger State Banner*, 6 May, 13 May 1871; *Mauston Star*, 11 May 1871.

Numbers: Schorger, "Great Wisconsin Nesting"; *Ninth Census of the United States of America* (New York: G. W. and C. B. Colton, 1870), 26–27.

"no longer": *Miss Leslie's New Cookery Book* (Philadelphia: T. B. Peterson and Bros., 1857), 541.

20 "the greed of man": Mershon, *Passenger Pigeon*, xii.

Emmett County: H. B. Roney, "Among the Pigeons," *Chicago Field* 10 (11 January 1879), 345–47; Martin, "All the Pigeons."

21 Sauk County and southern Wisconsin: I've relied on Western Historical Society, *The History of Sauk County, Wisconsin* (Chicago: Western Historical Co., 1880); Frederick Merk, *Economic History of Wisconsin during the Civil War Decade* (Madison: State Historical Society of Wisconsin, 1916), 15–58; Richard N. Current, *The History of Wisconsin*, vol. 2 (Madison: State Historical Society of Wisconsin, 1976), 452–64. On the economics of Midwest farming see Allan G. Bogue, *From Prairie to Corn Belt: Farming on the Illinois and Iowa Prairies in the Nineteenth Century* (Chicago: Uni. of Chicago Press, 1963), esp. chs. 8–10; Fred A. Shannon, *The Farmer's Last Frontier: Agriculture, 1860–1897* (New York: Farrar & Rinehart, 1945).

22 "Altogether": *Sparta Herald*, 18 April 1871; see also, e.g., Hartwick and Tuller, *Oceana County*, 81.

Game business: the few histories include Merritt, *Shadow of a Gun*; Bob Hinman, *The Golden Age of Shotgunning* (New York: Winchester Press, 1971), 17–34; David Kimball and Jim Kimball, *The Market Hunter* (Minneapolis: Dillon Press, 1969); Swanson, "Minnesota Game," 43–76; Tober, *Who Owns the Wildlife?* 52–57, 75–81. And I've drawn on dealers' advertisements in *Chicago Field*; merchants' ads in *Prairie Farmer*; city industry directories, e.g., Richard Edwards, ed., *New York's Great Industries* (New York: Historical Publishing, 1884).

23 *Mauston Star*, 18 May 1871.

24 Leah Hager Cohen, *Glass, Paper, Beans: Revelations on the Nature and Value of Ordinary Things* (New York: Doubleday, 1997), 225. Abstract value: while this contains echoes of Marx and the problem of fetishization, I have drawn more directly on Cronon's work on commodities as products of nature more than of social relations. See esp. *Nature's Metropolis*.

24–25 History of trap shooting: Hinman, *Golden Age*, 35–45; Edward Thomas, "Trap-Shooting in the Old Days," *Outing* 66 (June 1915), 368–70; Gwynne Price, *Clay Pigeon and Wing Shooting, and the Gun and How to Use It* (New York: American News, 1884); A. H. Bogardus, *Field, Cover and Trap Shooting*, rev. and ed. Prentiss Ingraham (New York: Orange Judd, 1884), 300–343 (hereafter short cites refer to this edition); "Marksman," *The Dead Shot*, 6th ed.

(London: Longmans, Green, 1892), 387–405; Albert W. Money, *Pigeon Shooting*, ed. A. C. Gould (New York: Shooting and Fishing Publishing, 1896).

25 Tournaments: *Turf, Field, and Farm* 12 (5 May 1871), 275; *Spirit of the Times* 24 (6 May 1871), 186; "The Pigeon Trade," *Milwaukee Sentinel*, 2 May 1871.

26 "The shooting"; "most intense": *Spirit of the Times* 24 (3 June 1871), 247.

   "any man," "I hereby": Bogardus, *Trap Shooting*, 302–4, 324–25.

27 "champion of champions": Thomas, "Trap-Shooting," 371–72.

28 "in good condition": Schorger, *Passenger Pigeon*, 162.

29 "Pigeon shooting": William Bruce Leffingwell, *The Art of Wing Shooting* (Chicago: Rand, McNally, 1894), 132. "It would not": "Marksman," *Dead Shot*, 387. "brought out," "nervy": Money, *Pigeon Shooting*, 21–22. "Perfect coolness," "A man of cool": *Dead Shot*, 399, 2. "Character, coolness": Money, *Pigeon Shooting*, 61. "Both cool": Leffingwell, 132. "of the most": Adam H. Bogardus, *Field, Cover and Trap Shooting*, ed. Charles J. Foster (New York, 1878), 12.

   Field shoot critics: Henry Hall, ed., *The Tribune Book of Open-Air Sports* (New York: Tribune, 1887), 427–28; Charles Hallock, *The Sportsman's Gazetteer and General Guide* (New York: "Forest and Stream" Publishing, 1877), 234–35.

30 "The heart beats": Elisha J. Lewis, *The American Sportsman* (Philadelphia: J. B. Lippincott, 1857), xxii.

31 "as cool as": Leffingwell, *Wing Shooting*, 132. Manhood: I've found esp. helpful Gail Bederman, *Manliness and Civilization: A Cultural History of Gender and Race in the United States, 1880–1917* (Chicago: Uni. of Chicago Press, 1995). On middle-class men in particular, see Mark C. Carnes and Clyde Griffen, eds., *Meanings for Manhood: Constructions of Masculinity in Victorian America* (Chicago: Uni. of Chicago Press, 1990); J. A. Mangan and James Walvin, eds., *Manliness and Morality: Middle-Class Masculinity in Britain and America, 1880–1940* (New York: St. Martin's Press, 1987). Sport-hunting: see John F. Reiger, *American Sportsmen and the Origins of Conservation* (New York: Winchester Press, 1975),

25–49. Influential works on cultural transformations of the late 19th century are T. J. Jackson Lears, *No Place of Grace: Antimodernism and the Transformation of American Culture, 1880–1920* (New York: Pantheon Books, 1981); Alan Trachtenberg, *The Incorporation of America: Culture and Society in the Gilded Age* (New York: Hill and Wang, 1982).

32 "they [are] rapid": John C. French, *The Passenger Pigeon in Pennsylvania* (Altoona, PA: Altoona Tribune, 1919), 179. "Those that escaped": "Pigeon Shooting," *New York Herald*, 24 May 1871.

"Imagine a thousand": Schorger, "Great Wisconsin Nesting," 33.

On the effects of urbanization and market expansion, I've found esp. helpful Cronon, *Nature's Metropolis*; Keith Thomas, *Man and the Natural World: A History of the Modern Sensibility* (New York: Pantheon Books, 1983); Raymond Williams, *Problems in Materialism and Culture* (London: Verso, 1980), 67–85; Yi-Fu Tuan, *Topophilia: A Study of Environmental Perception, Attitudes, and Values* (New York: Columbia University Press, 1974), 102–9.

35 Greatest numbers: "Tom Tramp," "A Pigeon Roost," *American Sportsman* 8 (3 June 1876), 149; Merritt, *Shadow of a Gun*; *Chicago Field* 9 (13 April 1878), 136.

The squab's trip: *Railroad Gazetteer* no. 19 (March 1871), 30, 32; Cronon, *Nature's Metropolis*, 443; Junius Henri Browne, *The Great Metropolis: A Mirror of New York* (Hartford: American Publishing, 1869), 406–12; James D. McCabe, Jr., *Lights and Shadows of New York Life* (Philadelphia: National Publishing, 1872), 489–90; Merritt, *Shadow of a Gun*, 75, 121, 221–23; Leopold Rimmer, *A History of Old New York Life and the House of the Delmonicos* (1898), 13; Lately Thomas, *Delmonico's: A Century of Splendor* (Boston: Houghton Mifflin, 1967), 52–53.

36 Delmonico's dishes: Charles Ranhofer, *The Epicurean* (New York: R. Ranhofer, 1905), 616, 730–31.

"For a pie": Rundell, *Domestic Cookery*, 112.

37 Menus and protocol: Ranhofer, *Epicurean*, 2–3; Alessandro Filippini, *The Table: How to Buy Food, How to Cook It, and How to Serve It*, rev. ed. (New York: Charles L. Webster, 1891), 21. History of American dining: I've relied on Richard J. Hooker, *Food and Drink in Amer-*

ica: A History (Indianapolis: Bobbs-Merrill, 1981); Michael and Ariane Batterberry, *On the Town in New York: From 1776 to the Present* (New York: Charles Scribner's Sons, 1973), esp. chs. 1–4; Harvey A. Levenstein, *Revolution at the Table: The Transformation of the American Diet* (New York: Oxford Uni. Press, 1988), esp. 3–22; Root and de Rochemont, *Eating in America*, esp. chs. 10, 27.

38 "ballotines," "cotelettes": Ranhofer, *Epicurean*, 1096, 1101. Delmonico's: Thomas, *Delmonico's*; Robert Shaplen, "Delmonico," pts. 1 and 2, *The New Yorker* (10 and 17 November 1956), 189–211, 105–37; Don C. Seitz, *The James Gordon Bennetts* (Indianapolis: Bobbs-Merrill, 1928); *New York Times*, 24 March 1871.

   Banquets: "Sorosis," *New York Herald*, 2 May 1871; ibid., 6 May 1871; ibid., 31 May 1871; yachting coverage, April and May 1871, *New York Herald*, *Spirit of the Times*, and *Turf, Field, and Farm*.

39 Meanings of food: I've consulted the overviews in Mary Douglas, "Standard Social Uses of Food: Introduction," in *Food in the Social Order: Studies of Food and Festivities in Three American Communities*, ed. Mary Douglas (New York: Russell Sage Foundation, 1984), 1–39; Kathy Neustadt, *Clambake: A History and Celebration of an American Tradition* (Amherst: Uni. of Massachusetts Press, 1992), 137–60; Jack Goody, *Cooking, Cuisine and Class: A Study in Comparative Sociology* (Cambridge: Cambridge Uni. Press), 10–39.

   Lower heights: e.g., Merritt, *Shadow of a Gun*, 183.

41 "the main body": William Bruce Leffingwell, "The Wild Pigeon," in *Shooting on Upland, Marsh, and Stream*, ed. W. B. Leffingwell (Chicago: Rand, McNally, 1890), 217, 236. Domestic pigeons: Martin, "All the Pigeons," 478–79; "Wild Pigeons," *Chicago Field* 13 (17 April 1880), 152. "I have often": William Bruce Leffingwell, "The Wild Pigeon," in *Shooting on Upland, Marsh, and Stream*, ed. W. B. Leffingwell (Chicago: Rand, McNally, 1890), 217. "we might expect": G. C. Tremaine Ward, "The Passenger Pigeon," *Auk* 18 (April 1901), 191–92.

42 "some thoughtful": Leffingwell, *Wing Shooting*, 148. "so nearly": Price, *Clay Pigeon and Wing Shooting*, xx.

Game birds: Peter Matthiessen, "The Wind Birds," pt. 1, *The New Yorker* 43 (27 May 1967), 40–42; Edward Howe Forbush, *A History of the Game Birds, Wild-Fowl and Shore Birds of Massachusetts and Adjacent States* (Boston: Massachusetts State Board of Agriculture, 1912), 317, 346, 426–28.

44 "Even now": Mershon, *Passenger Pigeon*, 2–3. "The sight": Childs, "Personal Recollections," 73.

45 Blaming the pigeons: Mershon, *Passenger Pigeon*, 68; Martin, "All the Pigeons," 479. Sightings: French, *Passenger Pigeon*, 207; Schorger, *Passenger Pigeon*, 211; "The Past Participle in Pigeons," *Saturday Evening Post* 183 (15 October 1910), 30; Gene Stratton-Porter, "The Last Passenger Pigeon," *Good Housekeeping* 79 (August 1924), 137–40; "Pigeon Poll," *Saturday Evening Post* 211 (14 January 1939), 80; Mershon, *Passenger Pigeon*, 153.

"murderous netters": "Backwoods," "In Wild Pigeon Days," *Forest and Stream* 44 (16 February 1895), 126. "nefarious, inhuman": "Scaup," "Destruction of Pigeons in Wisconsin," *Turf, Field, and Farm* 34 (9 June 1882), 379. "It wasn't done": Leffingwell, "The Wild Pigeon," 218. On class conflicts, see esp. Warren, *Hunter's Game*.

46 "until but": Martin, "All the Pigeons," 480. "progress": Merritt, *Shadow of a Gun*, 10–11. "man's greed," "heartless": Leffingwell, "The Wild Pigeon," 227.

47 "Alas": Mershon, *Passenger Pigeon*, 8. Pigeon nostalgia: e.g., G. Stanley Hall, *Life and Confessions of a Psychologist* (New York: D. Appleton, 1923), 94; James B. Purdy, "The Passenger Pigeon in the Early Days of Michigan," *Bulletin Michigan Ornithological Club* 4 (September 1903), 69–71. Rural nostalgia: I've drawn on Amy S. Green, "Savage Childhood: The Scientific Construction of Girlhood and Boyhood in the Progressive Era," Ph.D. diss., Yale University, 1995, ch. 3.

48 Bureau: "Pigeon Poll," 80. Sightings: Philip Hadley, "The Passenger Pigeon," *Science* 71 (14 February 1930), 187. "scores": "Pigeon Poll". "their strain": Courtney L. Zimmerman, "Where *Did* the Pigeons Go?" *Newsweek* 45 (4 April 1955), 6–8. "support the hope": Young, "Ecological Considerations," 65.

49 "In recent days": "Notes and Comment," *The New Yorker* 52 (18 October 1976), 29. Leopold, *Sand County Almanac*, 109.

51 "rapacity": Maitland Edey, "Once There Were Billions, Now There Are None," *Life* 51 (22 December 1961), 169. "The best example": Young, "Ecological Considerations," 235. "Supreme irreverence": Mitchell, *Passenger Pigeon*, 142. "Wanton greed": Richard Carrington, *Mermaids and Mastodons: A Book of Natural and Unnatural History* (New York: Rinehart, 1957), 214. "The epitome": Review of *The Silent Sky*, by Allan W. Eckert, *Time* 86 (15 October 1965), 125.

"Oooooh": Harold, "Passenger Pigeons." Leopold, *Sand County Almanac*, 109.

52 "When I can shoot": Mitchell, *Passenger Pigeon*, 107.

Chapter 2

57 Frank M. Chapman, *Autobiography of a Bird-Lover* (New York: D. Appleton-Century, 1935), 38–39.

58 Histories of the bird-hat episode: Robin W. Doughty's thorough *Feather Fashions and Bird Preservation: A Study in Nature Protection* (Berkeley: Uni. of California Press, 1975); Joseph Kastner, "Long Before Furs, It Was Feathers That Stirred Reformist Ire," *Smithsonian* 25 (July 1994), 96–104; Felton Gibbons and Deborah Strom, *Neighbors to the Birds: A History of Birdwatching in America* (New York: W. W. Norton, 1988), 107–25; Richard K. Walton, "Massachusetts Audubon Society: The First Twenty-Five Years, 1896–1921," draft (Lincoln: Massachusetts Audubon Society, 1986); Carl Buchheister and Frank Graham, Jr., "From the Swamps and Back: A Concise and Candid History of the Early Audubon Movement," *Audubon* 75 (January 1973); Frank Graham, Jr., *The Audubon Ark: A History of the National Audubon Society* (New York: Alfred A. Knopf, 1990), 3–73.

59 "in a most": Ellen Osborn, "What Is Now Visible in the New York Market," *Illustrated Milliner* 1 (October 1900), 34. "That there should": *Harper's Bazar*, 4 December 1897. "It will be":

"Notes," *Club Woman* 1 (November 1897), 5. Examples are from *Harper's Bazar, Illustrated Milliner, Delineator, Standard Delineator,* and *Millinery Trade Review.* On hat fashions, see Fiona Clark, *Hats* (New York: Drama Book Publishers, 1982); Stella Blum, ed., *Victorian Fashions and Costumes from Harper's Bazar 1867–98* (New York: Dover, 1974).

Cape Hatteras: Thomas Gilbert Pearson, *Adventures in Bird Protection* (New York: D. Appleton-Century, 1937), 50–52. Population declines: Doughty, *Feather Fashions,* 80–85; Peter Matthiessen, *Wildlife in America* (New York: Viking, 1959), 174–76; "Gull Family," in John K. Terres, *The Audubon Society Encyclopedia of North American Birds* (New York: Alfred A. Knopf, 1982), 457; Robert Porter Allen, *The Roseate Spoonbill* (New York: Dover, 1942), 3–9.

61   Membership: e.g., *First Report of the Massachusetts Audubon Society for the Protection of Birds,* 1897, Massachusetts Audubon Society archives (hereafter MAS MSS), Lincoln, MA (annual reports for the MA, CT, PA, and WI Societies are hereafter cited as *Report MAS, CAS, PAS, WAS*); *Second Report CAS,* 1899, Connecticut Audubon Society archives, Bridgeport Public Library (hereafter CAS MSS); *Second Report PAS,* in National Association of Audubon Societies archives, Rare Books and Manuscripts Division, New York Public Library (hereafter NAAS MSS). Audiences: e.g., Margaret Hamilton Welch, "Bird Protection and Women's Clubs," *Harper's Bazar* 30 (26 June 1897), 527; *New York Times,* 3 December 1897. Leaflets: e.g., Emma Lockwood, *Report,* 1899, Audubon Society of the State of New York, NAAS MSS; *Second Report PAS.*

William Dutcher, *Save the Birds!* pamphlet, Audubon Society of the State of New York, MAS MSS; Celia Thaxter, "Woman's Heartlessness," in *First Report MAS*; Lilli Lehmann, *An Appeal to Women,* leaflet, Audubon Society of the State of New York, NAAS MSS; *A Word for the Owl,* circular no. 11, 1897, Massachusetts Audubon Society for the Protection of Birds, MAS MSS.

Lacey Act: see Theodore Whaley Cart, "The Struggle for Wildlife Protection in the United States, 1870–1900: Attitudes and Events Leading to the Lacey Act," Ph.D. diss., Uni. of North

Carolina–Chapel Hill, 1971; Richard Littell, *Endangered and Other Protected Species: Federal Law and Regulation* (Washington, D.C.: Bureau of National Affairs, 1992), 19–26.

62 At the time, Miller, Croly, and many of the other women were prominent writers, editors, and activists.

63 Grinnell: Buchheister and Graham, "From the Swamps and Back," 7; John F. Reiger, *American Sportsmen and the Origins of Conservation* (New York: Winchester Press, 1975), 66–69.

"A score of ladies": "The Audubon Societies," *Bird-Lore* 1 (February 1899), 30. New clubs: Graham, *Audubon Ark*, 18. Rosters: *Audubon Society of the State of New York*, pamphlet, NAAS MSS; *Audubon Society of the District of Columbia*, pamphlet, ibid. The pattern was for the presidents to be men, the secretaries to be women: e.g., *Report MAS 1897–1902*, MAS MSS; *Fifth Report WAS*, NAAS MSS; "Report of the A.O.U. Committee on Protection of North American Birds," *Auk* 15 (January 1898), 81–114 (A.O.U. reports hereafter cited as "AOU Report"). Iowa was the major nearly all-female exception: *History and Records of the Audubon Society of the State of Iowa*, NAAS MSS.

64 Bridgeport: *Bridgeport Morning Telegram*, 25 April 1908; *Bridgeport Standard*, 20 April 1900. Iowa: *History and Records Iowa*. "not the least": *Club Woman* 1 (November 1897), 35. "gentlemen," "The Honorable": Pearson, *Adventures*, 74, 93. Connecticut: Miss Frances A. Hurd to Mrs William B. Glover, 1907, CAS MSS.

65 Women's clubs: see Anne Firor Scott, *Natural Allies: Women's Associations in American History* (Urbana: Uni. of Illinois Press, 1991); Karen J. Blair, *The Clubwoman as Feminist: True Womanhood Redefined, 1868–1914* (New York: Holmes & Meier, 1980). I've also used contemporary accounts: Mrs. J. C. Croly, *The History of the Woman's Club Movement in America* (New York: Henry G. Allen, 1898); a special issue on "Woman's Work and Organizations," in *Annals American Academy Political and Social Science* 28 (September 1906), iii–119; "President's Address," *Third Biennial: General Federation of Women's Clubs*, program book (Louisville: Flexner Bros., 1896), 14–25; Sophonisba P. Breckinridge, *Women in the Twentieth*

Century: A Study of Their Political, Social, and Economic Activities (New York: McGraw-Hill, 1933), 11–26.

Women *as* women in early conservation: see Carolyn Merchant's rare "Women of the Progressive Conservation Movement: 1900–1916," *Environmental Review* 8 (Spring 1984), 57–85. On gender roles and American women's interactions with nature, see Vera Norwood, *Made from This Earth: American Women and Nature* (Chapel Hill: Uni. North Carolina Press, 1993). And on gender study, I've benefited esp. from Joan W. Scott, "Gender: A Useful Category of Historical Analysis," *American Historical Review* 91 (December 1986), 1053–75; Natalie Zemon Davis, "'Women's History' in Transition: The European Case," *Feminist Studies* 3 (Winter 1975–76), 83–103; the comments and work of Michael Lewis Goldberg—see *An Army of Women: Gender and Politics in Gilded Age Kansas* (Baltimore: Johns Hopkins Uni. Press, 1997).

66 Saturday Morning Club: Katharine Farnam Harvey, notes on meeting places, Saturday Morning Club Papers, 1961, New Haven Colony Historical Society, New Haven, CT (hereafter SMC MSS). Ladies' Friday Musical Club: Madelon Price and Elaine Gernstein, per. com.

67 "competitive," "moral, nurturant": in Nancy F. Cott, *The Grounding of Modern Feminism* (New Haven: Yale Uni. Press, 1987), 19; Sara M. Evans, *Born for Liberty: A History of Women in America* (New York: Free Press, 1989), 69. "at no time": Rosalind Rosenberg, *Beyond Separate Spheres: Intellectual Roots of Modern Feminism* (New Haven: Yale Uni. Press), xv (quote refers to women). John Gray, *Men Are from Mars, Women Are from Venus: A Practical Guide for Improving Communication and Getting What You Want in Your Relationships* (New York: HarperCollins, 1992). "The home is": Olive Thorne Miller, *The Woman's Club: A Practical Guide and Hand-Book* (New York: American Publishers, 1891), 17, 14. Separate spheres: I've drawn esp. on Linda K. Kerber, "Separate Spheres, Female Worlds, Woman's Place: The Rhetoric of Women's History," *Journal of American History* 75 (June 1988), 9–39; Nancy F. Cott, *The Bonds of Womanhood: Woman's Sphere in New England, 1790–1835* (New Haven: Yale Uni. Press, 1975).

68 "While we have": Croly, *Club Movement*, 117. Parks: (Mrs. Chas. H.) Clara W. Raynor, "Federation of Women's Clubs in Florida," in *Makers of America*, vol. 2, Florida ed. (Atlanta: A. B. Caldwell, 1909), 45. "National housekeeping": see Scott, *Natural Allies*, esp. 141–58, 185–89; Paula Baker, "The Domestication of Politics: Women and American Political Society, 1780–1920," *American Historical Review* 89 (June 1984), 620–47.

69 Committees: see Croly, *Club Movement*; *Connecticut State Federation of Women's Clubs: Official Directory* (New Haven: O. A. Dorman, 1900). "one and all": Miller, *Woman's Club*, 12–13. "a new and more": Croly, *Club Movement*, 14. "great army": Welch, "Bird Protection." "marching": Miller, *Woman's Club*. "studied the universe": May Ellis Nichols, *A History of the Meridian* (Brooklyn, 1934), 12.

   Multiple membership: e.g., Mrs. Charles Cutting, *Study Club* (New Haven, CT, 1933); *CT State Federation*, 63.

70 Hemenway: Kastner, "Long Before Furs," 98; WEIU records, vol. 1, Arthur and Elizabeth Schlesinger Library on the History of Women, Radcliffe College, courtesy of Sally Deutsch.

   Joint membership: I cross-checked the names in *Fourth Report CAS* (in CAS MSS) and *CT State Federation*, both 1900. A cross-check of MA women in *Report MAS 1897–1902* and Croly, *Club Movement*, 588–674, also yielded a high percentage of matches. For other states, see T. S. Palmer et al., *Biographies of Members of the American Ornithologists' Union*, repr. from *Auk* 1884–1954 (Washington, D.C., 1954), 16, 56, 159.

   Fox and Noble: *CT State Federation*, 120–21. Morse: Croly, *Club Movement*, 593–96. New Haven: "Chronological List of Members, 1881 On," SMC MSS; "Subscribers to Lectures 1896–1901," record book, ibid.; Anna Porter, 75th anniversary history, 1956, ibid.; *CT State Federation*, 104–5, 15; Programs, 1898–99, 1900–1901, Fortnightly Club Papers, New Haven Colony Historical Society; "Members of the Fortnightly Feb. 17th 1890," ibid.; *Twenty-Fifth Annual Report of the Young Women's Christian Association of New Haven, Conn.*, 1905, YWCA Records, New Haven Colony Historical Society.

70–71 "not an isolated": "The Audubon Society at the General Federation of Women's Clubs," *Bird-Lore* 2 (October 1900), 166.
"ready, alert": *Annals American Academy*, 204.

73–74 "Do women": Mrs. Orinda Dudley Hornbrooke, "Bird Literature," *Club Woman* 1 (November 1897), 44. "The Federation": *Annals American Academy*, 204. "The twentieth century": Miller, *Woman's Club*, 113. "The greatest power": Raynor, "Clubs in Florida," 43. "The electric thrill," "carried away": Scott, *Natural Allies*, 111–12. "Civilization": Raynor, "Clubs in Florida." "She who rocks": Miller, *Woman's Club*, 22.

74 "fatuous, "brainless, "feather-headed": Joseph Collinson, "The Trade in Bird Skins," *Living Age* 19 (9 July 1898), 126–27. "shallow": T. Gilbert Pearson, "The White Egrets and the Millinery Trade," *Craftsman* 22 (July 1912), 420.

74–75 "selfish": "The Destruction of Birds: Cruel Thoughtlessness," *Our Animal Friends* 24 (June 1897), 217–18. "Pause a moment": *Bird-Lore* 1 (August 1899), 172. "If woman would": *New York Times*, 6 February 1898. Natural death: Hornbrooke, "Bird Literature," 44. "The frivolity": Miller, *Woman's Club*, 204.

75 Shops: e.g., "Fifth Avenue Millinery," *Illustrated Milliner* 1 (March 1900), 41–46.

76 "If there's anywhere": Pauline Phelps, *A Millinery Melee* (New York: Edgar S. Werner, 1904), 4. "A hat very often": Madame Rosée, *Handbook of Millinery*, 2d ed. (London: L. Upcott Gill, 1898), 50.
"Is my new": "Millinery Mirth," *Illustrated Milliner* 1 (January 1900), 45. "So you've bought": ibid., 1 (December 1900), 40. Complaints: e.g., "Success of the Theater Hat," ibid., 1 (December 1900), 52.

77 "feminine mind": "Millinery," *Standard Designer* 5 (April 1897), 62. "a federation": Lydia Avery Coonley-Ward, "Individuality in Dress," ibid., 6 (September 1900), 200. Pictures: e.g., *CT State Federation*. Dress Reform–fashion–womanhood: I've found esp. useful William Leach, *True Love and Perfect Union: The Feminist Reform of Sex and Society* (New York: Basic Books, 1980), 213–60.

78 "She feared": "Millinery Mirth" (January 1900), 45.

79 "vain, useless": Leach, *True Love*, 251. "The Pioneers . . . A History," in Pioneers program book (St. Louis, 1997–98), 2. "Her hats": *Harper's Bazar* 33 (27 January 1900), 69; and Croly cover in *Harper's Bazar* (3 March 1900). On working-class women's perspectives, see Kathy Peiss, *Cheap Amusements: Working Women and Leisure in Turn-of-the-Century New York* (Philadelphia: Temple Uni. Press, 1986), esp. 62–67.

"vulgar": "AOU Report," *Auk* 17 (January 1900), 53. "'real loidy'": "Hats!" *Bird-Lore* 3 (January-February 1901), 40–41.

81 "The exquisite": Frank M. Chapman, "The Passing of the Tern," *Bird-Lore* 1 (December 1899), 205. "What marvels": "Bird Study," *Club Woman* 8 (August 1901), 156. "reduce the glad": Henry Brown, "Trade and Sentiment," *Millinery Trade Review* 25 (January 1900), 108. "Every tern": *New York Times*, 2 April 1900.

Marie Antoinette: Kastner, "Long Before Furs," 99.

82–83 "Nature made her": in Brown, "Trade and Sentiment." "The place": "Notes." "I believe": "Bird Study," 156. "inartistic": "The Wearing of Egret Plumes," *Our Animal Friends* 24 (November 1896), 51. "a disgusting": "Notes." "Dead and mutilated": "Murderous Millinery," *Living Age* 251 (8 December 1906), 636. "Charnel houses," "Does any woman": Collinson, "Trade in Bird Skins," 126. Beauty–womanhood–natural look: see Lois W. Banner, *American Beauty* (New York: Alfred A. Knopf, 1983); Clark, *Hats*, 35–37.

83–84 "Have the milliners": Dutcher, *Save the Birds!* Lacey: *Congressional Record*, 56th Cong., 1st sess., 1900, 33, pt. 6:4871. "Birds are": "Bird Study." A.O.U.: see Cart, "Struggle for Wildlife Protection," 54–61.

84–85 "generosity": "'Bird Day,'" 50. *Citizen Bird*—in Peter J. Schmitt, *Back to Nature: The Arcadian Myth in Urban America* (New York: Oxford Uni. Press, 1969), 35; Olive Thorne Miller, *Little Brothers of the Air* (Boston: Houghton Mifflin, 1985); Marion Harland, "The Feathered Ishmaelite," *Harper's Bazar* 30 (31 July 1897), 632. "Much has": J. A. Allen, "An Ornithologist's Plea," *New York Times*, 18 November 1897. "wearisome bosh": "Here and There," *Millinery Trade Review* 25 (May 1900), 57. Nature-story craze: see

Schmitt, 33–55; Ralph H. Lutts, *The Nature Fakers: Wildlife, Science and Sentiment* (Golden, CO: Fulcrum, 1990); and on children, Amy S. Green, "Savage Childhood: The Scientific Construction of Girlhood and Boyhood in the Progressive Era," Ph.D. diss., Yale University, 1995. Sentimental fiction: I've relied on Ann Douglas, *The Feminization of American Culture* (New York: Alfred A. Knopf, 1977); and for more like-minded analyses, Jane Tompkins, *Sensational Designs: The Cultural Work of American Fiction 1790–1860* (New York: Oxford Uni. Press, 1985), esp. 122–46; Karen Halttunen, *Confidence Men and Painted Women: A Study of Middle-Class Culture in America* (Berkeley: Uni. of California Press, 1985).

86 "Can it be:" Louisa Jay Bruen, "Spare the Birds," *New York Times,* 1 March 1897. "There is very": *Millinery Trade Review* 22 (April 1897), 10. "killing is": "Personal," *New York Times*, 23 November 1897. Humane Societies: see James Turner, *Reckoning with the Beast: Animals, Pain, and Humanity in the Victorian Mind* (Baltimore: Johns Hopkins Uni. Press, 1980); Lisa Mighetto, *Wild Animals and American Environmental Ethics* (Tucson: Uni. of Arizona Press, 1991).

87 "feel wholly": *Audubon Society of the District of Columbia*, NAAS MSS. "This, however": "Plumage of Birds on Hats," *New York Times*, 4 May 1900. "should be compelled": Shawantum, "Our Game and Its Protection," *Recreation* 6 (May 1897), 359. On "civilization," see Gail Bederman, *Manliness and Civilization: A Cultural History of Gender and Race in the United States, 1880–1917* (Chicago: Uni. of Chicago Press, 1995), esp. 23–31.

88 "Without our": Hornbrooke, "Bird Literature," 44.

89 "Egret plumes": ibid. "harrowing": "Bird Study." "published": Brown, "Trade and Sentiment."

89–90 "The ground": May Riley Smith, *The Aigrette: An Appeal to Women*, leaflet, Audubon Society of the State of New York, NAAS MSS. "A woman": "Women and Egret Plumes," *Our Animal Friends* 23 (September 1895), 4. "Cruel thoughtlessness," "Murderous vanity": "The Destruction of Birds," 217, 218. "An act never": Pearson, "White Egrets," 419. "Why, to obey": Mrs. Kingsmill Marrs, *Does Fashion Make Women Heartless?* leaflet, Florida Audubon Society, NAAS MSS. "This is": Herbert

Keightly Job, *Wild Wings* (Boston: Houghton Mifflin, 1905), 144. "In the name": Smith, *The Aigrette*. "The reproach": *Must We Lose Our Birds?* "human ingenuity": "Personal."

90–91 Egret ecology: see Josep del Hoyo, Andrew Elliott, and Jordi Sargatal, eds., *Handbook of the Birds of the World*, vol. 1 (Barcelona: Lynx Edicions, 1992), 376–429. Siblicide: Douglas W. Mock, "Siblicidal Aggression and Resource Monopolization in Birds," *Science* 225 (17 August 1984), 731–33.

92 "The dried": Thaxter, "Woman's Heartlessness," 14.

"We never kill": F. W. H., "Men Are Culprits," *New York Times*, 29 November 1897.

93 Among the industry's women, shop owners receive almost no mention; and milliners use a defense of the factory workers to accuse Audubon women of destroying working-women's jobs: see Wendy Gamber, *The Female Economy: The Millinery and Dressmaking Trades, 1860–1930* (Urbana: Uni. Illinois Press), 1997. "Senator Hoar and the Workingwomen," *Millinery Trade Review* 25 (April 1900), 11–12.

"If women": Job, *Wild Wings*, 148. "a harmful": Buchheister and Graham, "From the Swamps and Back," 19. "the wretches": Mary F. Lovell, *The Wearing of Egret Plumes*, pamphlet, Humane Education Committee, Providence, NAAS MSS. "rough, untaught": "Where Grebe Skins Come From," *Bird-Lore* 2 (February 1900), 34. "barbarous stupidity": "The Destruction of Birds," 218. "no refinement": J. A. Allen, "Fashion's Cruelty and Bird Protection," *Our Animal Friends* 24 (April 1897), 177. "What can we": "Cruelty to Birds," *New York Times*, 20 July 1897. South Florida and plume hunting: e.g., Charles William Pierce, "The Cruise of the Bonton," *Tequesta* no. 22 (1962), 3–63; Charlton W. Tebeau, *Man in the Everglades: 2000 Years of Human History in the Everglades National Park*, 2d rev. ed. (Coral Gables: Uni. of Miami Press, 1968), esp. 75–95.

94 "The part," "Woman wants": Collinson, "Trade in Bird Skins," 127. "Why should we": "Notes," *Bird-Lore* 2 (October 1900), 163. Millinery district: *Where to Buy Millinery Goods* (New York: Millinery Trade Review, 1908), esp. 16–34.

"Suddenly": Chapman, "Passing of the Tern." "What fashion": "Disappearance of Our Native Birds," *New York Times*, 18 March 1896. "Dame Fashion": *Millinery Trade Review* 22 (April 1897), 10.

95 "The milliners": "The Bird Agreement Rejected," *Millinery Trade Review* 25 (September 1900), 34. History of economic ideas: I've consulted Robert L. Heilbroner, *The Worldly Philosophers: The Lives, Times, and Ideas of the Great Economic Thinkers*, 5th ed. (New York: Simon and Schuster, 1980), esp. 51–57; John Kenneth Galbraith, *Economics in Perspective: A Critical History* (Boston: Houghton Mifflin, 1987); Phyllis Deane, *The Evolution of Economic Ideas* (Cambridge: Cambridge Uni. Press, 1978).

98 "It is to": "Murderous Millinery," 637. "It lies in," "Ladies": "Urgent Plea for Birds," *New York Times*, 3 December 1897.

98–99 "home enlightenment," "Mama": Welch, "Bird Protection." Tactics: e.g., Julia Stockton Robins, *Pennsylvania Audubon Society*, leaflet, NAAS MSS; *Third Report CAS*. White Lists: e.g., "The Milliners 'White-List,'" *Bird-Lore* 2 (October 1900), 163–64; "Hats!" 40–41. Shows: e.g., "AOU Report," *Auk* 16 (January 1899), 71; "Reports of Societies," *Bird-Lore* 1 (August 1899), 138. Consumers' Leagues: see Maud Nathan, *The Story of an Epoch-Making Movement* (Garden City: Doubleday, Page, 1926); Scott, *Natural Allies*, 166–67.

99 Committees: e.g., *Report MAS 1897–1902*; Mrs. Lucy W. Maynard, "The Audubon Society of the District of Columbia," *Records of the Columbia Historical Society of Washington, D.C.* 35–36 (1935), 101. Male tactics: e.g., Pearson, *Adventures*, 74–82, 101–3; "AOU Reports," 1896–1902.

101 "salvation": Frank M. Chapman, *The Wearing of Herons' Plumes or 'Aigrettes,'* pamphlet, Massachusetts Audubon Society for the Protection of Birds, MAS MSS.

"burned": *Report MAS 1897–1902.* "Let us credit": "Hats!" 41. The battle continued after 1900 as the societies worked to pass state laws.

102 Steve Martin, *Picasso at the Lapin Agile and Other Plays* (New York: Grove Press, 1996), 77–78, 30–31.

Erosion of separate spheres: see Cott, *Grounding of Modern Feminism*; Rosenberg, *Beyond Separate Spheres*. Progressive legislation: see Baker, "Domestication of Politics"; Sarah Deutsch, "Learning to Talk More Like a Man: Boston Women's Class-Bridging Organizations, 1870–1940," *American Historical Review* 97 (April 1992), 379–404.

103 "We want to": Anne Raver, "Old Environmental Group Seeks Tough New Image," *New York Times*, 9 June 1991. See also Sharon Begley, "Audubon's Empty Nest," *Newsweek* 117 (24 June 1991), 57. 20th-century Audubon: see Graham, *Audubon Ark*. Endangered Species Acts: I've used Michael Bean, *The Evolution of National Wildlife Law*, rev. ed. (New York: Praeger, 1983), esp. 319–83; Kathryn A. Kohm, "Introduction" and "The Act's History and Framework," in *Balancing on the Brink of Extinction: The Endangered Species Act and Lessons for the Future*, ed. Kathryn A. Kohm (Washington, D.C.: Island Press, 1991), 3–9, 10–22.

104 Robert Bly, *Iron John: A Book About Men* (Reading, MA: Addison-Wesley, 1990); Clarissa Pinkola Estés, *Women Who Run with the Wolves: Myths and Stories of the Wild Woman Archetype* (New York: Ballantine Books, 1992).

Chapter 3

112 Terry Tempest Williams, *Refuge: An Unnatural History of Family and Place* (New York: Vintage Books, 1991), 89.

Some of my flamingo facts come from people who have showered me with stories and gifts (cited hereafter as PFI): Bruce Berger, my most prolific informant; Amy Green, Laurie Eckstein and Madelon and Elmer Price, who have made multiple contributions; and many others.

113 An excellent history of the pink flamingo is Colleen Josephine Sheehy, *The Flamingo in the Garden: American Yard Art and the Vernacular Landscape* (New York: Garland, 1998), 67–112.

114 Landscape architecture and ornamentation: I've relied on Philip Pregill and Nancy Volkman, *Landscapes in History: Design and Plan-*

ning in the Western Tradition (New York: Van Nostrand Reinhold, 1993), 223–52, 393–411; Elizabeth Wilkinson and Marjorie Henderson, eds., *Decorating Eden: A Comprehensive Sourcebook of Classic Garden Details* (San Francisco: Chronicle Books, 1992), ix–xiii, 146–48; G. B. Tobey, *A History of Landscape Architecture: The Relationship of People to Environment* (New York: American Elsevier, 1973), 127–59; Simon Schama, *Landscape and Memory* (New York: Alfred A. Knopf, 1995), esp. 339–43, 539–45, 567–73; George Plumptre, *Garden Ornament: Five Hundred Years of Nature, Art, and Artifice* (New York: Doubleday, 1989), 10–38, 103–30.

115 Destruction of villages: Ann Bermingham, *Landscape and Ideology: The English Rustic Tradition* (Berkeley: Univ. of California Press, 1986), 199; Nigel Everett, *The Tory View of Landscape* (New Haven: Yale University Press, 1994), 41.

116 "conceal every": in Bermingham, *Landscape and Ideology,* 11.

Nature, labor, power: I've drawn esp. on Bermingham, *Landscape and Ideology.* See also Keith Thomas, *Man and the Natural World: A History of the Modern Sensibility* (New York: Pantheon Books, 1983), 201–12, 242–54; Yi-Fu Tuan, *Dominance and Affection: The Making of Pets* (New Haven: Yale Univ. Press, 1984), 18–23, 172–76; Raymond Williams, *The Country and the City* (New York: Oxford Univ. Press, 1973).

118 Paintings: Bermingham, *Landscape and Ideology,* 14–33.

119 "Hudson River school": see Angela Miller's subtle, *The Empire of the Eye: Landscape Representation and American Cultural Politics, 1825–1875* (Ithaca: Cornell Univ. Press, 1993); Barbara Novak, *Nature and Culture: American Landscape Painting 1825–1875* (New York: Oxford Univ. Press, 1980).

120 Downing quotes: A. J. Downing, *A Treatise on the Theory and Practice of Landscape Gardening,* 8th ed. (New York: Orange Judd, 1859), 58, 60, 367. "invisible hands": Virginia Scott Jenkins, *The Lawn: A History of an American Obsession* (Washington, D.C.: Smithsonian Inst. Press, 1994), 119. Downing: see David Schuyler, *Apostle of Taste: Andrew Jackson Downing, 1815–1852* (Baltimore: Johns Hopkins Univ. Press, 1996); Gwendolyn

Wright, *Building the Dream: A Social History of Housing in America* (New York: Pantheon Books, 1981), 82–84.

120–21 Quotes: Downing, *Treatise*, 19, 63, 365, 410–11, 63 (emphasis in orig.).

122 Middle-class identity and Taste: I've found esp. helpful John F. Kasson, *Rudeness and Civility: Manners in Nineteenth-Century Urban America* (New York: Hill and Wang, 1990); Lawrence Levine, *Highbrow/Lowbrow: The Emergence of Cultural Hierarchy in America* (Cambridge: Harvard Univ. Press, 1988), esp. 171–242; and see Pierre Bourdieu's influential (if-you-have-enough-educational-capital) *Distinction: A Social Critique of the Judgement of Taste*, trans. Richard Nice (Cambridge: Harvard Univ. Press, 1984).

123–24 Frank J. Scott, *The Art of Beautifying Home Grounds of Small Extent* (New York: American Book Exchange, 1881), 105, 25; Michael Pollan, *Second Nature: A Gardener's Education* (New York: Atlantic Monthly Press, 1991), 59. Suburbia: I've relied on Wright, *Building the Dream*; John R. Stilgoe, *Borderland: Origins of the American Suburb, 1820–1939* (New Haven: Yale Univ. Press, 1988); Robert Fishman, *Bourgeois Utopias: The Rise and Fall of Suburbia* (New York: Basic Books, 1987), esp. ix–17, 145–47; Kenneth T. Jackson, *Crabgrass Frontier: The Suburbanization of the United States* (New York: Oxford University Press, 1985); and a concise history is John R. Stilgoe, "The Suburbs," *American Heritage* 35 (February–March 1984), 20–36. Olmsted: see Anne Whiston Spirn, "Constructing Nature: The Legacy of Frederick Law Olmsted," in *Uncommon Ground: Toward Reinventing Nature*, ed. William Cronon (New York: W. W. Norton, 1995), 91–113.

124 Ornaments: Sheehy, *Flamingo in the Garden,* 18–20; Ann Leighton, *American Gardens of the Nineteenth Century: "For Comfort and Affluence"* (Amherst: Univ. of Massachusetts Press, 1987), 230–34.

Three thousand acres: *American Decades (1950–1959)*, ed. Richard Layman (Detroit: Gale Research, 1994), 160–61. Fertility boom: see Landon Y. Jones, *Great Expectations: America and the Baby Boom Generation* (New York: Coward, McCann & Geoghegan, 1980).

125 "Better Things": in Jeffrey L. Meikle, *American Plastic: A Cultural History* (New Brunswick, NJ: Rutgers Univ. Press, 1995), 134. Plastics: see Meikle's comprehensive study; Stephen Fenichell, *Plastic: The Making of a Synthetic Century* (New York: HarperBusiness, 1996).

127 Union Products, Featherstone: Don Featherstone, interviews with author, 23 October 1991 (phone), 20 October 1992 (Leominister, MA), 25 July 1997 (phone) (hereafter cited as DF interviews). See also, e.g., Sue McElwee, "*Flamingo Plasticus*: A Species Not Soon to Become Extinct," *The Daily News* (Huntingdon, Saxton, Mount Union, PA), 18 June 1988; David Van Biema, "Lawn A-Mercy! Don Featherstone Rules the Roost in Plastic Flamingos," *People Weekly* 25 (19 May 1986), 126–27. *Sears, Roebuck and Co.*, catalog (Spring and Summer 1957), 1322.

   Sanford Gerard, *How Good Is Your Taste?* (Garden City, NY: Doubleday, 1946); Richard Gump, *Good Taste Costs No More* (Garden City, NY: Doubleday, 1951).

128 American lawns: see Jenkins' wonderful *The Lawn*; and not to be missed is Pollan, *Second Nature*, 19–21, 54–65.

129 Vance Packard's *The Status Seekers* (New York: David McKay, 1959) documented the postwar boundaries of taste and class.

   Catholic lawns: James Fisher, pers. com.; Joseph T. Manzo, "Italian-American Yard Shrines," *Journal of Cultural Geography* 4 (Fall-Winter 1983), 119–25.

130 South Florida: I've used Ann Armbruster, *The Life and Times of Miami Beach* (New York: Alfred A. Knopf, 1995); James R. Curtis, "Art Deco Architecture in Miami Beach," *Journal of Cultural Geography* 3 (Fall-Winter 1982), 51–63. Art Deco: see also Laura Cerwinske, *Tropical Deco: The Architecture and Design of Old Miami Beach* (New York: Rizzoli, 1981). Hialeah: Joseph Durso, "New Era Is Now Off and Racing at Hialeah," *New York Times*, 11 November 1991; John Crittenden, *Hialeah Park: A Racing Legend* (Miami: Pickering Press, 1989).

   Extinction: see Robert Porter Allen, *The Flamingos: Their Life History and Survival* (New York: National Audubon Society, 1956), 39–46.

131 Souvenirs: DF interviews; Sheehy, *Flamingo in the Garden,* 87. Flamingo Hotel: Jane and Michael Stern, *The Encyclopedia of Bad Taste* (New York: HarperCollins, 1990), 175. Las Vegas: see Alan Hess, *Viva Las Vegas: After-Hours Architecture* (San Francisco: Chronicle Books, 1993); Eugene P. Moehring, *Resort City in the Sunbelt: Las Vegas, 1930–1970* (Reno: Univ. of Nevada Press, 1989).

131–32 Tom Wolfe, "Las Vegas (What?) . . . (Can't hear you! Too noisy) Las Vegas!!!!" in *Literary Las Vegas,* ed. Mike Tronnes (New York: Henry Holt, 1995), 8. Pinks, "sassy pink": Karal Ann Marling, *As Seen on TV: The Visual Culture of Everyday Life in the 1950s* (Cambridge: Harvard Univ. Press, 1994), 40. Packard: *Status Seekers,* 72. Marling on Elvis: *As Seen on TV,* 195. On 1950s visual zeitgeist, I've used also Thomas Hine, *Populuxe* (New York: Alfred A. Knopf, 1986).

133 Real flamingos: Josep del Hoyo, Andrew Elliott, and Jordi Sargatal, eds. *Handbook of the Birds of the World,* vol. 1 (Barcelona: Lynx Edicions, 1992), 508–26.

133–34 Gillo Dorfles, *Kitsch: The World of Bad Taste* (New York: Universe Books, 1968), 14, 300, 302; Clement Greenberg, "Avant-Garde and Kitsch," in *Mass Culture: The Popular Arts in America,* ed. Bernard Rosenberg and David Manning White (Glencoe, IL: Free Press, 1957), 102, 98. A scholarly review is "On Kitsch," *Salamagundi* no. 85–86 (Winter-Spring 1990), 197–312.

Dwight MacDonald, "A Theory of Mass Culture," in Rosenberg and White, *Mass Culture,* 59, 72–73; "Mass culture threatens": Bernard Rosenberg, "Mass Culture in America," in ibid., 9; Greenberg, "Avant-Garde," 102; Dorfles, *Kitsch,* 30. A history of the debate is in Herbert J. Gans, *Popular Culture and High Culture: An Analysis and Evaluation of Taste* (New York: Basic Books, 1974), 19–64.

135 Union Products: DF interviews. MacDonald: "Theory of Mass Culture," 72. On the quest for authenticity, I've benefited esp. from the comments and work of Philip J. Deloria: see *Playing Indian* (New Haven: Yale Univ. Press, 1998); and on its history, see also T. J. Jackson Lears, *No Place of Grace: Antimodernism and the Transformation of American Culture, 1880–1920* (New York: Pan-

theon Books, 1981). On Nature in postwar popular culture, see esp. Alexander Wilson, *The Culture of Nature: North American Landscape from Disney to the Exxon Valdez* (Cambridge: Blackwell, 1992); Andrew Ross, *The Chicago Gangster Theory of Life: Nature's Debt to Society* (London: Verso, 1994); Susan G. Davis, *Spectacular Nature: Corporate Culture and the Sea World Experience* (Berkeley: Univ. of California Press, 1997).

136   Wolfe: "Las Vegas." Whyte: William H. Whyte, Jr., *The Organization Man* (New York: Simon and Schuster, 1956). Titles: in Fishman, *Bourgeois Utopias*, 200; Scott Donaldson, *The Suburban Myth* (New York: Columbia Univ. Press, 1969), 11. Florida and Las Vegas: Sterns, *Encyclopedia of Bad Taste*, 8, 122–23, 171–76; Hess, *Viva Las Vegas*, 10. "Little Boxes," by Malvina Reynolds, was made popular by Pete Seeger.

137   "lifeless," "Are you": Ted Williams, "The Joe-Pye-Weed Is Always Taller in the Other Person's Yard," *Audubon* 83 (July 1981), 109–10. "people refuges," "great pasture": Jim Wilson, "Plant Prairie Grass," *Horticulture* 54 (March 1976), 24. One practitioner: Williams, "Joe-Pye-Weed," 110. Natural-lawn movement: see also Jenkins, *The Lawn*, 159–61, 170–81; Jim Russell, "How to Quit Mowing Your Lawn Without Going to Jail," *Family Handyman* 29 (March 1979), 85–89; "Grow a Prairie of Your Own," *Changing Times* 35 (March 1981), 17–21.

139   *Sears, Roebuck and Co.*, catalog (Spring and Summer 1972), 810; ibid. (Spring and Summer 1970), 1024–26.

139–140 Charles A. Reich, *The Greening of America* (New York: Random House, 1970), 234–35, 6–9, 376–77; Robert Gottlieb, *Forcing the Spring: The Transformation of the American Environmental Movement* (Washington, D.C.: Island Press, 1993), 100. Nature and 1960s movements: I've relied on Gottlieb, *Forcing the Spring*, 86–114. Counterculture and New Left: e.g., David Burner, *Making Peace with the 60s* (Princeton: Princeton Univ. Press, 1996), 113–66; David Farber, *The Age of Great Dreams: America in the 1960s* (New York: Hill and Wang, 1994), esp. 167–211; James J. Farrell, *The Spirit of the Sixties: Making Postwar Radicalism* (New York: Routledge, 1997), 137–70, 203–31.

140–41 "everything gone": in William Grimes, "From Bakelite to the Pink Flamingo," review of Meikle, *American Plastic*, *New York Times Book Review*, 14 January 1996. Joan Didion, *Slouching Towards Bethlehem* (New York: Washington Square Press, 1968), 127. Greenberg, "Avant-Garde," 105–6; Dorfles, *Kitsch*, 97. "do away with": Charles Fenyvesi, "A Landscape Revolution," *Washington Post*, 26 May 1988. Gary Snyder, *Turtle Island* (New York: New Directions, 1969), 67. Reich, *Greening*, 234–35. New Left: Meikle, *American Plastic*, 260.

141 *Sears, Roebuck and Co.*, catalog (Spring and Summer 1968), 1049. John Waters, *Trash Trio: Three Screenplays* (New York: Vintage Books, 1988), 1–91.

142 Waters quotes, *Variety*: John Waters, *Shock Value* (New York: Thunder's Mouth Press), 2, 21 (Cadillac on p. 16). Canby: "Where Does 'Flamingo' Road Lead?" *New York Times*, 6 May 1973.

Baltimore: *Current Biography Yearbook*, 1990, s.v. "Waters, John." Waters's own memoirs are in *Shock Value*.

144 "We were united": Jancee Dunn, "John Waters," *Rolling Stone* no. 762 (12 June 1997), 42. *Desperate Living*: Waters, *Trash Trio*, 105. "To understand": ibid., 2.

144–45 Claes Oldenburg, in *Modern Dreams: The Rise and Fall and Rise of Pop*, ed. Institute for Contemporary Art (Cambridge: MIT Press, 1988), 105–6. Pop art and Warhol: I've consulted Robert Hughes, *The Shock of the New* (New York: Alfred A. Knopf, 1981), 341–65; Dick Hebdige, "In Poor Taste: Notes on Pop," in Institute for Contemporary Art, *Modern Dreams*, 76–85; Marco Livingstone, *Pop Art: A Continuing History* (New York: Harry N. Abrams, 1990), esp. 63–91, 115–39. Plastic Inevitable: see Andy Warhol and Pat Hackett, *POPism: The Warhol '60s* (San Diego: Harcourt Brace Jovanovich, 1980), 143–200; Mark Booth, *Camp* (London: Quartet Books, 1983), 169.

145 Susan Sontag, *Against Interpretation* (New York: Farrar, Straus & Giroux, 1961), 275, 279. Camp: I've found useful Andrew Ross, "The Uses of Camp," in *Camp Grounds: Style and Homosexuality*, ed. David Bergman (Amherst: Univ. of Massachusetts Press, 1993), 54–77; Bergman's introduction in ibid., 3–16. See also the

essays by Bergman, Jack Babuscio, Esther Newton; Booth, *Camp*; Philip Core's encyclopedia *Camp: The Lie That Tells the Truth* (New York: Delilah Books, 1984).

145–46 Elaine Cannel, *Good Taste: How to Have It, How to Buy It* (New York: David McKay, 1978); also, e.g., Stanley Schuler, *Make Your Garden New Again: How to Relandscape, Replant, and Develop Your Property* (New York: Simon and Schuster, 1975), 26. Union Products: DF interviews.

147 *Rolling Stone*: Ann Marie Thigpen, essay in *The Great American Lawnscape: Yard Art*, cur. Thigpen and Karen Valdés (Gainesville, Univ. of Florida, 1992), 17. *The Cat's Pyjamas: Swell Stuff*, catalog (vol. 7), 5. 1980s flamingo revival: e.g., Elizabeth Sporkin, "Those Tacky Birds Are Taking Wing," *USA Today*, 30 September 1985; Van Biema, "Lawn A-Mercy!"; Ken Franckling, "Pink Flamingos Perch Atop the Status Ladder Again," *Boston Herald*, 4 September 1986.

Port Huron: in Farber, *Age of Great Dreams*, 192.

148 *Cat's Pyjamas*, 2. A definition of yuppies, by material criteria and by sensibility, is in Barbara Ehrenreich, *Fear of Falling: The Inner Life of the Middle Class* (New York: Pantheon Books, 1989), 196–243. And see Marissa Piesman and Marilee Hartley, *The Yuppie Handbook* (New York: Long Shadow Books, 1984), for an at-a-glance description.

Travel: PFI; "Bad Taste at 31," *Economist* 308 (24 September 1988), 32. Hiking: PFI. Housewarming, moving: e.g., "Couple's in the Pink After a Little Fowl Play," *Chicago Tribune*, 23 May 1988; Sporkin, "Tacky Birds"; PFI. Birthdays and holidays: e.g., James Dempsey, "Flamingos Make Quite a Statement," in newspaper file at Union Products (hereafter cited as UPNF); "A Gift that Keeps on Giving," *Plain Dealer*, 26 December 1987, UPNF; Cynthia Pasquale, "Yard Art," *Denver Post*, 15 December 1989. "I've never seen": Elaine Viets, "Birthday Bash for Pink Flamingo," *St. Louis Post-Dispatch*, 26 July 1988.

149 Thefts: e.g., PFI; "Flamingo Park," *Newsweek* 100 (9 August 1982), 65; Bella English, "Lawn Thefts Bottom Out," *Boston Globe*, 5 October 1988. Lawn jockeys: PFI.

149–50 Artists, shows: e.g., PFI; Susan Segal, *A Pink Flamingo* (Berkeley: Ten Speed Press, 1989); Denise Laffan, "That Front-Lawn Friend, the Flamingo, Is 30," *Sunday Patriot-News* (Harrisburg, PA), 11 September 1988. Art Deco: see Barbara Capitman et al., *Rediscovering Art Deco U.S.A.* (New York: Viking Studio Books, 1994). Christo: Dominique G. LaPorte, *Christo*, trans. Abby Pollak (New York: Pantheon Books, 1985), 57; Marina Vaizey, *Christo* (New York: Rizzoli, 1990), esp. 132–39. Massachusetts: DF interviews.

151 Nostalgia: e.g., Sporkin, "Tacky Birds"; PFI. Antique stores: DF interviews; Laffan, "Front-Lawn Friend."

152 Stores: Sporkin, "Tacky Birds"; Holly D. Remy, "Pretty (Popular) in Pink," *Arizona Republic*, 14 August 1988; Berkeley Pop Culture Project, *The Whole Pop Catalog* (New York: Avon Books, 1991), 256; William E. Geist, "Where Did All Those (Plastic) Flamingos Go?" *New York Times*, 21 July 1983. *Cat's Pyjamas*; *Archie McPhee: Outfitters of Popular Culture*, catalogs, collector's eds. 25–27 (1992, 1993).

152–53 Fads: e.g., DF interviews; Elaine Viets, "The Latest for Lawns," *St. Louis Post-Dispatch*, 2 April 1989; Diane White, "Fleece in Our Time," *Boston Globe*, 30 August 1989. Features: Sporkin, "Tacky Birds"; Van Biema, "Lawn A-Mercy!"; UPNF. Clubs: e.g., Virginia Morris, "Guilford Flamingos Are Still in the Pink After 30th Bash," UPNF; Viets, "Birthday Bash"; Laffan, "Front-Lawn Friend." Waters: Sporkin, "Tacky Birds"; John Waters, *Crackpot: The Obsessions of John Waters* (New York: Macmillan, 1983), back jacket leaf. Featherstone: Paula Della Valle, "Flamingo Is Bird of Pink Paradise," *Evening Gazette* (Worcester, MA), 19 May 1987; Edward Engel, "These Birds of a Feather Don't Bother with a Feeder," *Sentinel & Enterprise*, 22–23 April 1989, UPNF. "We're trying": DF interviews.

155 Major texts in the Culture Wars include Allan Bloom, *The Closing of the American Mind: How Higher Education Has Failed Democracy and Impoverished the Souls of Today's Students* (New York: Simon and Schuster, 1987); Dinesh D'Souza, *Illiberal Education: The Politics of Race and Sex on Campus* (New York: Free Press, 1991); William J. Bennett, *The De-Valuing of America: The Fight for Our Culture and Our Children* (New York: Summit Books, 1992); Stanley Fish, *There's No*

Such Thing as Free Speech . . . and It's a Good Thing, Too (New York: Oxford Univ. Press, 1994); Lawrence W. Levine, *The Opening of the American Mind: Canons, Culture, and History* (Boston: Beacon Press, 1996); Henry Louis Gates, Jr., *Loose Canons: Notes on the Culture Wars* (New York: Oxford Univ. Press, 1992); David A. Hollinger, *Postethnic America: Beyond Multiculturalism* (New York: Basic Books, 1995). DeGeneres: e.g., Bruce Handy, "Roll Over, Ward Cleaver" and "He Called Me Degenerate?" *Time* 149 (14 April 1997), 78–85, 86; Bernard Weinraub, "DeGeneres's Companion Puts Studios on the Spot," *New York Times*, 28 April 1997.

156–57 Travel: Laffan, "Front-Lawn Friend"; DF interviews. Geese: e.g., Marge Colborn, "Don't Count the Flamingos," *Gannett News Service*, 28 October 1991; Sharon Strangenes, "Gaggle Me with a Spoon," *Chicago Tribune*, 23 June 1991. Rushing: "Yard Art: The Good, the Bad, and the Unbelievable," lecture, Missouri Botanical Garden, St. Louis, 27 April 1997. Campers: PFI. Holidays, etc.: e.g., "40 Flamingos," *Wisconsin State Journal*, 17 February 1993; "On Stagnant Pond," http://www.osp.sitecrafters.com; Marilyn Goldstein, "The Endangered Pink Flamingo," *Newsday*, 10 August 1990. Flamingo Surprise: http://www.flamingosurpris.com/; "Buy, Buy Birdie!" *New York Times Magazine*, 19 May 1996. *Shocking Gray: The Catalog of Family Values* (1993–1994), 9. Pink Flamingo Publications: http://www.pinkflamingo.com (saw 27 June 1997). Matt and Bonnie Taylor, *Neon Flamingo* (New York: Dodd, Mead, 1987); Marc Savage, *Flamingos* (New York: Perfect Crime, 1992); Bob Reiss, *Flamingo* (New York: St. Martin's Press, 1990); James Lee Burke, *A Morning for Flamingos* (Boston: Little, Brown, 1990). Gay Games: "Buy, Buy Birdie!"

157–58 IgNobel: Philip J. Hilts, "Presenting the IgNobels, UnPrizes Satirizing Weak Science," *New York Times*, 5 October 1996. Smithsonian: Marca Woodhams, pers. com. "On Stagnant Pond." Museums: Thigpen, *Yard Art*; 1991 exhibit, Boise Art Museum; and see Myles Aronowitz, "Out Front," *New York Times Magazine*, 13 February 1994. Pez: *ABC World News Tonight*, TV broadcast, 4 June 1997. Jell-O: William Glaberson, "Celebrating a Jiggly Dessert's Place in History," *New York Times*, 27 July 1997. Plastics

Center: see http://npcm.plastics.com/. Sterns, *Encyclopedia of Bad Taste*, 182; Berkeley Pop Culture Project, *Whole Pop Catalog*.

158–59 Signings: e.g., Loretta Grantham, "Pink Flamingos: Real Yard Birds," *St. Louis Post-Dispatch*, 25 June 1997. Sundance: http://sundancefilm.com/. "Well, I eat": Karen Hershenson, "John Waters Remains Unabashed About His Signature Filth, 'Pink Flamingos,'" *Knight-Ridder Tribune News Service*, 17 April 1997; "They *hated*": James Grant, "He Really Can't Help Himself," *Los Angeles Times*, 10 April 1994; "We're very proud": Jane Sims Podesta, "Spotlight on . . . John Waters," *People Weekly* 47 (14 April 1997), 20. "With all the": "Many Happy Returns," *Entertainment Weekly* no. 375 (18 April 1997), 46.

159 Princeton: Richard D. Smith, "A Spacious Alternative to Gothic Dormitories," *New York Times*, 18 October 1995. Anti-flamingo complaints and restrictions abound: e.g., Dianne Saenz, "The Case of the Shanghaied Flamingo," *Washington Post Magazine*, 3 May 1987; David S. Hilzenrath, "Neighbors See Red Over Flamingos," *Washington Post*, 5 November 1988.

Earthmade Quality Products, catalog (1997), 44, 31; *Gardener's Supply Company*, catalog (1997), 32–33. Lawn-ornament boom: e.g., George O'Brien, "Splendor in the Grass," *New York Times Magazine*, 21 June 1992; Barbara Whitaker, "Why Those Backyards Are Looking Like Versailles," *New York Times*, 23 June 1996; Christopher Mason, "'Honey, They Stole the Birdbath,'" ibid., 19 June 1997.

164 Factory: DF interviews; visit on 20 October 1992.

165 Allen Lacy, *The Gardener's Eye, and Other Essays* (New York: Atlantic Monthly Press, 1992), 151–52. See also Pollan, *Second Nature*. Featherstone: "On Stagnant Pond."

Chapter 4

167 "Wow!": "What Is The Nature Company?" The Nature Company press kit (Berkeley, CA, 1994). See also Pete Dunne, "In the Natural State," *New York Times*, 7 May 1989.

168   Stanley W. Angrist, "It's All in the Earn-Out," *Forbes* 141 (25 April 1988), 52. Demographic: e.g., CML Group, Inc., "Annual Report Pursuant to Section 13 or 15(d) of the Securities Exchange Act of 1934" (for the fiscal year ended July 31, 1993), Securities and Exchange Commission Form 10-K, 5; Gordon Bock, "CML Group: Soaking Up Those Yuppie Dollars," *Business Week* (16 June 1986), 75–76.

Baby-boomer marketing strategies: e.g., Landon Y. Jones, *Great Expectations: America and the Baby Boom Generation* (New York: Coward, McCann & Geoghegan, 1980), 218–29; Thomas Frank, *The Conquest of Cool: Business Culture, Counterculture, and the Rise of Hip Consumerism* (Chicago: Univ. of Chicago Press, 1997).

169   Wrubel quotes: informational handout for employees (current March 1994), 1–3 (hereafter cited as handout). *Business Week*: Bock, "CML Group," 75. Stores: "The Nature Company Profile," press kit; CML Group, *Annual Report* (Acton, MA: 1993), 2.

169–70 "Ahhh!": Kathryn Jackson Fallon, "Wet Seals and Whale Songs," *Time* 137 (3 June 1991), 45. "Why, on earth": Dunne, "Natural State."

A harsher, less ambivalent critique of The Nature Company is Neil Smith, "The Production of Nature," in *FutureNatural: Nature, Science, Culture*, ed. George Robertson et al. (London: Routledge, 1996), 35–54.

170   Discovery sale: see Marianne Wilson, "Discover Your World at Discovery," *Chain Store Age* (1 April 1998), 39 on Lexis/Nexis.

171   twelve thousand: handout, 3. All products mentioned here were marketed February 1993–August 1994. Store size: CML Group, "Annual Report," 5.

172   Items the company will *not* sell: handout, 2; store entrance plaques; Maureen O'Brien, "The Nature Company Jumps into Japan," *Publishers Weekly* 238 (17 May 1991), 37. Terms: e.g., handout, 1–3; "What Is The Nature Company?"; CML Group, *Annual Report*, 10; interview with store manager, 23 June 1994 (hereafter cited as interview). Real items: Liz Lufkin, "Natural History Gets Hip," *San Francisco Chronicle*, 18 December 1986; *The Nature Company*, cata-

log (Holiday 1993), 14, 48, 32 (hereafter, catalogs cited as *TNC*); "in line with": *TNC* (Fall 1994), sale section, A-B.

173 "Each product": "What Is The Nature Company?" "relates": handout, 3. "layers": *TNC* (Holiday 1992), 43.

174–75 *Glacier Bay* CD: *TNC* (Summer 1994), 27, 5. "tales": Allene Symons, "Marketing Nature Tie-ins at Nature Company," *Publishers Weekly* 231 (1 May 1987), 37. "give me the": *TNC* (Summer 1994), 15 (uppercase mine). "might have come": *TNC* (Holiday 1994), 48. "for days off": *TNC* (Summer 1994), 7. Henry David Thoreau, *The Selected Works of Thoreau*, rev. and with a new introd. by Walter Harding (Cambridge: Houghton Mifflin, 1975), 43.

   Countermodern meanings of Nature: I've benefited from William Cronon, ed., *Uncommon Ground: Toward Reinventing Nature* (New York: W. W. Norton, 1995), and have drawn especially on the essays by Cronon, Candace Slater, Richard White, Susan G. Davis and Giovanna Di Chiro.

176 "vary according": *TNC* (Fall 1994), 21. "one-of-a-kind": *TNC* (Holiday 1994), 53. "Jet": *TNC* (Holiday 1994), 28. "Our Dakota": *TNC* (Holiday 1994), 51; "sculpted by": *TNC* (Fall 1994), 21. "Our Nature Company": *TNC* (Summer 1994), 26–27; "tools": *TNC* (Fall 1994), 2.

177 "enhance people's": CML Group, *Annual Report*, cover. "products": "CML Group (20½)," report on company by Adams, Harkness & Hill, 22 March 1994, 4. *Business Week*: Bock, "CML Group," 75. "Pachelbel," "weaves": *TNC* (Summer 1994), 27. "moodtape": *TNC* (Holiday 1993), 3. "perfect for": box notes for Ron Roy, producer and director, *Tranquility* (Studio City, CA: Ron Roy Productions, 1986). "Clearly": "CML Group (20½)," 4.

178 New Age: I've found helpful Paul Heelas, *The New Age Movement: The Celebration of the Self and the Sacralization of Modernity* (Oxford: Blackwell, 1996); Susan Love Brown, "Baby Boomers, American Character, and the New Age: A Synthesis," in *Perspectives on the New Age*, ed. James R. Lewis and J. Gordon Melton (Albany: State Univ. of New York Press, 1992), 87–96.

   "Authenticity": front cover of The Nature Company folder, 1994. "create moods": Leighton Taylor, *Glacier Bay: Last Great*

Places on Earth, pamphlet (Berkeley: The Nature Company, 1991), 3, accompanies Dennis Hysom, CD of same title (vol. 2, The Nature Company Audio Library). "will open": *TNC* (Summer 1994), 26–27.

179 "Kids are": *TNC* (Summer 1994), 36. Nature and a Real Self: I've drawn heavily on Susan G. Davis's comments and work: see "'Touch the Magic,'" in Cronon, *Uncommon Ground*, 204–17; *Spectacular Nature: Corporate Culture and the Sea World Experience* (Berkeley: Univ. of California Press, 1997).t

"Pretend," "if the kid": *TNC* (Summer 1994), 18, 14.

183 Stores: in The Nature Company catalogs.

Joan Didion, *The White Album* (New York: Simon and Schuster, 1979), 180. Wright: in Thomas Hine, *Populuxe* (New York: Alfred A. Knopf, 1986), 9. Shopping-center design: I've drawn on Barry Maitland, *Shopping Malls: Planning and Design* (New York: Nichols, 1985); Margaret Crawford, "The World in a Shopping Mall," in *Variations on a Theme Park: The New American City and the End of Public Space*, ed. Michael Sorkin (New York: Hill and Wang, 1992), 3–30.

184 1980s malls: e.g., Barry Maitland, *The New Architecture of the Retail Mall* (New York: Van Nostrand Reinhold, 1990); Robert Davis Rathbun, *Shopping Centers and Malls*, orig., Book 2, and Number 4 (New York: Retail Reporting Corporation, 1986, 1988, 1992). On mall logic, I've drawn especially on Jon Goss, "The 'Magic of the Mall': An Analysis of Form, Function, and Meaning in the Contemporary Retail Built Environment," *Annals Association American Geographers* 83 (March 1993), 18–47; idem, "Disquiet on the Waterfront: Reflections on Nostalgia and Utopia in the Urban Archetypes of Festival Marketplaces," *Urban Geography* 17 (1996), 221–47; Crawford, "World in a Shopping Mall."

"star-filled": "Restaurants, Nightclubs & Food," Mall of America press kit (Bloomington, MN, 1994).

185 Stores: "The Nature Company Stores," press kit.

187 Pittsburgh Airport: interview.

188 "ALASKA": *TNC* (Summer 1994), 27. "Escape to": Taylor, *Glacier Bay*, 6. Best-selling: interview.

191 "dappled forest": Fallon, "Wet Seals," 45. Design strategy: interview. "I suppose": Dunne, "Natural State."

192 "There's nothing": Lufkin, "Natural History Gets Hip."

193 Didion, *White Album*, 186. "Invitees": The Urban Land Institute, *Dollars & Cents of Shopping Centers: 1990* (Washington, D.C.: Urban Land Institute, 1990), 4. Three hours: Crawford, "World in a Shopping Mall," 14. Forty-five percent: Rathbun, *Shopping Centers*, orig., 7.

194 Sales quotas: CML Group, *Annual Report*, 2; also, e.g., Urban Land Institute, *Dollars & Cents*.

195 "we bought": Dunne, "Natural State."
    Shopping–TV: Goss, "Magic of the Mall," 18.

196 Sex: in ibid. A wonderful review of consumer-culture theory is Jean-Christophe Agnew, "Coming Up for Air: Consumer Culture in Historical Perspective," in *Consumption and the World of Goods*, ed. John Brewer and Roy Porter (New York: Routledge, 1993), 19–39. On commodities and identity, I've been influenced esp. by Mary Douglas and Baron Isherwood, *The World of Goods: Towards an Anthropology of Consumption* (London: Allen Lane, 1979); Grant McCracken, *Culture and Consumption: New Approaches to the Symbolic Character of Consumer Goods and Activities* (Bloomington: Indiana Univ. Press, 1988); Mihaly Csikszentmihalyi and Eugene Rochberg-Halton, *The Meaning of Things: Domestic Symbols and the Self* (Cambridge: Cambridge Univ. Press, 1981). Agnew persuasively advocates a middle ground on the question of whether consumers vs. producers control meaning. A scathing critique of the popular emphasis on consumer agency is Thomas Frank and Matt Weiland, eds., *Commodify Your Dissent: Salvos from the Baffler* (New York: W. W. Norton, 1997).

197 Best-selling: *TNC* (Fall 1994), sale section, A.

198 "Thoreau": *TNC* (Summer 1994), 22.
    Wrubel: Lufkin, "Natural History Gets Hip." "Green marketing": e.g., Jacquelyn A. Ottman, *Green Marketing* (Lincolnwood, IL: NTC Business Books, 1993); "Selling Green," *Consumer Reports* 56 (October 1991), 687–92; and for an excellent critique, Robert Goldman and Stephen Papson, *Sign Wars: The Cluttered*

Landscape of Advertising (New York: Guilford Press, 1996), 187–215.

199 My analysis here is informed both by Agnew's insistence that, while celebrating consumerism as an imaginative act, we not forget economic power and the social relations of production, and by William Cronon's insistence that we should not forget that commodities are products not only of human labor but of nature: Agnew, "Coming Up for Air"; Cronon, *Nature's Metropolis: Chicago and the Great West* (New York: W. W. Norton, 1991). A wonderfully readable work on alienation and fetishism is Leah Hager Cohen, *Glass, Paper, Beans: Revelations on the Nature and Value of Ordinary Things* (New York: Doubleday, 1997).

200 Strategies: David Guterson, "Enclosed. Encyclopedic. Endured: One Week at the Mall of America," *Harper's* 287 (August 1993), 54. Cohen, *Glass, Paper, Beans*, 13. "magical space": handout, 3.

201 "Although": handout, 3. Countries: E. J. Muller, "Global Strategies for Small Shippers," *Distribution* 90 (October 1991), 29; Byron Greer, "Nature Company Expansion in High Gear," *San Francisco Chronicle*, 13 July 1987. Distribution: CML Group, "Annual Report," 7. Where the money goes: handout, 4; O'Brien, "Nature Company Jumps into Japan," 37, 38. Salaries, stockholders: CML Group, company records, *Disclosure* database, April 1994.

Agnew, "Coming Up for Air," 33.

202 Bush: Jack Anderson and Michael Binstein, "Cuff Links and Trade Deal Come Undone," *Washington Post*, 3 February 1992.

Susan E. Kuhn, "The Best & Worst Stocks of 1992," *Fortune* 127 (25 January 1993), 20–23; Gary Belsky, "Seven Growth Stocks to Spice up Your Blue-chip Portfolio," *Money*, iss. 13 (Forecast 1993), 79. CML began to lose money in 1994, had its revenues peak in 1995, and posted its worst year in 1996: CML Shareholder Direct, http://www.shareholder.com/cml; Stock Reports on America Online.

203 "folks with": Bock, "CML Group," 75. "a great deal": Angrist, "Earn-Out," 52. Davis, *Spectacular Nature*.

205 Field stations: CML Group, *Annual Report*, 10; interview.

"a gracious": "What Is The Nature Company?"

Chapter 5

208 Plumbing: Bill McKibben, *The Age of Missing Information* (New York: Plume, 1992), 18. Four hours: "TV-Free America Announces: The 3rd Annual National TV Turn-Off Week!" leaflet (Washington, D.C.: TV-Free America, 1996); but see, e.g., Ed Papazian, ed., *TV Dimensions '95* (New York: Media Dynamics, 1995), 75; Suzanne Hamlin, "Time Flies, but Where Does It Go?" *New York Times*, 6 September 1995; Robert Hughes, "Why Watch It, Anyway?" *New York Review of Books*, 16 February 1995. 93 percent: "Reader Poll Results," *TV Guide* 44 (17 August 1996), 14.

209 Fish Channel: "Ask TV Guide," *TV Guide* 42 (7 May 1994), 3. Greening: e.g., Louise McElvogue, "Jaws, Claws and Cash: Show Biz Jungle of Wildlife," *New York Times*, 29 September 1997; Rick Schindler, "The Year of the Animal," *TV Guide* 45 (4 January 1997), 39; Mark R. Orner, "A Realist History of *Nature*: A Case Study Involving a Realist Historical Interpretation of Public Television's Natural History Series *Nature*," M.A. thesis, University of Massachusetts, 1990, 51.

209-10 Guy Lyon Playfair, *The Evil Eye: The Unacceptable Face of Television* (London: Jonathan Cape, 1990); Marie Winn, *The Plug-In Drug*, rev. ed. (New York: Penguin Books, 1985); Newton N. Minow and Craig L. LaMay, *Abandoned in the Wasteland: Children, Television, and the First Amendment* (New York: Hill and Wang, 1995); Winn, *Unplugging the Plug-In Drug* (New York: Viking, 1987); William F. Baker and George Dessart, *Down the Tube: An Inside Account of the Failure of American Television* (New York: Basic Books, 1998); David Marc, *Bonfire of the Humanities: Television, Subliteracy, and Long-Term Memory Loss* (Syracuse: Syracuse Univ. Press, 1995); Hughes, "Why Watch It, Anyway?"

Poll: Elizabeth Kolbert, "Americans Despair of Popular Culture," *New York Times*, 20 August 1995. Jean Baudrillard, *Simulacra and Simulation*, trans. Sheila Faria Glaser (Ann Arbor: Univ. Michigan Press, 1994), 27–32: he argues TV is often "hyper-real," or intentionally constructed to seem real. TV as anti-Reality: for just a few examples, see Michael Medved, *Hollywood Vs. America: Popular Culture and the War on Traditional Values* (New York: HarperCollins, 1992); Sara Rimer, "With TV Off, Real Life Asserts Itself," *New York Times*, 1 May 1996; McKibben, *Missing Information*. See also TV-Free America's literature: e.g., *TV-Free America's 1997 TV-Turnoff Organizer's Kit*, booklet (Washington, D.C., 1997).

210–11 McKibben, *Missing Information*, 68–85 (quotes on 22, 77). Charles Siebert, "The Artifice of the Natural," *Harper's* 286 (February 1993), 43; Ron Powers, "The Medium Is the Message," *Audubon* (September–October 1994), 78.

213 A critique of the "zombie hypothesis" is David Gauntlett, *Moving Experiences: Understanding Television's Influences and Effects* (London: John Libbey, 1995). TV and reality: I've found esp. useful John Fiske, *Television Culture* (London: Methuen, 1987). As with Fiske, much work in TV studies argues producers' intent as hegemonic and demarcates it from consumers' readings far more cleanly than I do. But I'll argue it is useful to look for shared broad meanings—particularly for the yuppie demographic, so heavily involved in TV production. Also, however empowering ideas of nature on TV may be, they can at once be deeply felt.

214 Meg Greenfield, "Great Donuts—Great TV," *Newsweek* 115 (14 May 1990), 80. On double pleasures in modern life, I've benefited from the comments and work of Philip J. Deloria: see *Playing Indian* (New Haven: Yale Univ. Press, 1998).

215 "treacle": Richard Zoglin, "Frontier Feminist," *Time* 141 (1 March 1993), 64. "frontier hooey": Tom Shales, "Dr. Quinn: Hokum on the Range," *Washington Post*, 1 January 1993; "hackneyed": Jonathan Storm, "Dr. Quinn, Medicine Woman Puts a Superwoman in the 1800s," *Philadelphia Inquirer*, 1 January 1993. "in a word": Frank Ahrens, "'Dr. Quinn': An Unhip Hollywood Square," *Washington Post*, 2 September 1995. Success: e.g., Monte Williams, "Saturday Night Audience Ripe for the Picking," *Advertising Age* 64 (24 May 1993), s–18; Lisa Schwarzbaum, "Love, Medicine, and Miracles," *Entertainment Weekly* no. 230 (8 April 1994), 28–30.

216 TV westerns: the scarce work includes Gary A. Yoggy, *Riding the Video Range: The Rise and Fall of the Western on Television* (Jefferson,

NC: McFarland, 1995); J. Fred MacDonald, *Who Shot the Sheriff? The Rise and Fall of the Television Western* (New York: Praeger, 1987). Landscape in film westerns: see Jane Tompkins, *West of Everything: The Inner Life of Westerns* (New York: Oxford Univ. Press, 1992), 69–87; and a major treatment of the genre is Richard Slotkin, *Gunfighter Nation: The Myth of the Frontier in Twentieth-Century America* (New York: Macmillan, 1992).

218 Sets: Wolf Schneider, "Strong Medicine: The 'Lead-Off Hitter' for CBS' Saturday Night Lineup Proves That the Family Drama Is Alive and Well," *Hollywood Reporter*, 17 May 1996.

220 Why cancel: e.g., Gail Pennington, "Many St. Louisians Cry Foul Over 'Dr. Quinn' Cancellation," *St. Louis Post-Dispatch,* 2 June 1998.

221 Army: e.g., Terrence Rafferty, "One Thing After Another," *New Yorker* 66 (9 April 1990), 86; Richard Zoglin, "Like Nothing on Earth," *Time* 135 (9 April 1990), 96–97; Jim Collins, "Television and Postmodernism," in *Channels of Discourse, Reassembled*, ed. Robert C. Allen (Chapel Hill: Univ. North Carolina Press, 1992), 345; a special *Twin Peaks* issue of *Literature/Film Quarterly*, vol. 21 (October 1993).

222 A different reading of the owls, in context of the spotted-owl controversy, is Andrew Ross, *The Chicago Gangster Theory of Life: Nature's Debt to Society* (London: Verso, 1994), 189–91.

223–24 "a small town," "immutable," "forming," "melts": Michael Leahy, "Snoqualmie Notebook: Our Man Visits the Real Twin Peaks," *TV Guide* 38 (7 April 1990), 62. "snow-capped," "majestic": Florence Fabricant, "The Jewel in the Crown of Twin Peaks Country," *Wine Spectator* 16 (5 July 1991), 44. Salish Lodge: ibid. Interstate etc.: Leahy, "Snoqualmie Notebook," 60; and see "Out of the Woods," *New Yorker* 66 (10 September 1990), 36–38.

225 "Quality TV": see esp. Robert J. Thompson, *Television's Second Golden Age: From Hill Street Blues to ER* (New York: Continuum, 1996). On self-reflexivity see also, e.g., Mimi White, "Ideological Analysis and Television," and Collins, "Television and Postmodernism," in Allen, *Channels of Discourse*, 194–96, 334–36; Robert Goldman and Stephen Papson, *Sign Wars: The Cluttered Landscape*

of Advertising (New York: Guilford Press, 1996); and don't miss David Foster Wallace, *A Supposedly Fun Thing I'll Never Do Again: Essays and Arguments* (Boston: Little, Brown, 1997), 21–82.

226 ABC ads: Jamie Malanowski, "TV Is Good. But How About Those Ads?" *TV Guide* 45 (11 October 1997), 12; "Mocking the Mockers," *New York Times*, 20 August 1997.

227 Pilot, demographic: Miriam Horn, "TV's Leap into the Unknown," *U.S. News & World Report* 108 (23 April 1990), 56. Quotes: in Collins, "Television and Postmodernism," 343. Bravo: Rich Brown, "Bravo to Run Complete *Twin Peaks*," *Broadcasting* 123 (18 January 1993), 99.

"unapologetically": Frank Ahrens, "Hollywood Square." Demographics: Papazian, *TV Dimensions*, 226.

228 Tourism: e.g., "Out of the Woods," 36–38; Fabricant, "Jewel in the Crown," 41–44; Leahy, "Snoqualmie Notebook," 60–62.

229 "We're real": Scott Nance, *Exposing Northern Exposure* (Las Vegas: Pioneer Books, 1992), 17.

Demographic: Papazian, *TV Dimensions*, 226; Marcy Magiera, "CBS, Universal License 'Exposure,'" *Advertising Age* 63 (30 November 1992), 3, 52.

Northern Exposure, too, received a lot of scholarly attention: e.g., "Popular Culture Meets *Northern Exposure*: Three Perspectives on the Popular CBS Program," in *The Mid-Atlantic Almanack* 3 (1994).

231 Location: Bryan Di Salvatore, "City Slickers," *New Yorker* 69 (22 March 1993), 40–41, 46; Tom Gliatto et al., "Faked Alaska," *People Weekly* 36 (18 November 1991), 44; "A Town Goes Alaskan for 'Northern Exposure,'" *New York Times*, 17 June 1991; Louis Chunovic, *The Northern Exposure Book* (New York: Citadel Press, 1993), 28.

232 "Alaska": Susan Littwin, "Alaska on a Shoestring," *TV Guide* 38 (21 July 1990), 8. "We used it": Richard Zoglin, "A Little Too Flaky in Alaska," *Time* 137 (20 May 1991), 64. Deborah Starr Seibel, "Northern Exposed," *TV Guide* 41 (23 January 1993), 19; Chunovic, *Northern Exposure*, 11 (quotes), 31; Gliatto et al., "Faked Alaska," 44.

233 Critical success:"'Exposure' No. 1 with Critics—Again," *Electronic Media* 11 (7 December 1992), 18. *Northern Exposure* and "quality TV": see Betsy Williams, "'North to the Future': *Northern Exposure* and Quality Television," in *Television: The Critical View*, 5th ed., ed. Horace Newcomb (New York: Oxford Univ. Press, 1994), 141–54.

The nature look: e.g., David Hiltbrand, "Picks and Pans," *People Weekly* 34 (16 July 1990), 7.

236 Except where noted, commercials here aired 10 May 1994–1 September 1998. Greening trend in ads: see Goldman and Papson, *Sign Wars*, esp. 156–60, 191–92.

237 Infiniti: *Advertising Age Best TV Commercials of 1989*, videocassette (New York: Crain Communications, 1989).

In fall 1994, a prime-time spot on ABC, CBS, NBC or Fox cost from $60,000 to $320,000, dependent on ratings: "Hot Spots," *Variety*, 29 August 1994. In 1996, Toyota RAV4 and Nissan Pathfinder campaigns cost, respectively, $50 to $60 million and $30 to $40 million: "Japanese Sports-Utilities Kick Off at Super Bowl," *Advertising Age* 67 (29 January 1996), 36.

On ads' mechanics of meaning, I've found especially helpful Goldman and Papson, *Sign Wars*; Michael Schudson, *Advertising, the Uneasy Persuasion: Its Dubious Impact on American Society* (New York: Basic Books, 1984); Roland Marchand, *Advertising the American Dream: Making Way for Modernity, 1920–1940* (Berkeley: Univ. of California Press, 1985).

238 Goldman and Papson, *Sign Wars*, is a terrific look at these strategies; see also Leslie Savan's lively *The Sponsored Life: Ads, TV, and American Culture* (Philadelphia: Temple Univ. Press, 1994). Ads and nature: I've benefited also from Judith Williamson, *Decoding Advertisements: Ideology and Meaning in Advertising* (London: Marion Boyars, 1978), 103–37.

239 On whether TV watchers "believe" commercials, see Schudson, *Advertising*; Papazian, *TV Dimensions*.

242 Gas guzzler: Keith Bradsher, "What Not to Drive to the Recycling Center," *New York Times*, 28 July 1996.

245 On nature shows, see esp. Alexander Wilson, *The Culture of Nature: North American Landscape from Disney to the Exxon Valdez* (Cambridge: Blackwell, 1992), 116–55.

248 "Some of the": *TV Guide* 44 (23 March 1996), 107.

249 *Nature*,George Page, and the nature-show style: see Orner, "A Realist History of *Nature*," esp. 72–74. Genre's history: see also Peter Steinhart, "Wildlife Films: End of an Era?" *National Wildlife* 18 (December–January 1980).

A less forgiving analysis is Graeme Turner, "Nostalgia for the Primitive: Wild Life Documentaries on TV," *Australian Journal of Cultural Studies* 3 (1985), 62–71.

250 Campaign: "Japanese Sports-Utilities."

250–51 McKibben quotes: "The Age of Living Vicariously," in *TV-Turnoff Organizer's Kit*; *Missing Information*, 229, 231. Siebert, "Artifice," 44; "Letters," *Harper's* 286 (May 1993), 77.

251–52 "Cheers and Jeers," *TV Guide* 44 (2 March 1996), 10. "factual re-creations," "We would rather," "You can't feed": Mindy Sink, "The Call of the Wildlife Show," *New York Times*, 15 April 1996; and see McElvogue, "Jaws, Claws and Cash."

252 See TV-Free America's quarterly newsletter, *The TV-Free American*; *TV-Turnoff Organizer's Kit*.

254 "demand no": *V70,* catalog (New Jersey: Volvo Cars of North America, 1997), 4.

ACKNOWLEDGMENTS

I began this book for many reasons, and kept going for many more. Among the rewards of finishing is the chance to thank formally the people whose guidance and support proved so essential along the way. It's a pleasure to begin with William Cronon, who advised this project through its parallel life as a history dissertation: anyone who knows his work will recognize the depth of my intellectual debts, but Bill advanced my progress in countless ways, and spearheaded a committee that fostered remarkable support for an unorthodox project in the Yale History and American Studies departments. Ann Fabian ignited my incipient interest in how people make meaning, and gave me the benefit of her great knack for the important questions. John Demos taught me to think creatively about history and writing, and helped usher the project into its life as a book. Howard Lamar's knowledge of history and gracious encouragement of his students are legend.

I had wonderful earlier teachers, too, and I must thank especially Gary Gerstle, who introduced me to history with such conviction that he made it impossible to ignore; John McPhee, who taught me some ABC's of writing, but most useful of all, that it must be accurate and that it is very hard work; and Arch McCallum, whose passion for birds and wild places made a permanent impact.

Many friends helped create *Flight Maps*. Phil Deloria worked out every major idea here with me, and many minor ones, and has been a marvel of a reader, brainstormer, like mind, intellect, critic, fan and friend. Amy Green plowed with an infallible eye through a mountain of drafts, and her friendship has literally sustained me. Michael Goldberg has demanded, as a constant friend and reader, to save me from my mistakes. Although I've acknowledged all their ideas in the notes, I'm sure they also appear here via osmosis. I also thank Cindy Ott, who has been such a terrific friend and colleague in all ways; Peg Burns, who kept me going with her great good sense and insight (and cooking); and Alice Wexler, whose L.A. welcome made it so much easier for me to finish the book.

Among more friends who came to my aid—with comments, conversation, enthusiasm, filmfests and cookies, and with guidance through my mystifying new worlds of publishing and Los Angeles—I thank especially Dianne Andrews, Tom Andrews, Bruce Berger, Susan Buchsbaum, Cathy Corman, Elizabeth de Forest, Giovanna Di Chiro, Joanne Gernstein, Andrew Hurley, Reeve Huston, Jane Kamensky, Carl Nightingale, Leila Philip, Gunther Peck, Marita Sturken, Kirsten Swinth and Liz Varon.

I received comments on earlier chapter versions from conference and seminar participants whom any young scholar would feel fortunate to hear from: Margaret Crawford, Simon Schama, Yi-Fu Tuan, Richard White, Donald Worster; the 1994 Reinventing Nature seminar at the Humanities Research Institute at UC-Irvine; the 1994 Narrating Histories workshop at CalTech; James Farrell and his 1996 faculty workshop at St. Olaf College; the 1996–97 Nature and Culture seminar at the University of Kansas; and the 1996–97 Animals and Human Society seminar at the Shelby Cullom Davis Center for Historical Studies at Princeton University. At the Humanities Research Institute, I found the book's heart: I thank especially Susan Davis, who with Giovanna Di Chiro kept asking, "But *whose* nature?" Alane Mason catalyzed my efforts by editing and publishing an early flamingo polemic at Harcourt Brace; and William Cronon and W. W. Norton published an earlier essay on nature stores. At Yale, Nancy Cott guided Chapter Two through its first version. In the last stages, the remarkable Research Scholar program at the UCLA Center for the Study of Women supplied critical access to library and computer resources.

For guidance in the archives, I thank Chris Aschan for her extensive efforts at UC-HRI, Martha Cohen at the Massachusetts Audubon Society, Jim Campbell at the New Haven Colony Historical Society, Jennifer Lee at UCLA Interlibrary Loan, and Mary Witkowski at Bridgeport Public Library. The Mid-County branch of the St. Louis County Library moved mountains of books for two years from the system's collections. Many people went beyond the call of duty to help me with illustrations and the permissions to use them: as some may not wish to be thanked by name, I thank them as a group. Don Featherstone graciously gave me interviews—as did Nature Company staff—and toured me through his factory. As a student, I was supported by a four-year Mellon Fellowship in the Humanities, by a Yale University fellowship, and by UC-HRI.

Special thanks to Faith Childs, my agent, for great energy, insight and compassion, and for my confidence that I'm in such capable hands. Basic Books has made my first-book experience a pleasure: if publishing has gone mad, as all the jeremiads protest, I wouldn't know it. I thank Don Fehr, my editor, for his faith, and for his patience and persistence when each was appropriate. Richard Fumosa put *Flight Maps* together from many and changing pieces, and John Kemmerer expertly handled phone calls, troubles, and a FedEx blizzard. And I thank the folks at Basic and the Perseus Books group who put the book together and are seeing its way in the world—among them, Stephen Bottum, Matthew Goldberg, and Arlene Kriv.

My nephews and niece—Jacob, Ian, Micha, Gabriel, Danny, Shlomit, Yishai—gave me joy; and while all of them can talk now, none has ever said "Is it finished yet?" My brothers, Grant, Jonathan and David, and sisters-in-law, Frances Wu, Naomi Schacter and Jane Higgins provided homes away from home, did cheerleading, and read drafts. I take heart that the memory of each of my aunts—Celia Biederman, Bernice Laba and Marlene Tashma—must be in here. Last and most, I thank my parents, Elmer Price and Madelon Tashma Price, for their love and support. They've always been my closest-at-hand models for intellectual curiosity, independent thinking and a sense of what's important. Among the most important of the many things this book turned out to be, it is a gift to them.

INDEX